THE REMINISCENCES OF

The WAVES
Volume I

U.S. Naval Institute • Annapolis, Maryland

Copyright © 1971

Recollections

of

Captain Mildred McAfee, USNR (Ret.)

(Mrs. Douglas Horton)

U. S. Naval Institute
Annapolis, Maryland
1971

DECLARATION OF TRUST

The undersigned does hereby appoint and designate as his (her) Trustee herein, the Secretary-Treasurer and Publisher of the United States Naval Institute to perform and discharge the following duties, powers, and privileges in connection with the possession and use of a certain taped interview between the undersigned and the Oral History Department of the United States Naval Institute.

1. Classification of Transcript.

   (✓)a. If classified OPEN, the transcript(s) may be read or the recording(s) audited by the qualified personnel upon presentation of proper credentials, as determined by the Secretary-Treasurer of the U. S. Naval Institute.

   ( )b. If classified PERMISSION REQUIRED TO CITE OR QUOTE, the user will be required to obtain permission in writing from the interviewee prior to quoting or citing from either the transcript(s) or the recording(s).

   ( )c. If classified PERMISSION REQUIRED, permission must be obtained in writing from the interviewee before the transcribed interview(s) can be examined or the tape recording(s) audited.

   ( )d. If classified CLOSED, the transcribed interview(s) and the tape recording(s) will be sealed until a time specified by the interviewee. This may be until the death of the interviewee or for any specified number of years.

2. It is expressly understood that in giving this authorization, I am in no way precluded from placing such restrictions as I may desire upon use of the interview at any time during my lifetime, nor does this authorization in any way affect my rights to the copyright of my literary expressions that may be contained in the interview.

Witness my hand and seal this 7th day of May 1971.

Mildred McA. Horton

I hereby accept and consent to the foregoing Declaration of Trust and the powers therein conferred upon me as Trustee:

R Y E Bowhig

Preface

This manuscript is the result of two tape-recorded interviews with Mildred McAfee (Mrs. Douglas Horton) in Randolph, New Hampshire in August, 1969. These interviews were conducted by John T. Mason, Jr. for the Oral History Office in the U. S. Naval Institute.

Only minor emendations and corrections have been made to the manuscript. The reader is asked therefore to bear in mind the fact that he is reading a transcript of the spoken word rather than the written word.

Interview with Mildred McAfee Horton
At her home in Randolph, New Hampshire
Date: Monday, 25 August 1969

By: John T. Mason, Jr.

Q: Mrs. Horton, I can't tell you how happy I am to be here tonight and to meet you in the flesh, to get to know this wonderful person who headed the WAVES in its initial stages. I wonder if you would tell me something about the origins of the idea for women serving in the Navy proper.

Mrs. H.: I'm afraid I don't know much of the history of it, except that the Army began to take women into the service six months before the naval law was altered so that women could come into the service, and my understanding is that the Navy resisted very much the whole idea of having women in the service, but that when they began to see that the manpower shortage might prevent their doing some of the things they needed to do without drawing on womanpower, they then decided to establish it on a little different basis, however, from the basis which the Army had tried. The theory from the very beginning, I understand, was that if women were going to be in the service, they were going to be in the Navy and under the control of the naval officials, rather than being an auxiliary corps that would run its own ship.

Q: That, of course, was the set-up in World War I, wasn't it? Where they were somewhat auxiliary to the whole naval service?

Mrs. Horton - 2

Mrs. H. My understanding is that the Yeomanettes were brought in to do some clerical work, but I think there were no commissioned officers and I'm not sure that the enlisted women were actually enlisted into the Navy. I don't know the mechanics of that. The thing that has interested me is that we thought the Yeomanettes were a very imaginative and interesting group of women, but that they looked awfully funny in those old-fashioned uniforms, until the other day I ran across a picture of us in the Navy, and within these 25 years the styles have changed, so we...

Q: Time passes on...

Mrs. H.: Time passes on and skirt...

Q: Was the idea of the WAVES, was it influenced in part, perhaps, by the British experience with the WRENS?

Mrs. H.: I'm sure that many of the details of it were. The Chief of Naval Personnel, Admiral Jacobs, went to Canada and, whether on purpose or as a byproduct of his trip, he viewed some of the British WRENS in Canada - Canadian WRENS - and the byproduct of that visit was his absolute insistence that the women of America in the Navy must wear black stockings because they looked so handsome as they marched past him on review. So we had to fight that battle. One of the first we fought. The battle of the black stockings.

Q: And tell me how it worked out. I mean you said something at dinner about this.

Mrs. H.: Yes, well, he was determined that we should wear them because they looked some handsome on the Canadians, and we were equally determined not to because, at that time, black stocking were simply not being worn by american women. I tried to buy some in Washington and couldn't find any except the sheerest of sheer things that would have worn out in half a day.

Q: Only acceptable in a nunnery.

Mrs. H.: Well, no, the only kind I could find were more acceptable in a night club. I mean, very, very sheer. But I was making no dent on him at all about this when, one day, he said finally, "All right, you won't have to have black stockings." I asked him what had happened because his wife and his daughter had been quoted to me several times by him as saying they were protesting it on our behalf, but he was not listening to them either. And finally he said that he had been seated at dinner the night before at some dinner party next to a man who had told him that the same chemical was used for the dye in black stockings as was needed for gunpowder, or ammunition of some sort. So he said that rather than jeopardize the war effort, he would allow us to wear tan stockings. So silly.

Q: Well, tell me about your first connection with the WAVES. How did you get drawn into the picture?

Mrs. H.: It was shortly after Pearl Harbor, I guess, sometime that winter, the man who was working on personnel in Admiral

Mrs. Horton - 4

King's office, then Chief of Naval Operations, had been a dean of engineering at Columbia. You can find his name, but it just escapes me. I can't think of it at the moment. Anyway, he had enlisted Miss Gildersleeve at Barnard and a professor, Miss Reynard, - Reynard the Fox, she used to call herself - to help him consider the question of women in the service. And so Miss Gildersleeve at Barnard called a conference of the executives of a large variety of women's colleges - I think the deans of several co-educational colleges - quite a group of women were present at a meeting at Barnard. I don't have the date of it and I don't know that I have any record of it, but at that time we were told that there was the likelihood that women would be admitted to the Navy, and that it was their hope that we would encourage recruiting for this. The officer who told us about this, as I recall it, was a man by the name of Hartenstein, who was at the University of Pennsylvania until he had joined the Navy. Bert Hartenstein. His name was Paul B., and I don't know why he was called Bert, but that was it. And he talked very enlighteningly about the kinds of things which women might be asked to do, and then the meeting adjourned. And the next I knew...

Q: You had come down for this meeting...

Mrs. H.: I just came down from Wellesley to hear what it was all about.

Q: This was called on the spur of the moment, I believe.

Mrs. H.: Yes, fairly quickly, as I recall it, and in response to the emergency and we were all eager to do our bit, and everybody was eager to know what would happen to colleges and the students in them, and so on. I don't recall, really, the very next thing I heard except that I think it was by way of Miss Gildersleeve, who wrote me to ask if I would accept this appointment, and it never...

Q: They had this new organization?

Mrs. H.: They were going to have this new organization, and I think it was right at that time that it was explained to me that the Navy had decided that it was going to have somebody at the head of this organization who was not politically related or known, They had decided to try to get a college president on the principle that the Navy knew enough about the Navy, but they didn't know much about girls, and that somebody who had been working with young women would be the kind of person they'd look for.

Q: And you say the college president had to be the president of a women's college.

Mrs. H.: Well, that's the only kind of woman president there is, I guess. And, furthermore, this was the real trick of it, the Congress had limited the rank to that of a lieutenant commander, and one thing which we had been insisting upon at this meeting, and which the Navy was entirely in sympathy with, was that women should not have special privileges, they should

Mrs. Horton - 6

conform to the regulations, and that meant that the director, who was to be the only lieutenant commander - this high-ranking, impressive thing, see - must be within the ages of a lieutenant commander being brought in from civilian life. I happened to be the one within the age bracket who was young enough to fall in that low rank.

Q: That was a factor, then...

Mrs. H.: I'm sure it was, oh, yes...

Q: I believe from what I've read, that another very important factor - and a much more important one, perhaps - was that you could bring to the organization a kind of prestige and respectability.

Mrs. H.: The theory definitely was that in appointing anybody to be the head of this, they wanted to assure the parents and boy friends of girls that they would be looked after in the Navy. That this was not going to be a wild show, but it would be respectable, and the president of a woman's college - the reason they chose that category to begin with, was with the thought that somebody who had been accustomed to dealing with girls and was in a position which had respect attached to it would enhance getting the right kind of person into the service.

Q: Were women at that moment enrolled in the Army, as WACS and the Marine Corps?

Mrs. H.: Yes - no, not the Marine Corps, just the WACs. They were the only one when we started up, and I think it's fair to say that the limitations of this general intent of a category to select from, and the age bracket, were really the things which made them approach me about it. In her autobiography, Miss Gildersleeve had a reference to this selection of me in this position, and was incensed and said she simply could not understand why it was that the Trustees of Wellesley College raised a real question about whether I should be released from my commitment to them for the sake of doing this.

Q: And did they?

Mrs. H.: The thing that happened was that she came up to Boston to talk with them about my going to the Navy. If I remember correctly, I had had no direct communication from the Navy, and it hadn't occurred to me that this advisory woman who had been called in a consultative - for consultation - was really authorized by the Navy to appoint an officer. So that as we talked with her and when the Trustees talked with her, they were very skeptical about whether this new venture was one that was really going to be bought by the Navy. You see, they thought it was...

Q: Thought it wasn't official.

Mrs. H.: ...entirely unofficial. Moreover, I remember one of our Trustees had a son in the service and he said to me, "You don't want to get mixed up in anything where your rank is that

Mrs. Horton - 8

of a lieutenant commander. That's not enough to carry any weight." And I had no notion, I didn't know the ranks at all. I knew nothing about it.

Q: Well, had you expressed your willingness to...?

Mrs. H.: No, I hadn't expressed anything. They came and asked if I would do this, you see, and the enquiries that we were making seemed to Miss Gildersleeve just utterly unpatriotic. I mean you ought to be ready to jump the minute you're asked. But we weren't at all sure who was asking. Well...

Q: You hadn't been really completely informed of the background on it.

Mrs. H.: No, so when she was there with us, I said that I certainly was willing to go to Washington and talk with the Chief of Naval Personnel and find out what it was all about. So, I did go, and I talked to Admiral Jacobs. I've often laughed at him, and with him, on this, but I said, "Now, I don't know a thing about ranks in the Navy, but one of my Trustees has said that he thinks it's debateable whether really I ought to leave a position which really has as much responsibility as the presidency of the college, for something at this rank of lieutenant commander." And he said, "Why, think nothing of that. In the Navy anybody who's in charge of anything, is the ranking officer there. In a little small boat it might be an ensign, but his word is law. And this is just a technical congressional requirement. It doesn't mean a thing. You'll be in charge, and this will be your baby."

Mrs. Horton - 9

Well, the fact of the matter was that for me and for many - scores - of the women who came in, this matter of rank really didn't mean anything. It just didn't matter.. I mean if it was a job...

Q: You came to do a job.

Mrs. H.: We came to do a job and we didn't know enough to know that rank would make any difference. I remember how perfectly appalled we were very early in the game when, at one of the first training schools, they sent out word that the school would be commanded by a man officer, and then there would be a woman executive officer, and there was to be a woman who was to be in charge of the actual instruction in the skill, whatever it was, I think it was secretarial skills, and the girl in the PROCUREMENT office worked slavishly to find the right people and sent them down. One qualified to be a general administrator, and one to be a teacher, and they got there and found to the horror of everybody that the teacher outranked the executive by one day, and the young man who had been assigned at his first step from civilian life to be the commanding officer of this thing simply said, "We can't do this in the Navy. We simply can't do this. The ranking officer with seniority has got to count in this." And we thought it was just asinine, so silly. But I noticed that very soon after, people began to be sensitive about seniority, and then they soon caught the spirit about it, but at first it just literally made no difference.

Mrs. Horton - 10

Q: You were fresh from civilian life. This rank was written into the law was it?

Mrs. H.: It was written into the law.

Q: Was it an idea born on Capitol Hill, or was it born in the Navy itself?

Mrs. H.: Oh, I think it probably was mutual. My impression is that Capitol Hill did not do anything which the Naval officials actively resented, at this point. I mean they - for an instance, almost immediately the issue came up of going overseas, and one of the requirements was that WAVES would not go overseas.

Q: This was written into the initial law?

Mrs. H.: This was written into the law, yes. And it was hard on recruiting. I think a lot of people wanted to get overseas. They knew that the Army was sending women overseas, the Red Cross was sending women, that nurses could go, and why the WAVES? One of the reasons was the Chairman of the House Naval Affairs Committee...

Q: Was this Carl Vinson?

Mrs. H. Carl Vinson, who was, as you know, a Southern Georgia gentleman, and I got the very definite impression that he just wanted to protect these young girls, see, and on one occasion, I - it was either to him or to Senator Walsh, who was the Chairman of the Senate Naval Affairs Committee - that I made

Mrs. Horton - 11

some comment about how it did seem that they could leave it to the Navy to decide these things, instead of tying it into law, and got definitely the impression from one or the other of them that it was in the law because the Navy wanted it there, rather than because anybody else did. And I think that's / probably true Certainly, after the war was over and they had been relaxed so that we could go to the American theatres, which meant Honolulu, at that time, I was going to Japan. This must have been after the - it must have been '46, I guess, and got...

Q: After you ceased being...?

Mrs. H.: Yes, I was out of the service. But I got in touch with Admiral Nimitz in Guam - no, no, no, that's wrong, that's another trip.. I had gone to Honolulu, and the war was virtually over, it was not yet over - this was before I was out of the service - and was in Honolulu and I tried to reach, I did reach, Admiral Nimitz to ask if now that the fighting was really pretty well subsidizing in that part of the world, if the girls couldn't go out to Guam, at least. And he just said, no, I'm not going to have them there. And then it was on a later trip, after the war was over, and after I was out, that I went to Japan on an educational mission and saw Guam and saw Johnson Island, saw all these places, and was grateful that I didn't have to build up the morale of the young things going out there. They were horror holes, really.

Q: It was that initial legislation which made them a part

Mrs. Horton - 12

of the Naval Reserve. I believe the man who sponsored it in the House was Melvin Maas. Did you have connection with him?

Mrs. H.: Not really directly. I had very little connection with the legislature, except with Margaret Chase Smith, who was on the House Naval Affairs Committee, and we had a captain in BuPers who handled all the legislation and introduced me to the intricacies of legislation as I had never met them.

Q: You were a babe in arms in terms of...?

Mrs. H.: Oh, absolutely. I was as green as grass. I remember on one occasion there was a question about - I guess it was about WAVES going overseas, was coming up for discussion and I went up with him, up on the Hill. They didn't even mention it. It seemed to me there was no discussion of this issue, which was the one which I was to comment on because it was so important. It was all a question of, "Well, I'd just as soon go along with that," whatever "that" was, "if you can sponsor this or the other thing, see." I came down off the Hill with him and said, "That was really discouraging." "Oh, no," he said, "not at all discouraging. We got everything we wanted." I was startled and said, "How did we get what we wanted?" And he said, "Well, you see, they were all agreeing that they could approve this bill if the men who were sponsoring it would approve theirs." He said, "I don't think there's any question it will come through all right," which it did.

Q: In the parlance of Capitol Hill, that's called log-rolling,

I suppose.

Mrs. H.: Well, I think in the parlance of Capitol Hill, it's called negotiating. In THE STICKS it's called log-rolling. But it was my introduction to the technique of legislation. Very enlightening. Very interesting.

Q: In its initial stages, I believe that Senator David Walsh was very emphatically opposed to the whole idea, wasn't he?

Mrs. H.: Yes. I think so, and he did it on the score of protecting womanhood, I think, which we all thought was a little unnecessary to pick on us to be protected. We didn't think we were any worse - in any worse danger - than any of the others. But I'm sure that they reflected a very great hesitation within the Navy about doing this, and BuAir had had a lot of experience with other nations in air things, and wanted very much to have women get in quickly. BuPers was the one that would have to administer it, and Admiral Jacobs finally got I think really quite excited about it, and he kind of felt that he was the grandfather of the whole thing, and he was very helpful and wanted very much...But, at the moment, my impression is, and this is all a vague memory, but my impression is that BuPers didn't really covet having BuAir take the lead in this...

Q: Who was head of BuAir? Towers?

Mrs. H.: Yes, Towers. Anyway, it was some, certainly weeks, if not months after I'd been there that suddenly, I went to

Mrs. Horton - 14

Admiral Jacobs and I said, "It seems to me a little bit funny that we aren't finding out what people want women to do, instead of just getting women trained to do something." And he said, "I think you're right. I think you ought to go round to thse Bureaus and find out what they'd like to have you do." And he arranged for me to go and visit the chiefs of all the various bureaus, and when I got to Admiral Towers, I think he was on my first go-around, I was perfectly astonished at the violence with which he spoke, saying "Where have you been all this time? We've been clamoring for these WAVES and nobody's ever listened to us to know who we want and so on." Then they asked for the largest single number in time.

Q: Why hadn't he come directly to you?

Mrs. H.: Well, because, you see, I was a lieutenant commander in the Bureau of Naval Personnel, and this rank business which made not one hill of beans difference to me, definitely made people recognize that, so far as the general policy was concerned, that was being done way up in some echelon that I never came in contact with. I had direct access any time I wanted to the Chief of BuPers. Admiral Jacobs' door was open to me any time I wanted it. That he kept firmly in the picture. But I've often thought he didn't make it very plain outside of the Bureau, and within the Bureau, he was much more explicit to me, making me feel perfectly comfortable about going to him, than he was explaining to everybody else what the relationship of this strange new thing was going to be.

Q: He must have understood thoroughly the impediment of that low rank in terms of...

Mrs. H.: Well, I think he did, except that womanhood had its privileges too. I mean regardless of rank, I got incredible privileges which nobody else, at that rank, would ever have, which of course was infuriating to a lot of people who had worked very hard for that rank. But I've always remembered the time when a man from Marshall Field was brought in to help re-organize the Bureau of Personnel, which had expanded enormously, of course. A nice boy. I can't remember what his name was. But he came to all the offices and got the feel of what the Bureau was doing. When he came to me, he - the one remark he made somewhere was that he was talking about the relationship of this enterprise to all these others, and I remember vividly saying, "I think this is right. I think it would be fine. I guess I'll ask these men to come in and we'll talk the whole thing over." He said, "Miss McAfee, you go to see them." That was my introduction to rank. I mean, I - it never occurred to me. At Wellesley I telephoned people and they came in to see me.

Q: They came to you, yes.

Mrs. H.: It just hadn't dawned on me about this and so on. I was perfectly willing to go hat-in-hand, that was all. But this kind of - we really were simply plunged in, and this Bert Hartenstein who had explained all this to the group of women to begin with, I finally discovered had been in the Navy

Mrs. Horton - 16

for three weeks before he began talking about what we were going to do about these women. And he was assigned in the training - no, in the Office of Procurement Division - to help on the recruiting, and was a most helpful factor in the whole thing. I've always been indebted to him for this.

Q: But limited because he didn't...

Mrs. H.: Because he only had three weeks to go on. He didn't know much more about it than we did, and we knew nothing. It was really just awful.

Q: Could we revert back to Wellesley and to the final permission given by the Board of Trustees...?

Mrs. H.: They were very happy to do it when it became clear that it really was a request from the Navy. Now, the negotiations on this included the explicit understanding that I would go for a year...

Q: This was a year's leave of absence that you were taking?

Mrs. H.: That's right. And that I would be in the Navy for one year, and again, you see, we didn't know anything about how you do things in the Navy.

Q: And you had no idea of the extent of the war, either.

Mrs. H.: No, of course not. And the theory was that I would get it set up and then go back to Wellesley.

Mrs. Horton - 17

Q: This was a terrific compliment to your administrative ability, wasn't it, to go down there and set it up in a year?

Mrs. H.: Well, theoretically, but, of course the point is that it wasn't my administrative ability. I mean it had to be geared in to the going Navy, you see. I used to say that my function was to be the dangling link on the chain of command. To make enough noise so that things could get done, but I really, really had no authority, see, except the authority of influence with Admiral Jacobs, who could get things done, and with a perfectly remarkable group of women, who by chance were attracted into this thing to begin with, and were simply remarkable in their ability to work themselves into the positions where they could really be influential on things.

Q: When you went to Washington, you didn't actually divest yourself of the authority you had as president of Wellesley? This was carried with you in a very intangible way, perhaps.

Mrs. H.: Exactly, and of course the trouble is that many times I used it without ever knowing it was abnormal, see, because I thought this is what you did when you were organizing something, you just go ahead and do something about it. This is the thing which I think was the most perplexing to a lot of the people in the Navy, that this bunch of women came in here and, with no axe to grind at all, we just went on about our business. The men were perfectly astonished over the fact, for instance, that the first group of yeomen were good workers in the offices, and they'd never seen a woman working in an office before. I didn't understand this until I went out to an Army and Navy Club night one Saturday night and saw these gorgeous creatures who were the Navy wives whom/men thought of as women, see. And these little girls who'd been hard-working secretaries for years, and years, and years, were glad to get out of an office and into the Navy and do something for the war, were simply fine stenographers. The men were simply astonished because it hadn't occurred to them that they really would be skillful, and in that particular category, obviously the boys, many of them, had no interest in being yeomen from the point of view of running a typewriter. They wanted to get out where the action was. And when these girls came in knowing there wasn't any better action than this for them, they did a perfectly stunning job, and ~~people were just genuinely~~ a lot of the commanding officers were just genuinely surprised because they'd never seen women in this kind of action.

And since we knew it was temporary for us, we were the women accepted for volunteer emergnecy service, and we weren't going to be there for ever or stay there...

Q: It's a very clever title, I must say.

Mrs. H.: And you know how it evolved, don't you?

Q: No. Tell me.

Mrs. H.: There was a classification for officers called VS - Volunteer Specialist, who'd come right from civilian life into

Mrs. Horton - 19

the Navy.

Q: That's what the W...

Mrs. H.: And, of course, the W was for women. And then the question was what should the women be called in the service. I was extremely high-minded about this and I said, I think they should just be called by their ranks and just women in the service, in the Navy - until I saw a headline in a Washington paper, early in the summer, I think just after the legislation had passed, "Goblettes Come to Town."

Q: Goblettes?

Mrs. H.: Yes. Navy gobs. At that point I bought the nickname WAVES, which had been going around the office as a possibility because the thing with WVS, it would either be Waves, Wives, Wolves, or Woobs, you see, and Waves seemed appropriate for the Navy. And then they attached the words, Women Accepted for Volunteer Emergency Service.

Q: The Goblettes! How dreadful.

Mrs. H.: You know the story from Hawaii, don't you? Somebody out there, right after the thing began, said he didn't know just what the letters were supposed to stand for, but he thought they probably were "Women Are Very Essential Sometimes."

Q: That's a very apt interpretation.

Mrs. H.: Yes, very.

Mrs. Horton - 20

Q: Tell me about the induction ceremony for you, and the use they made of this in terms of publicity for the new organization and that kind of thing.

Mrs. H.: Well, the induction ceremony was simple, but very gracious and very nice because it was in the office of the Secretary of the Navy.

Q: Knox, was that?

Mrs. H.: Knox, yes, and I think Admiral King came in, two or three high ranking people were there for my swearing-in. Then there was a press conference right afterwards, and of course I'd nothing to say. I didn't know anything about anything, though I had been in Washington. I think I'd been there about a month before the legislation passed, and it was well known that when it did pass I was going to be the commissioned officer, but it was very nebulous because I didn't have any status at all for the first few weeks.

Q: You merely had a desk.

Mrs. H.: I had a desk, and I think there was a - I did have a civilian secretary, but I didn't have much to write, really. The theory was that we were finding people who would be the nucleus of our organization, and that was done by way of naval districts and the appointment in each naval district, often by a committee which had been appointed by Miss Gildersleeve, see, in the setting-up of this thing, or by invitation of somebody in the Navy, to find civilian women who would find the officer or the person who could be commissioned to be the ranking officer in that district. I went down to New Orleans to interview half a dozen people, but in most of the areas that appointment was made by somebody other than me. And they became the, let me see, Senior Woman Officer, I think we called them, in the district, whose business then was to set up the recruiting and the program. Early in the game, it was decided that all women would be enlisted or commissioned through the Office of Procurement officers, and not the recruiting officers.

Q: The enlisted personnel and the officers as well?

Mrs. H.: Enlisted personnel were going to be procured through the same officers. That caused some consternation round through the Bureau because, again, I didn't know enough about it to know what was the matter. But the procurement [recruiting] forms and so on, of course, were geared to recruiting officers, and we had to modify the ordinary officer procurement for taking in enlisted women. It did one thing which was what we hoped for, which was that it brought women in to offices which were very much more attractive, more appealing, than the Post Office recruting station.

Q: Psychologically it...

Mrs. H.: And, psychologically, it brought a fine group of women in. We are greatly indebted to the Army on their experience, because when they started in it was the first time

Mrs. Horton - 22

women had been taken into any of the services, and they had opened the doors and said to everybody, we want you to come in. They had established recruiting offices, I guess in the regular Army ones, I'm not sure about that, in any case, lines had formed for blocks around the Army headquarters of girls who wanted to come in, or women, anybody, who had not been cleared at any point, see. The reporters had a field day with those WACs people who were not in the Army, the Army had nothing to do with it except it offered to let them apply. But the stories were picked up from the clowns in these lines, so that one of the first things that was suggested to us, and I think Bert Hartenstein relayed it to us, was that instead of having people just come to volunteer, they must write to the Procurement Office, and they must give their name, and their age, and their occupation, and if the basic facts looked promising, they would then be sent an application form together with a time - an appointment - for an interview.

Q: It was a culling process.

Mrs. H.: It meant there were no lines. Nothing happened ~~on behalf of the Navy~~ over which the Navy had no control, and they came on the half-hour or whatever the time was, and were interviewed by this one woman who had some kind of experience. For instance, we had the Director of Personnel at Macys who had been interviewing people for years. She came early in the game. We had somebody, I think she was even then at Katie Gibbs School. We had a woman who'd been the dean of women at Wilson College in Pennsylvania. We had somebody who'd been in business interviewing applicants for years in her own profession. So that the women who were selected in these first posts were people who knew how to size other people up pretty well. And when the first people were brought into the service, I've forgotten how many women officers we wanted, but there were many more who qualified as officers. who could not, at that time be taken, and so they just enlisted. I mean, it was that simple. So that the first 60 or 75 per cent, I think, or something like that of the first group of enlisted women were qualified as officers.

Q: I read somewhere, somebody's remark, that at Smith College in the initial class or classes the number of degrees outnumbered the number of people.

Mrs. H.: I wouldn't be at all surprised. Yes, I think that's true. That was one of the most startling and really grim experiences, because we really had very high-powered women there, and when they got there, nice Captain Underwood, who was a wonderful person - everybody loved him dearly eventually, or they did at once, as soon as they knew him - he decided that the way to train these women as officers was to put them through the kind of training that a man would get at Annapolis, or some place, in six weeks, you know, 30 DAY WONDERS be. But the point was that they were to be drilled and they were to march and do all the things that would be done on a naval station. And you got the dean of women of Purdue University, and you got the head of the great

Mrs. Horton - 24

housing development at Stanford University, and you got people who had been accustomed to giving orders all their adult life, mature women. And suddenly they found themselves squads in this mass experience, and it was really excessively hard for them to take. They were wonderful sports about it, they did just beautifully. And they then went out to be the heads of all the other projects, you see, and they certainly had lived through what other people had to live through.

Q: Would you talk a little about the incentive, the motive, which brought this plethora of talent at the initial stage?

Mrs. H.: I think it was a case of the nation being at war, men being drafted, everything being revised for the sake of the war, and here was a very direct way in which a woman could get into something which was really going to foster the war effort - further the war effort. The fact that men were drafted and women weren't meant that a great many people had to weigh very heavily whether or not they really were wanted. But when they were convinced, as many of these leaders were, that they were needed to get the thing off the ground, I think it was just a sheer case of responding to what they believed was really the real need and they wanted to be in on it.

Q: Now, this was fostered by the way in which the publicity on the WAVES was handled, wasn't it?

Mrs. H.: Yes. I'm sure this is true.

Q: And what role did you play in that?

Mrs. H.: Well, we very soon got into it by way of getting the person who subsequently became another director of the WAVES, who was the head of public relations at Mt. Holyoke College, and we got her in quickly to ride herd on the publicity.

Q: Who was this?

Mrs. H.: This was Louise Wilde, who came in right after Jean Palmer, as I remember, and she at once became liaison with me with the official public relations people, and I remember one of my most vivid moments was when they were going to make a movie. She had talked with these people about it, and she talked with me, and she was greatly distressed because there was so much cheesecake in it, and it was appealing to an adventure that we couldn't possibly guarantee. I mean, it wasn't exciting for the people once they got into it. There was an awful lot of drab stuff. And when they showed it to me, I said, "I just won't buy that. We cannot have this thing which will make them think they're coming in to get their man and to have a thrill, because we can't come through with it, and we'll soon ruin their career." The men doing this were simply infuriated, and they said my girl had gone along with it, and Billy had, because they were the big boys and they outranked her and all the rest of it. But that was one of the cases where I remember very vividly that I appealed to the Admiral on it, and he supported me in withdrawing this thing, because it was just completely misrepresenting the thing that had to be done. But they soon got the idea, and one such episode convinced them all that this was not the way to...

Q: Well, at that period, public relations as handled by the Navy was a very embryonic kind of thing anyway, wasn't it?

Mrs. H.: Yes, there was nobody who really knew how to do it at that moment. The fact that so many of these women who began it were level-headed, really, but not at all sissy, I mean they were very good sports, all of them, and popular women, meant that it was quite clear that somebody was going to see to it that it wasn't going to be any riff-raff crowd, you see. But the real secret of that was that the Navy, at no point, thought in big terms to begin with. It was going to be small and grow gradually. Well, we eventually had, I think I'm right, at one point we had 86,000 women on duty at one moment.

Q: I believe that was when you gave up the command, wasn't it?

Mrs. H.: Yes, pretty nearly. About then. But the...

Q: Why had they not anticipated this great growth and this great response?

Mrs. H.: Because I really think there was so much internal resistance to it, that it had to prove itself before people would plan for it. And the way it proved itself was something which, now, I would think that they would have anticipated. You know that when a Navy man in command of a station judges his own people, they are always tops. "My people are wonderful. We don't want WAVES, in general, but my WAVES are fine." And this possessive admiration of "my ship" and "my station" really, [MEANT] as soon as WAVES got out of training and on somebody's station so they were his girls, he was all for them. It really was simply fantastic. This is true of the old chiefs. The chiefs just died at the thought of having women.

Q: Yes.

Mrs. H.: And then their girls came along and the chiefs just melted. And "their girls" were all right, and as long as "their girls" were all right, over at the next station they heard that some of these people could do something, and they took them on. But it was just part of the whole Navy psychology that once they belonged, they were all right.

Q: I suppose this is an inappropriate kind of footnote, an inappropriate reference, but this "show me" [this] necessary "show me" aspect of it, was suitably handled by you who came in from Missouri.

Mrs. H.: That may be. The point is that I wasn't the one to be shown.

Q: No, but you were proving the merit of the organization.

Mrs. H.: Well, of course, I think the most unhappy feature of my experience in the Navy was receiving the plaudits and credit for so much for which I was not responsible, and knew I wasn't responsible. This is a very painful position - to be receiving all kinds of honors all over the place, when really you knew that it was back-door diplomacy if you had anything to do with it at all, because we really were incorporated into the services. It was not a case of my undertaking to establish something outside of this framework, and it was within the framework. You see, every girl who went out to a station was under the command of the commanding officer of that station. Now, we had a woman there who was liaison between the girls and the commanding officer to interpret them to him and him to them, but she wasn't in command. I think once we had seven WAVES in my office, and I was in command of those, but I had no command of the rest of it. I didn't want to command. I mean it was very satisfying, very gratifying to us, to be able to say, we're not auxiliary, we're in the service. But it was hardly fair for me to get the red-carpet treatment...

Q: Yes, but that's a part of the obligation and responsibility of leadership, isn't it?

Mrs. H.: Well, I took it with great satisfaction. I had a very interesting time, but it was frustrating, really, not to be able to accomplish the things you wanted to, except by such very indirect methods- I think I may confess to a memorable experience, when we were sensing the fact that things were going very badly. We weren't getting anything much accomplished to speed things up the way we wanted to, and so on...

Q: This was during the initial months?

Mrs. H.: No, I think it was near the end of a year or two, and we were accepted enough now to feel the limitations of what we could do and accomplish, you see. And I remember, we had a coffee mess every morning in my office, when the people came in. We had a WAVE officer in each of the Bureau departments.

Q: Who had this idea?

Mrs. H.: I wouldn't know where we got it, but it worked. We got people appointed to each of the offices to be the contact between my office and the...

Q: Your eyes and ears...

Mrs. H.: That's right. And one or two of them seemed to be very skillful, and the rest were bungling it. I was rushing things, and trying to get the things accomplished, and wasn't getting to first base. And we had a coffee mess every morning when we talked about what we'd got to get done, then we'd go out to do it. Of course, this was subversive in the Navy, in a way. I mean, the Navy didn't have anybody like me in the chain of command, and it was very disconcerting to everybody. So, we sat there one day and I remember vividly that we solemnly agreed that we were going at this wrong, it wasn't right. We could go on having just as many ideas as we wanted to, but under no circumstances must they come from my office to those offices, by way of these girls, except indirectly, and it would be the fine art of each of these young women, fine intelligent young women, to get the idea to the man in charge so he thought it was himself, and never to say this was the combined judgment of all these women.

Q: Women are awfully skilled at this, anyway, aren't they?

Mrs. H.: I remember we, all of us, felt positively embarrassed about this. How perfectly stupid to resort to this technique when we were there to do a job - how stupid. But we tried it, and, boy, it worked fine. We just had a peaceful and lovely time from then on. And felt pretty silly with it, but the real fact of it was, you see, that these offices were headed by people who were on the way up. We didn't care whether we went up or not, but some of these men did know that their professional careers depended on what happened, and if they had ideas which could work, that helped their career. And we didn't have a career, we didn't care. I was waiting and trying to get out instead of trying to get up. There was nothing noble about this, it was just a good technique. It worked fine.

Q: I suppose there is a weakness in the military system, whether it's Navy or what-have-you, in that a man doesn't occupy a billet very long. I mean he's there only such a brief time, then he goes on to something else.

Mrs. H.: Yes, he has to make his mark.

Q: Tell me, Mrs. Horton, about the advisory committee that

came into being even before the legislation. Tell me about its role, the scope of things, how it functioned during the years.

Mrs. H.: Well, we had a little trouble deciding that, too.

Q: You say the WAVE organization had a little trouble?

Mrs. H.: Yes, but the real virtue of it was its public relations value - working a little bit both ways - but by having this group of very distinguished women, they were fine people who were on the advisory committee, and bringing them into the Navy Department about once, or, maybe twice - no, once a year, I guess, we made some trips with them to take them to the establishment and so on where they would not otherwise have gone, and this meant that they then went back as spokesmen who could interpret the Navy very favorably, and I think they rendered a very real service at this point.

Q: Did they represent the various naval districts, too?

Mrs. H.: Yes, yes. It was all done by naval districts. And when I say we had trouble defining it, it was deciding what would be a profitable way to spend their time when they came down to offer advice. We didn't always know, but I think we had some very good trips and some very interesting conversations. But, you see, one of the complications about this, really, again was that if you weren't in the service, you didn't really realize how external civilian advice was, and this was their war effort. They wanted to render service. But they really were kind of apart from it, and how to maintain their interest and respect them respectfully and so on, and yet know that they really couldn't accomplish very much was the trick that complicated the life of some of us sometimes.

Q: So, what it boiled down to was that it was really in the area of public relations.

Mrs. H.: That was the place at which they really made their greatest contribution. Now, after the war was over and Mrs. Rosenberg - Mrs. Rosenberg?

Q: Anna Rosenberg.

Mrs. H.: ...was Secretary of...

Q: Of Manpower.

Mrs. H.: ...of Manpower, oh yes, she convened another committee which I think is still going strong. It was called Dacowits. A women's "Advisory Council On Women In The Services." Mrs. Rosenberg asked each of us who had been the head of the wartime services to be a member of that committee. I remember on one occasion, and I was then in the role of being the civilian advisor, see, one of the civilian doctors after the war, was talking about the fact that there were a great many health matters which could very profitably be studied about the group of women then in the service. I remember Oveta Culp Hobby saying to her, "I worked for four years in the Army to try to get something like this accomplished and didn't get to first base, and you just can't do it from outside." And the reason

Mrs. Horton - 33

I remember it so vividly was that I remember saying to Oveta that this was the first time I ever heard her imply, even, that she couldn't get anything she wanted out of the Army. She used to make us very annoyed because we'd be frustrated, and she'd always sound as though the Army just did anything she wanted to have done, and when she admitted publicly that for four years she worked on something she hadn't done, I resigned from Dacowits. I said, "I've achieved my objective now. I don't want to serve any more." I was very fond of her. She's a great girl. And she was wonderful on morale. It really was true that she built up the most incredible attitude of military acceptance of things, which some of the rest of us found it very hard to accept.

Q: Tell me a little more about that committee. I mean some of the specific things they did. I mean where they went with you, and that kind of thing.

Mrs. H.: I remember one trip down to Jacksonville, Florida, and the reason I remember that so vividly was that I was called back from it for a meeting with the Secretary with one of our Trustees who was there to try to extract me from the service.

Q: Thought you'd served long enough.

Mrs. H.: Yes, because at the end of the first year, it was perfectly plain to me, as to everybody else, that it was

Mrs. Horton - 34

ridiculous to leave now because nobody else was being allowed to leave, and it would have been very bad for morale for me who had been a symbol of membership to quit at this particular point, so I did stay on for a second year.

Q: And a third year.

Mrs. H.: Yes, but I think the second year - I think it was at the end of the second year - that I flew back from Jacksonville - may be it was Pensacola, I guess it was down in Florida, we'd taken the whole advisory committee down there, and I flew back for this conference with one of the Trustees and Secretary Knox, where we evolved the plan of letting me go back for one weekend a month to Wellesley for that second year. Kind of kept my finger in it, and then, the third year, I went back for one week a month, and then they let me out.

Q: What sort of arrangement did you have at Wellesley? Whom did you have as your understudy?

Mrs. H.: We had a troika, but we didn't call it that. We had three people, one of the Trustees was a gorgeous person who lived nearby and she took part of the work that was involved in keeping the Trustees informed of what was happening. She spent a lot of time on the campus. And then a dean worked with the faculty - kept the faculty going, and the dean of students kept the student program going. And Mrs. Haffeneffer is the trustee who worked closely with the business people. So that the people who were doing it anyway in connection with the faculty and students just maintained their own responsibility, and Mrs. Haffeneffer took on this other thing, and the three of them together made decisions which affected all of them.

Q: This was a terrific burden for you, wasn't it?

Mrs. H.: Well, it wasn't the first year, I paid no attention to it. I was so completely swamped with the Navy that I didn't even know what was happening, and they did a beautiful job with it. They were three people who were personally very congenial and worked together very nicely, and of course in war time everything was geared to doing what was necessary for the sake of the war effort and so on. It got to be, I think, quite a strain on them. In the second and third years, I could pick up a little of it but not much, I went back after I was married - I went back for four years to give the other two a chance to get leaves of absence.

Q: Was the student body somewhat reduced during the war?

Mrs. H.: No. The women's colleges held up remarkably, partly because we made a great case of it that getting an education was one of the contributions you could make to the war effort. The men's colleges and co-educational ones were awfully badly disorganized with no men there, and my memory is that there was no falling-off at all, we had fine numbers to select from because the services weren't taking girls in - as officers, certainly - until after they'd finished college. And then the options for girls were not as great as they might have been if the draft system had prevailed...

Q: What you said earlier would indicate, and I think my recollections bear this out, that the opportunity given women in a structured kind of service in war time was something they welcomed and they demonstrated a kind of willingness and patriotism which almost outshone the men.

Mrs. H.: Well, of course, it was a willingness and a patriotism which did not involved the risks which it did for the men. I remember I had several conversations with people who wanted us to go all out for big veterans' rights and things, which all seemed utterly unreasonable. I mean I couldn't get any excitement up among the women for this, because...

Q: Veterans' rights?

Mrs. H.: Yes...They had the pensions and things which everybody else had, but for special wartime services and so on, it really was kind of silly when you were shore-bound to talk about having made these enormous sacrifices because most of us weren't sacrificing anything to be there, and were actually finding a rewarding experience in moving into a different area. A good many of the people who started in on this were women who had, as I had done, worked pretty largely with women's organizations, and this was a help in dealing with the women who were coming in, but it was also an interesting experience for people who had been doing that, to get into a man's world, which was a brand-new experience.

We kept saying all the time that we never had realized how completely the Navy was a man's world. There was no doubt about it. And that was an interesting experience to have. We didn't mind that at all... But of course to the enlisted women, the young ones, the young girls, the whole thing had a kind of exhilarating novelty to it, which didn't really apply to the young officers as much as it did the girls. Indeed, I think the hardest group, from the point of view of a sense of achievement, was this young junior officer group, because there is a sense in which that is the lowest form of life in the service anyway, and when it was a woman doing it, too, it was very hard. But it was very gratifying to find even during those first four years how many women rose above this. I think it was in New York - the whole personnel office was being managed by a woman officer who was responsible for placement of hundreds of men. That was an administrative job...

Q: She had the responsibility.

Mrs. H.: She had the responsibility, exactly. And they got to be instructors in several of the schools and were holding very important offices in communications and a lot of the other things, which was gratifying.

Q: Are you able, in reflection, and perhaps from contact with people, are you able to make any assessment of the value which this experience had for some of these junior officers in later life in their later careers?

Mrs. H.: I think it had an enormous value in convincing people that they could do things that they had never done before. So many of these officers were sent out to do jobs which only in the Navy would they have ever been asked to do, and they found they could do them. One of our prize stories was of a station where they needed a dietician - mess hall director - and a recreation director, and they looked hard and fast for these two billets to be filled, and they finally found a recreation director, sent her out, and the commanding officer said, "I need a dietician much more than I need a recreation director, so you will run the mess hall." She said, "I've never done anything like this in my life before." He said, "You're in the Navy. You do it." And she did it so well that when they finally sent the mess hall director out, he said, "We're very well pleased with what we have. You can take care of the recreation picture." This kind of gross mis-assignment of people, yet convinced a great many of them that they had capacities, interests, and skills which they had never dreamed they had and which they would never have thought would appeal to them. So that I think, vocationally, it did something to limber up people up and make them feel that they were much more adaptable than they thought they were.

Q: In the years that have followed, then, this group of women who had this broader experience in a man's world, so to speak, did they in turn go out and broaden the base of women's activities in the world at large?

Mrs. H.: That's my impression, that they have done that very

Mrs. Horton - 39

decidedly. The ones whom I knew best, naturally enough, are the ones that I've followed most closely have been the ones in the field of education because that's where I met them. Otherwise, many of them who had never done administrative things have stepped into administration where they did have to adapt to new situations, as they had not expected to do originally. The present dean of Douglas College of Rutgers University, for instance, Marjorie Foster, is a girl who did a good job at - I don't remember what her job was in the service - but I took her back to Wellesley to do some fund-raising, as I recall, public relations, or something. She moved on from there and got her doctorate, went up to be assistant at Mt. Holyoke, and now is the dean at Douglas, a very important and big position. She would have done it under any circumstance probably, but the Navy opened up doors to her which she hadn't otherwise opened. And I think the group of people I've seen most often in New York, like Jean Palmer, are people who have built themselves into big jobs, whether they were big jobs to begin with or not.

Q: Can we in the way of prognosis, can we anticipate that perhaps one or more of these women with this broader experience will eventually become presidents of universities and colleges? And occupy places which heretofore have been occupied only by men?

Mrs. H.: Well, I think that may be coming sometime, but I don't think it's here directly, and I think one of the complications has been that we're still facing the fact of the marriage which diverts people from one profession or another, and a great many of these WAVES are/wives now instead of WAVES, and are not necessarily going along in the professions. But I'm not so sure that with the lack of the war and the patriotic incentive, there are corresponding numbers of people in the present military services to maintain this pattern of moving into bigger positions. I just don't know that. I'm not in touch with the present pattern. But out of 86,000 people who had the gumption to volunteer for this, because it all had to be voluntary, except me, I think, I was the only one drafted, as far as I know...

Q: And drafted without your knowledge.

Mrs. H.: Yes. With that many people involved, the chances were great that some of them would move on into big positions. But I think for all of them - I mean from the very least of them, the least efficient, I mean, the experience of being part of a big enterprise was one of the very great rewards, and that this encouraged a great many of them to go into something that was big enough to excite them next time. They weren't going to be satisfied with just ~~little~~ pesky little jobs.

Q: That was the broader basis that they acquired.

Mrs. H.: Yes. Yes, that's the broadening. And, of course, in war time there's just no doubt about the fact that it was an extremely satisfying thing to be part of a Navy which was doing so many dramatic things, and it was one of the things we tried to build in, and I think it was the thing that appealed as much as anything to the women - to be reminded of the fact that because it was such a big and complex and complicated enterprise, each little cog in it was important to the whole business. And these little girls who looked like such babies but were proud to be Link trainers and training the sailors to go off to sea enlarged their own feeling of the significance of being part of something bigger than themselves.

Q: Well, isn't this a concept which is much more readily understood by a woman than it is by a man. I mean, to be a part of a chain, to be a link...

Mrs. H.: I don't know. Of course, my contact with so many men in the church makes me think it's part of me too - I mean a ministerial husband who's just as conscious of being significant as part of the whole enterprise of the church, as I ever was in the Navy. I just don't know. I haven't had any experience on whether it's a masculine or feminine trait. But it certainly worked with a lot of girls in the Navy, I'm sure.

Q: I want to ask you a question which may not be easy of answer. I don't know. You were awarded the Distinguished Service Medal for your service to the Navy, to the WAVES, and again you personified all the women in your organization, but in the award citation, it said that you had succeeded nobly in translating experienced-based theories into the total effort of the war. Now, I hope you will discuss that. Experienced-based theories - I assume that these are ideas which you had gleaned from your college experience and which you felt were applicable in this larger enterprise.

Mrs. H.: I think the only kind of things - I had forgotten that phrase entirely - but I had a lot of theories about the way in which women could be persuaded to do their best work. For instance, I kept insisting that barracks should have enough elbow room so that a girl could get off by herself if she wnated to. I kept insisting that it was important for a woman officer to be present when a girl was being disciplined, not in order to protect the girl, but to protect the Navy, because these little girls with their big blue eyes would look at these big, big sailor men and say, "Oh, Sir, I'm so sorry. I didn't mean to," and he would melt. The girls would be getting away with murder and jeopardizing their standing in the service. I looked at girls as human beings and not just as little cuties. I knew out of experience they were as different and as varied as any boys, and that they needed to be held up to certain standards or they would soon run off with the place. I think the experience and the theory of how you deal with women to get them to do their best work would have grown out of experience, and I think perhaps that's what they had in mind.

Q: Well, that's a tremendous contribution because anybody who's had anything to do with women's groups...

Mrs. H.: It is a help to know how women get around doing things, and, for example, we brought in every year to Washington the ranking woman officer in each of the districts and spent a day on conversation and conference with them about the problems that they were facing in getting girls to fit into the picture adequately. Now I don't have any memory, ever, of having thought of that as anything particularly unique because you always have alumnae come back or you have a group of women in a conference or something. But the fact of the matter is that it was something new in the Navy. I mean there - they were bringing people in constantly for conference, of course, but administrative people, just keeping the wheels going. The custom was to tell the boy down the line what was going to happen and the experience of dealing with women made me know that they like to talk about things and are not really very responsive to instruction without full debate...

Q: Without the democratic process.

Mrs. H.: Exactly. This, I think, helped to grease the wheels. Here was the place where Admiral Jacobs and his successor, Admiral Denfeld, were

Mrs. Horton - 44

very, very helpful because they let me do things like this. ~~I mean they - oh~~, I think one of the most astonishing things which they tolerated, really, was ~~that on~~ the whole racial business, I had been in the service for weeks before I knew that the procurement officers were not recruiting any black WAVES, then called Negroes, you remember. And the local Negro people in the Urban League and the NAACP, I suppose.

Q: Yes, that was in existence.

Mrs. H.: They began inquiring about this: why could there not be any women, Negresses, ~~and~~ I couldn't see any reason at all why there couldn't, and began inquiring. Did you ever know Chris Sergeant? Does that ring any bells? You've probably heard of Dr. Sergeant, who was the pastor of St. Bartholomews. *Church in NYC* Well his son, Chris, who has since died, ~~I believe~~, was in the Navy and he was down in the Policy Control Department. He was concerned about this, because he thought it was unfair not to give Negroes a chance. But it was just an adamant, unbroken rule of the Navy that ~~only the people who~~ - that black men would be ~~was~~ cooks and bakers, and it was explained to me carefully that they had plenty of cooks and bakers, so women couldn't replace them ~~and therefore they couldn't~~ - You see we had to replace men in the service - and that didn't satisfy some of the Negroes...

Q: Yes, ~~but that seems to have disappeared~~.

Mrs. H.: I remember that on at least one occasion, we invited a whole group of Negro women to come in and meet with some of the ranking officers in BuPers to discuss this whole business...

Q: Were they leaders in Negro organizations?

Mrs. H.: Yes. And even at the time I realized that this was really a very gracious thing for these men to do because it was something that was not customary, at least, to have civilians coming in to question the policy of the Navy, Yet they sat through a long morning of conversation, undertaking to explain what to many of the Negro people was inexplicable, but it was a very generous and gracious thing of these men to be willing to talk to this bunch of women.

Q: This was at the time, too, when racial questions and agitation really hadn't come to the fore, was it not?

Mrs. H.: No, they were just beginning. Indeed, the first year when this question came up, the Negro women and the Negro people with whom I discussed it were extremely understanding about the whole thing. When Roosevelt was about to be elected for the fourth term, which was two years later, with very little notice, indeed I think it was one Friday afternoon, the Secretary's office called over to my office and said, "The President has ruled that beginning next week, we will admit Negro women." And it was thus suddenly thrust upon us. But just before then, we'd been talking about it a little bit and I had discussed with some of the women who had been most understanding in the first year about what we would do when

Mrs. Horton - 46

we did admit Negro women, which we presumed would happen pretty soon. The question that I was posing was, what shall we do for the training of these girls? Would it be better to have a training school for Negro women in a state university where they would be the only military units, so that it would be military but not conspicuously racial? Or would it be better to put them in a big co-educational university where there were already many Negro students? Or should we take a place like Greensboro College down in North Carolina and have a training school there corresponding to what Smith was up here? I was very much interested because one of the people who had been most helpful and understanding at first, over the telephone said, "I will never give advice which perpetuates segregation, and I simply have nothing to say to you about this." In those two years the thing had moved to that point of - and then she went on. She said, "Our men have been fighting a war for two years, we're fighting for freedom", and I'm not going to play with the segregation idea..."

Q: This was a colored woman?

Mrs. H.: A colored woman in Washington, and she said if you can't take them in as human beings, we're not going to be interested at all. So when the President suddenly decided that this would happen, it was announced quickly that we would accept officers and - we wanted officers particularly to help supervise the women - the Negro women - at Hunter in the basic training school, where there was to be no segregation except that there would be a company of 250 women, and they would have all the privileges of the station, they would eat in the same mess, everything there, which was a simply incredible achievement from the point of view of where we'd been in the Navy. But with the word that this was what was going to happen, the whole thing was boycotted, and we got only two applicants for Negro officers, and one was a graduate of Mt. Holyoke and one was the graduate of Hunter. They came in and were willing to work as secretary or something, and they came to help work with us. The 250 women to be taken into the company at Hunter were way short - I think there were only 25 or something like that - and some of the boys in the Bureau who thought it was a cockeyed idea anyway, promptly said, "Well, goodie, now we've kept - the Secretary said we could have a company and we can't get the company, so we won't have any." And I said, "I think the Secretary said that we would admit Negro women, so I think we'd better ask him what to do about this."

Q: This was Forrestal?

Mrs. H.: This was Forrestal, and - oh, I love this story very much, I tell it quite often. I think both Admirals Jacobs and Denfeld went over with me to ask the Secretary about this, and we told him the story, and he said, "Could we admit those 25 girls without isolating them, putting them into any company they came in?" I said, "I'm sure we can do it because all the officers there - the women officer - have been accustomed to dealing with interracial groups, and would be glad to do it, but," I said, "I think you'll have to give the order because it is so strange to Navy practice, but if you'll give the order, I'm sure it will go all right." He thought for a moment and then he said, "When I was a freshman at Dartmouth, there was a perfectly fine Negro boy in my class. He was a great runner and they all liked him very much. If Dartmouth College can do it, surely the United States Government can manage this." And it worked, just perfectly.

We sent the same Louise Wilde down to see how it was being handled, and we found that somebody had brightly suggested that they would keep all the Negro girls together in one spot and after twenty white girls came in, they'd put in one Negro. Miss Wilde was able to scotch that. The Negro girls simply went in and took their places with everybody else. This was at Hunter. I telephoned down that night to see what had happened and Captain Amsden said, "It has been wonderful, the way it's worked." He said, "The only episode that we remember was when one white girl went down to the 'mate of the deck' in the apartment house and said, 'I think there must be some mistake because I find that my roommate is going to be a Negro girl,' and the officer of the deck said, 'Well, we're in the Navy now, and we're all citizens.' So," Captain Amsden said, "the white girl went upstairs and helped her roommate make her bunk."

Q: She got her orders. Can you give me the background for the President's order.

Mrs. H.: I'm a little cynical about it. I think it was the

Negro vote. The timing was such that it certainly looked as though...

Q: Well, as I remember the history of the development of all this agitation, Frances Perkins had something to do with it originally.

Mrs. H.: This I don't know, but I'm sure there were many people in government who were kind of ashamed ~~of it~~ the way it was being handled. I have always just assumed since it was quoted to me as coming from the President's office rather than just as basic naval policy, I think it entirely good policy and very good judgment.

Q: That's another example of the broadening of the base through the wartime experience.

Mrs. H.: That's right. There's no doubt about that. That moved it very fast then.

Interview No. 2 with Mildred McAfee Horton

at her home in Randolph, New Hampshire

on Tuesday morning, 26 August 1969

By John T. Mason, Jr.

Q: Mrs. Horton, last night when we broke off you had been telling me about the several experienced-based theories which you had put into operation in the WAVES in Washington, and they pertained largely to ways of handling women effectively in groups. Do you have, in reflection, anything else to add to that particular paragraph?

Mrs. H.: Well, I doubt it, except perhaps to comment on the fact that, so far as I was concerned, I wasn't thinking in terms of theory. It was not a case of, you know, feeling this is a policy which we ought to adopt on this situation. It was just practice. It was the experience which led me to do some of these things without theorizing about them, I'm afraid.

Q: That brings up this question - tell me how you went about your job, this new job, this tremendous challenge that came your way.

Mrs. H.: I'm afraid it was rather a case of standing by and seeing what hit me, because the first few weeks in the Bureau of Naval Personnel in the Arlington Annex are a muddle of complete confusion to me. I was tucked away in a little office somewhere, where it seemed to me there was no way of finding out what the whole thing was all about. This was just taking each step at a time, and my first assignment - my first responsibility - was this business of just getting enough women there to start doing something, and what they were to do was as vague to me as it was to all the rest of the Navy at the time. Finally, my memory is that we did get a handful of people who then were my eyes and ears and got around through the Bureau and found where the strategic points were where the problem of adapting women to it was going to be met. I'm afraid it was a very unsystematic kind of thing because everybody was rushing around like mad as the war was expanding, and they didn't have time to brief me on anything much, and I just stayed around and tried to see what was happening which affected women. For instance, one interesting little episode that I recall was that the matter of uniforms was being handled in Admiral Jacobs' office by a young aide to the Admiral. My memory is that I asked him what was happening about uniforms and that he said, "We're having a showing of them this morning," which I had not heard one word about. As I recall it, it was with some reluctance that he said, "you can come and look at them, if you want to." As though I wouldn't want to! When I got there, Mrs. Forrestal was there...

Q: The wife of the Secretary?

Mrs. H.: Yes, and she, you remember, had been working with <u>Vogue</u> magazine and I think we must credit her with having gotten Mainbocher to design these uniforms. But my great contribution to the cause was that when I got there, the design was basically the design which came through, but the stripes were red, white, and blue, and it looked just like a comic opera costume. I struck, I said, "This we cannot do." Furthermore, we had a very pretty, light-blue-colored shirt which was to go with this outfit, and we talked about the fact that it would be much better looking, and people would feel more comfortable in it as a working uniform and not as a show piece, if the braid could be the same color as the shirt. We were told emphatically that there just wasn't enough gold braid in the country, and could never be during the war, to let women wear gold braid, and we said, "ok, we didn't care," discovering later that this was a terrible slap in our face which we didn't even know enough to know was a slap in the face. We didn't mind a bit.

Q: This would be putting you on the same level.

Mrs. H.: Yes. I mean this was too awful. But we liked our uniform very much as it was because it was a handsome-looking thing, and the fact that it did not have the gold braid still meant that it was all synchronized to be a very good-looking color combination. The first shirts which Mainbocher and, with Mrs. Forrestal's help, I'm sure, had designed were handsome blouses, open at the neck, and you wore them over your head. They were simply impossible to iron. Made for the trade, see, where there were little maids around to do your ironing for you. So that very shortly we had to change this handsome thing to be the workable open shirt that you can really get hold of.

This, I think, was rather characteristic of the early stages. Everything had been gotten under way before there were any women around, and it just didn't occur to these people to defer to us, but by just listening around and finding out what was happening we got ourselves into these things, and eventually worked out the technique of the job which really had to be that of a kind of over-all consultation. I spoke, I think last night of the young man from Marshall Fields who came to help re-organize the Personnel Bureau, and I have one vivid memory of one session which he had with the heads of all the departments and, of course, I was the only woman present. Each of them had written out a job analysis for himself. My job analysis consisted entirely of being in touch with these various departments to interpret what was happening there, from the point of view of the women that they were trying to incorporate in it. And when they got all around, with all the Departments represented, Admiral Jacobs asked if there was any comment from anybody about overlapping, and so on. And in all good faith but to the embarrassment of some of them - I hadn't meant to be embarrassing, I said, "My only problem is that I'm supposed to be liaison with all these people, and no one of these men has mentioned having any responsibility for seeing that I get information. How do I get it?" And the Admiral said, "Each of you must write in that you are to keep the Director of the Women's Reserve informed." But this was rather par for the course that it wasn't in the thinking of the naval official to bother

Mrs. Horton #2 - 54

with trying to incorporate women into it.

Q: All this you really had to earn, didn't you? I mean this kind of recognition...

Mrs. H.: You didn't even earn it. You just had to kind of demand it, I guess. Subsequently, and in the last years, it got to be very smooth. It was all understood. The first way how to get hold of a job, as you put it, in those first months was really a trial and error process of just trying to create what the relationships would be. I think there's no doubt that when we first went in, all of us who were there knew we wanted to adapt to the Navy, but supposed that we would be much more responsible than we really finally came to be, we found that it worked very much more effectively to get the other people to do it, rather than to claim it ourselves. Really, as I look back on it, the only things that we really initiated were those things which were the patterns for relationships among the women which would help to get things running smoothly. So that from the point of view of making Navy policy on one thing and another, we really weren't doing it, and we didn't make any claim to do it, and didn't intend to.

Q: And this is where you said your advisory board was really of very little value because they were on the outside.

Mrs. H.: They were magnificent from the point of view of public relations, but they really were even more helpless than we were in determining what was going to happen inside the service.

Mrs. Horton #2 - 55

This was normal, I think.

Q: Was Elizabeth Reynard of any help at this time? She had been in Washington for a year or so.

Mrs. H.: That's right. She was a professor at Barnard, very close to Dean Gildersleeve, who with - I wish I could think of his name, you'll easily find it, the dean, I believe it was of engineering, at Columbia who became the personnel consultant in CNO - in the office of CNO. It will come to me some fine day, but I cannot get his name right now. Elizabeth Reynard was British - by ancestry and she had been in touch with the WRENS and was a professor of English with a poetic and romantic imagination. She had very poor health, but absolute devotion to the Dean and to the project of serving the nation. And she had been in Washington for some time before I got there, and was trying to find a way to do things and so on. She came up one time to see me at Wellesley before I went down, and told me about the way the women were guarding the shores of Great Britain and that we probably ought to look for a lot of people who could ride horseback and ride up and down the coasts and save the Navy from invasion and so on, see. Well, before I ever got there, I knew that this wasn't going to be the kind of thing that women did, but she dramatized the business. I heard her speak one time to a gorup of recruits coming in, and she said, "You'll sometimes wonder why we use this nautical terminology and talk about the wall as a bulkhead, and the stairs as ladders," she said, "There may come a time when you have to be the person who speaks to the Navy man to save his life and you'll have to use his terminology," and so on. She dramatized the thing so that I think she always thought that I was just a very stodgy old creature - administrative type - because I couldn't buy this kind of fervor and drama, shall we say. Her field was English literature and she read widely and she wrote very beautiflly. She had a fine gift of writing, and, personally, my feeling has always been that she was miscast in the role of undertaking to administer this business, but her imagination sparked some very fine things. She developed down in New York at the recruit training school at Hunter a perfectly fabulous program of training. She went to - all the bureaus and the division heads and so on and she got samples of ships and she got up pictures and designs and so on, and had a fascinating museum at Hunter to help these girls get some understanding of what the Navy was all about.

Q: Indoctrination.

Mrs. H.: That's right. Indoctrination. She worked very closely and very effectively with Captain Amsben, the director there, who I think relied much more directly on Miss Gildersleeve as the chairman of this advisory committee than we did nationally, because she was right there on the spot. She adopted the Hunter recruit training school, and

Elizabeth Reynard ~~just~~ gave her life's blood to this business, but she had to be in a particular kind of niche to make it effective, just because she was such an enthusiast and she was impractical in many ways because she simply hadn't ~~this~~ ordinary experience. The girls who came in from business had positive hysteria over the files which she had begun to set up for us; these were women who had applied to come into the Navy and she set up a file drawer which was then found by some of these people who were working on personnel, and the files were catalogued ~~by~~ as "good prospects," "bad prospects," "impossible." Well, you don't - you just don't set up a filing system like this. It was a little confusing. She had been there first and she was the one who stimulated a lot of people about things, and I think she was always a little bit unhappy because we presently did transfer her back to New York where she could do something creative in this reserve school. Because, frankly, I found it very confusing to have her dealing with these administrators who didn't understand her techniques.

Q: This was in essence, then, in dealing with Miss Reynard, and the professionals who came in, this was a contrast between the idealist and the professional, wasn't it?

Mrs. H.: I think, in part, yes. It was also a somewhat temperamental - personalities - difficulty, because I guess maybe it's idealism, but it's also professionalism and amateurism, really, in an administrative situation. But the whole service was very much indebted to her because she really did a stunning

Mrs. Horton #2 - 58

job on this New York recruit school, which became very famous.

Q: Well you, as the chief administrator of the organization, were responsible for bringing in these women from outside who had aptitudes and so forth in placing them in the right spot.

Mrs. H.: We had to look at the people who were doing various things, and my memory is that Grace Cheney, for instance, started in the New York headquarters and we brought her in to Washington. Tova Wiley was recruited out on the West Coast, but was so good that we very soon brought her in to Washington, and several of the other people, I think, came direct. There was a group of about 12 women who were never indoctrinated, who arrived in Washington and, in one way or another, got involved in my office, and then they moved out from various places. I don't really remember where all of them came from. There was one bitter letter which came in the office, as people were writing in to say that they wanted to come in to the service. They had to conform to the technical requirements, of course, of the Navy, and we often had to write back and say that we couldn't accept them. One wrote back in reply to a letter of regret that we couldn't use her, that apparently you either had to be a college classmate of Miss McAfee or an employee of Macy's in order to enter the service.

Q: Quite a contrast, isn't it?

Mrs. H.: Yes, but it really didn't work that way. Much of this

Mrs. Horton #2 - 59

was just plain volunteering of people who said they were ready to work and had a record of effectiveness elsewhere.

Q: They sort of came to the surface.

Mrs. H.: They just sort of surfaced and were tapped for this, that, or the other thing. It was a very unsystematic procedure, but it worked very nicely.

Q: This leads me to a question about the setting up of these training centers, Smith, and Hunter, and some of the others. Would you devote your attention to that for a little while.

Mrs. H.: I remember with great interest the decision to go to Northampton for this training, because the President of Smith had been there only a little while, Mr. Davis, a delightful person, and apparently the Navy had written to the various colleges to ask if any of them would be interested in having a training center for women, and Smith and Vassar replied. Vassar had as its president at the time, President McCracken who had been there for years, and I sat in on the meeting where this was to be discussed and decided. And I was highly entertained because I'd known Pres. McCracken all through my undergraduate days and for years after, and I remember his saying, "Now, we have a ~~great~~ big central dining hall where we serve hundreds of students and we can arrange it so that the Navy can have it at certain hours, but of course our students will have to have priority. We'll have to arrange the timing on this." President Davis, in effect, said to the Navy, "Anything that you want, we'll just be delighted to do."

Mrs. Horton #2 - 60

Finally, I turned to him and said, "President Davis, have you discussed this with any of your administrative officers?" "Oh, no," he said, "but they will be glad to do anything they can for the service." So they went to Smith. It was very fine for the Navy, because really Smith did come through with all this, but I was entertained by the fact that we took the alumnae house from Smith and several dormitories, as I recall it, and, of course, the inn in Northampton was turned over to the Navy. This was not under the auspices of Smith, but it became the big barracks for the Waves, and I think Vassar never really seriously regretted not having this horde of outsiders coming in. This was, as I recall it, a response to the places that were big enough so that it could be done. When the time came finally for a supply corps training center for the men, that was set at Wellesley without my knowledge at all. I just heard it was going to be there, and I inquired around to know what they planned to do. They planned to use buildings in the very center of the campus, to reach which you have to go through the whole campus, at that point I reverted to my type and said, "You may certainly have buildings and we would be glad to have you come, but you can't have those buildings. It's absurd. There are satisfactory buildings right by the main road where you can have your own private life without complicating ours." And they bought that, too. But this was all being done by the whole training division, which was locating training schools all over. When it came to the first recruit schools, one of them was established down in Millidgeville, Georgia. I can't imagine why.

Q: Oh, down in Fred Vinson's home town.

Mrs. H.: ~~I just can't imagine why, and~~ Why there was a naval establishment there was plain only to those who knew whose home town it was. Then we had one out at Cedar Falls early in the day. I don't know quite why that was, but...

Q: Cedar Falls - that was in Iowa?

Mrs. H.: Uh huh, Iowa. Again these were set up, you see, by the training division, of which at that time Arthur Adams was the director. He had been the president of the University of New Hampshire and of the American Council of Education. I think he had been or was going to be - no, he had been, I guess. He's now back at the University of New Hampshire as ~~dean, assistant to the presidet,~~ consultant to the president. We had funny times with the training division because we all talked the same language, except one boy in the training division who came in one day and said, "You know, Miss McAfee, you'll have to learn the difference between training and education." And I said, "What is the difference?" He said, "At Annapolis, everybody has to achieve a minimum of training and experience, and the thing you have to do in teaching them is to get everybody up to that level. If a man can do better than that, that's fine, but this is what you have to have. And," he said, "I suppose in education you try to get everybody to go as far as he can himself go. But that's education, not training." I have never known whether the boy spoke from any

Mrs. Horton #2 - 62

knowledge at all, but this was the explanation given me. So we had a good time with the training division. But the allocation at Hunter was again a shock to President Shuster, I'm sure, because we thought New York would be a good place for this and he had an uptown campus and I think I recall correctly that he was glad to aid the Navy, but he had no intention of giving up the whole uptown Bronx campus but found he had done so by the time they all moved in. And this was a brilliant installation. It really was a beautiful place, which Captain Amundsen directed, but he had very able assistance in Elizabeth Reynard and a host of very able women who went with him and a fine group of men, of course.

Q: Well now, Smith was entirely for officers.

Mrs. H.: Yes. That's right, and it had an extension over at Mt. Holyoke finally. It got too big for Smith, and so we took Mt. Holyoke, too.

Q: Did they acquiesce?

Mrs. H.: Oh, yes, they were very glad to do it. The story that came out of Mt. Holyoke I've used many times because it was a wonderful story. We were marching around in very military fashion to expedite things, because it was quicker to march a group here and there than to have them go at their own pace. Finally the superintendent of buildings and grounds came to the commanding officer s and said, "We're finding that the old buildings here are being threatened by this marching in unison, so will you ask your women to break step when they come into the buildings, lest the foundations be shattered. See what a splendid illustration this is of our united womanhood - I worked it into the ground.

Q: To what extent did you direct and design the kind of training at Smith, or to what extent did the Navy boys...?

Mrs. H.: Oh, the Navy did it entirely. Once the women got there and they were taken on to the faculty, they began to have a voice in what would happen, but the actual course of instruction was entirely planned by Captain Underwood and his cohorts, as I knew it. No, my role up there, as every place else, was to go - every other month I went to their graduation exercises and stayed long enough so that I got acquainted with some of the women and began to pick out the ones that they were picking out as the leaders for future reference, and try to encourage them in what they were going to be doing and so on. But, again, I insist that if I was influential, it was all influence—it was no responsibility.

Q: And the indoctrination course took two months, I take it.

Mrs. H.: Yes, I think that was it - almost two.

Q: And tell me this: with marching and reviews and all that, this implies a very great deal of regimentation, doesn't it?

Mrs. H.: That's right.

Mrs. Horton #2 - 64

Q: And, it seems to me that women don't always take to regimentation...

Mrs. H.: We were all simply astonished at the way they went for it. Of course, the marching, the drilling and things, they loved, for the rhythm of it. There was never any problem about the actual drill. They loved it. They had beautiful drill teams and their flag-bearers and things, you know, this just - the rhythm and the swinging and the drama of that was very satisfactory. Now, as I spoke yesterday of the first group that went up to Northampton, the regimentation for them was overwhelming because they hadn't been warned that this was going to be a regimented...

Q: And they were largely academic.

Mrs. H.: They were academic and they were - experienced or business - unprepared for it. Once they were prepared for it and the next groups knew what they were getting into, I think the discipline of it went with incredible success. We none of us anticipated that women would take to this. On as simple a matter as the uniform, we were all of us really uncertain what would happen to women in uniform. I mean, no choice of what kind of clothes you'd wear. An order went up on a bulletin board - today you will wear such-and-such a thing - we thought it would be perfectly ridiculous. I think all of us got to the place where it was a profound satisfaction, not to have to be bothered with clothes. We felt well dressed, and not to have to think of what you're going to wear was just a fine way to save time and bother.

Q: It brought on a certain amount of freedom, then.

Mrs. H.: Exactly. It was very reassuring, and one of the things which rather disconcerted us was that some of the people who left came back in because they liked the discipline.

(Interruption)

Q: Well, you were talking about the whole subject of regimentation and training at Smith, particularly, for the officer class.

Mrs. H.: I think the experience of the actual training program was one of satisfaction in knowing the proper way to behave under military circumstances. It was good to know if there was going to be a review what the responsibility of the officer was in connection with it, and it was not true that after the training there was this kind of routine regimentation. We all expected some kind of military control. I've never quite forgiven Admiral Jacobs because the first time I asked him a question about what I should do about something he said, "Well, use your judgment." I was appalled because I thought that he was going to take all the responsibility of telling me what to do, though I didn't want him to. I wanted to tell him, but it was normal thereafter for the officers in the shore-bound Navy to have really a remarkable degree of freedom and independence, and I think the regimentation which made them feel that they were part of the Navy and were able to participate in the things that were characteristically and dramatically Navy, was something to which they all got reconciled very quickly. One of the events which will always be riveted in my memory was the time when we had, I think it was something like 25,000 WAVES - I guess not, at this time, I guess it was 2,500 at the time, in Washington, right there, and to celebrate the first anniversary, Frances Rich, who by that time was in my office, had organized a parade at the Washington Monument, where we had all the big brass to speak to these women. I'll never forget the actual effect of this - the scene of it - as we stood at the Monument and saw these women coming from all over the city of Washington, marching, and forming a regular pattern of company marching. Well, this is the kind of thing that made them know they were a part of the Navy, and it was a very dramatic and exciting kind of thing, which you couldn't do if you hadn't been trained to do it. We always enjoyed the story on that occasion of Tova Wiley, who had never been indoctrinated, but being the next ranking officer - I was with the powers that be up in the grandstand, but she had to be the person leading the whole procession. And she didn't know a thing about marching, because she had never gone through this discipline, see. But she was flanked, right behind her, by a group of people who knew her well and knew the whole situation and, I think the story was that, on one occasion, she said by the right flank when it was quite plain that they had to go left, so they just went left and the whole procession following after. We got along very well this way. The prize story on

Mrs. Horton #2 - 67

that was the first group at Northampton, where Captain Underwood had singled out Elizabeth Crandell as the person to be the executive officer of it. She's the one who'd been in charge of the big women's residence at Stanford, and they marched back from the inn up to their quarters two or three times, and suddenly, one day, Capt. Underwood turned to her and said, "Now, you take these women back," and all the boys who were the instructors were waiting up at the inn and saw this, but she'd never conducted a drill in her life. She got them started all right because they'd all lined up before, and they marched up the main street, and there was a car in the way. She knew they had to get around it. She didn't know what the word was for it - the men were out of hearing by that time - and so she just turned round and said, "Ladies, use your judgment," which they did, and they all got around and it looked very fine from a distance. We adapted to situations like this.

Q: What about the non-officer groups at Hunter? Did they take more readily to training and regimentation?

Mrs. H.: No. I think again they were able at Hunter to build up a great sense of pride in the whole enterprise. It was big. It was dramatic in that they saw themselves as part of this great big outfit, and Captain Amundson was a genius on getting people like Madame Chiang Kai-Chek to come and review the troops. I think every two weeks he had some big review of some sort, that they sensed at once the necessity of getting ready to do this kind of thing. I think the first day or two, for most of them, was a perfectly appalling experience when suddenly they lost their identity and became just a member of this squad or that squad, but they very shortly got into the idea that this enhanced their own importance. Moreover, at Hunter, and again at Northampton, everybody recognized the fact that this was a big shift from the ordinary experience of girls and there were women officers around who picked them up when they fell down, they deliberately had a kind of personnel supervision, which was not characteristic of the Navy in general, I think. Though I think probably the Chiefs in the regular Navy did much the same thing for boys. But relatively few dropped out, once they were there they were glad to be there.

Q: These people caught them before they got too...

Mrs. H.: Yes, yes, they kind of kept in touch with the situation. It was broken down into small units, and people from one class would stay over for another class to break in a new company and that kind of thing.

Q: But on the whole, the morale was reasonably high, wasn't it?

Mrs. H.: It seemed to be. I was always conscious of it. Now there were a few spots where it was notoriously bad. I never quite got into it much at Corpus Christi, but that was a great big, sprawling outfit where the women were, as I recall it, in a very small minority and doing rather dull jobs, and it was physically uncomfortable.

Q: With the Air Force, were these?

Mrs. H.: Yes, with the Air Force, but it was physically a bit uncomfortable because they grew so fast they couldn't build them good barracks and that kind of thing. That's the kind of thing where Frances Rich was very good. We'd send her down to a hot spot and she'd talk with the captain and then they'd try to do something for the women.

Q: She shared your philosophy that they should have adequate space and all that.

Mrs. H.: Yes, and she had a very - well, she's a very personable person, as you will see - oh, you're not interviewing her. She had been a starlet out in Hollywood, at one point...

Q: She's the daughter of...

Mrs. H.: Of Irene Rich, and she went to Smith College and came to Smith to be in the Navy. She has a very gracious, very pleasing way with people, and was a great asset to the Navy really in the way in which she'd get on with the brass and make the whole service look appealing to these people, and I finally took her on as a kind of - I didn't rate an aide, but she served as an aide. She went with me on several trips and was extremely helpful in getting all arrangements made and things for me, and was a very good trouble shooter for the Navy's low spots. And then I finally got to spending a good deal of the time going out to all stations, whether there was good or bad morale. One of the things that was extremely

Mrs. Horton #2 - 70

helpful to us was the fact that - there is a chivalry built into this Navy, you see, that "you've got to be nice to those women," and while they were on the station the girls were part of the whole outfit. When I would come they would be - in the first place they'd be very gracious to me personally - but then they would arrange to let the WAVES all get off duty for a while and we'd have a Navy pow-wow and then, of course, we'd have a big dinner which would kind of enhance their stature on the station because they'd get special treatment . I went down one time to Quonset Point here in wherever it was...

Q: Rhode Island.

Mrs. H.: Rhode Island, and my own niece had left college - the only girl I ever advised to leave college - but she was a student at Oberlin and all the men had gone and it was just dull for her. She got very fed up with it, and so she came in as an enlisted woman, and she was stationed at Quonset, and she told me that WAVES - the officers - were not allowed in the women's barracks. I think I spoke to the commanding officer about this and he said, "Yes, we'll have to invite her up to our house and you can see her there." But there was one time I broke ground - I knew it was a rule but that struck me as so silly that I stopped by the WAVE barracks as we went out and on that station there was a great social cleavage between enlisted and officer. It didn't really apply very much at many of the stations. I mean the men officers thought the enlisted women were kind of cute, and they didn't always observe

Mrs. Horton #2 - 71

all these technicalities. Of course, they didn't go to the officers' mess, but - I think the morale was helped by the fact that, by and large, they were given very good treatment on the stations.

Q: But where there were low spots, it was usually equated with the kind of work they were performing?

Mrs. H.: It was partly work, because there was so much dull monotony. There was so much standing by without really enough to do. That was very hard on them, and then sometimes it really wasn't unpleasant work, I mean, they weren't assigned mean, OR difficult jobs, except that often what they were doing seemed to be just meaningless. It was just a routine something in an office or clinic. But the air stations were, by and large, very popular because they were really doing things that they saw were important. They were doing repair of machines or the Link trainers, where they knew that they were really training pilots, and where it was so evidently important jobs, the morale was fine.

Q: Anything that pertains to the air and flying has its own built-in...

Mrs. H.: Satisfaction, yes. The places - every once in a while they'd be assigned to a new station which hadn't yet gotten its recreation facilities, didn't have its swimming pool, didn't have anything to do in leisure hours, see, that got to be a problem. Then they had to make their own entertainment, and they did it with remarkable success obviously.

Mrs. Horton #2 - 72

But it was never very hard to build them up again to the idea that you had to have people standing by in order to be there when the crisis develops. I remember one girl - this was an officer - who was a mathematics major at Wellesley. She joined the service, and I met her in Washington early in the day, and I said, ""how are you getting on?" And she said, "It's perfectly awful. Any moron could do my job." And I immediately replied - this was a phrase that was used very often, and I always replied that you were supposed to do it better than a moron, but she said there was nothing to do better, it was just a dull job, and she said, "I came into the service to use my technical skills as a mathematician." I said, "Well, is it something that has to be done?" And she said, "Oh, yes, somebody has to do it." And I said, "Is there anybody else there to do it?" And she said, "No, but why should I do it?" So, I said, ""Well, because/if it has to be done you're the person to do it. That's the way it gets done." At which she drew herself up and said, "Miss McAfee, I wish you wouldn't be philosophical about my life." which I've always thought was a very good lesson for me. But we did find cases like this where - when it got too desperate, well, they applied for transfer and so on.

Q: Were there cases the opposite side of the coin, so to speak, where they got more or less out of their league? In other words, where a job was basically a male job and yet they had to perform it and it was stretching themselves to do it?

Mrs. H.: I think they didn't use the women that way very much,

Mrs. Horton #2 - 73

except that I remember one that was a physical out-of-their-league situation, which was a story we loved to tell, about two girls going to a naval base some place inland, where they were to replace two boys, who really didn't care about going out to sea very much and they didn't want these girls to take over their job. The girls were assigned to a kind of warehouse, as I envisage it, and they got there just before the lunch hour for the boys, and these great big strapping men said, "look, the job that you've got to do is to get these truck tires stowed away up in that loft," and they knew they couldn't do it. The girls couldn't even lift them. And they went off gleefully, chuckling to themselves, and the girls looked around, and when the men came back the tires were all up there, and they said, "How on earth did you do it?" And one of the girls said, "We rigged a pulley, of course." They just established a leverage, see, and pulled them into the loft and then stowed them. Once in a while we ran into this kind of thing. Rather rarely, I mean they didn't usually ask of them a place where the brain could have sufficed in lieu of the brawn. But you see the demands got big enough so that there were plenty of jobs for them at the point where their skills could operate, and we ran into very little of this. And if it was happening there was a space in the station where it was happening where they could be put in something that they could cope with.

Q: And someone told me, I've forgotten the source, about the girls who were initially assigned to prepare parachutes, to pack them, and so forth. Then, according to the regulations,

Mrs. Horton #2 - 74

they were supposed to go beyond this...

Mrs. H.: Well, no, the story, as I recall this, was that they couldn't pack the parachutes - they couldn't meet the requirements for the parachutes unless they took a ~~directed~~ PARACHUTE jump. That was it, and my memory is that there was some problem about letting women jump. I mean, it wasn't just that the girls hesitated, because many of them thought that would be fun to do, but that there was some regulation that the parachute must be - you must jump it with a man as the weight, you see, that would it...

Q: Oh, yes.

Mrs. H.: ...and so, since they couldn't jump, they weren't allowed to do parachutes, and they were sorry about this. I do remember that. Which reminds me of this weight of a man on the parachutes. We had trouble in one of the naval districts one time. They couldn't fill their quota. They sent some fine girls to the Navy but there weren't enough of them from the proportion that was presumably assigned to that area, and we discovered that some boy in the office had overlooked the directives which had come out and had just gotten the general idea that women must replace the men, and so he had insisted that the women who would be accepted must meet all the physical requirements of the men - height, weight, everything. And they just couldn't find enough women who were of the brawn to do it, so we only had a little handful, but they were Amazons, they were superb looking women. We ran into that kind of thing occasionally, but not very often.

Q: You cited several instances where the Navy Regs were interpreted by newcomers - males - newcomers to the service who were not very flexible in the applications.

Mrs. H.: That's right. And of course naval officers - any good officer - knows when to break the rules. The boys didn't any more than we did, and we were scared of them. One of my first introductions to Navy Regs was by way of teaching - the Navy is literal about such stuff on occasion - because I was never indoctrinated, I had to do what other civilians did coming into the Navy, which was to go through Navy Regs and take the written test, which was not a test of my knowledge because I just had to find the answer in the Regs and write it down. And the girl who administered this to me was a young ensign in the office, her father was a captain in the Navy, a perfectly lovely person, and she was following her instructions, and there came a point at which a regulation had been modified and was on my desk as a correction of the Navy Regs in the book which I was working from, and so when I came to the answer, I wrote the new regulation in. She marked it wrong and she said, "I can't give you any credit on that because it isn't the way it is in the book." Though it had been superseded, you see. I'm afraid I got out of the Navy without ever having finished the whole course, which struck me as rather ludicrous on the whole, but there was a kind of literalness about us all which I think was normal in the situation.

Q: Well, I suppose there has to be a certain rigidity in a structured...

Mrs. H.: Oh, yes, there's no doubt about that.

Q: Military structure. Tell me, were the WAVES given any latitude in choosing the kind of work to which they were assigned?

Mrs. H.: Yes, they were given very interesting vocational tests at Hunter for this, and at Northampton they were allowed to express a preference, and you know, if there wasn't a right vacancy there, they didn't get it. But there was an effort really made to...

Q: There was a conscious effort to match them up to a given job?

Mrs. H.: Very conscious effort. The girls in Washington who was our representative in the office of procurement and placement of officers was the girl who had been handling personnel at Macys, and went back to become a Vice President of Macys eventually, though she's now retired from that. But she knew the value of this kind of placement and with the staff there worked very well to try to assign right personnel to jobs. It didn't, as I say, always work because if when the person got there, there was something more urgent, she got put into it, but I think they all felt that there was an opportunity at least to express their preferences.

Q: Tell me about some of the administrative knots that you

had to untangle as you went along.

Mrs. H.: Oh, dear, I don't really remember specific instances because usually it was a case of trying to find out what was already in the works, and to get a voice in on the thing that was being done. For instance, on this parachute business, on this kind of thing there would be a sudden statement that women could not any longer be assigned to this, and then it was the role of trying to find out what the reason for it was and how to explain it and interpret it, rather than deciding de novo we will not do this kind of thing. I can't remember the countless things - except, for instance, this business of determining what would happen about women who became pregnant in the service. They weren't allowed to become pregnant, but some of them did without our approval, and how to phrase the directives, how to work out the procedures by which this could be conveyed to everybody what to do in a specific case, was the kind of thing that took a lot of time and consultation with the various people that might be affected by it. I remember one episode of hearing that there was rather lax discipline in the big barracks in Washington, and I had no authority over it, you see, there was nothing I could do about it except try to find out what was happening and why.

Q: Potomac River Command?

Mrs. H.: Yes, Potomac River Command. I don't remember who the man who ran it was at all, but I remember going down and saying that I'd like to go to a mast and hear how it was being administered, and being perfectly appalled by the reporting of the episode where an MP had arrested a girl and boy as they had presumably been having intercourse on the front lawn of some place or other in Washington, and the captain kept saying, "Did you actually see this occur?" Then the poor little MP said, "Well, no, I didn't actually see it occur, but it was obvious that's what they were doing." So he said, "Well, then, we can't do anything about this." I went storming back to the Bureau of Personnel and I said, "Look, OK, you couldn't hold her on that but you could certainly hold her on conduct unbecoming an officer." He wasn't doing this, you see. But the way I had to do this was to see it, to hear it in action, and then get somebody topside to do something about it, which they did, and it was straightened out presently, simply because it was beginning to get out of hand through this kind of literalism and unwillingness to involve any maintenance of standards. But this kind of thing was the way we did go about it - had to go about it. I'm trying to think of other instances of specific cases of shaping the policy. We spent three years working at it very hard, but I can't think what they were, nor what we did with it. There were the constant little needling things, getting the new uniforms and getting the - oh, one question for the first six months that we spent hours on, was what does a woman do about saluting? You don't salute in the Navy unless you have your hat on. An officer takes off his hat when he goes in a house, but a lady doesn't. What should she do when the Star Spangled Banner was played? It was this kind of crucial matter in the

World War situation which absorbed our time and attention, but we consoled ourselves as we did all these youngsters down the line that somebody had to do this and we were the ones that had to do it. My memory is that we got very badly involved because a few of the commanding officers ordered that the women take their hats off when they came into the officers' mess, and that solved their problem, but it didn't solve the problem for others because, at other stations, they were allowed to keep them on if they wanted to. There was no hard and fast rule about it. And if their hat was on, then, you saluted, and if it wasn't, you didn't. I remember the anguish which I suffered going into a hotel, up in a roof garden or something, there in Washington for dinner one night, and the Star Spangled Banner was played and I was there with my hat on - what did I do? I don't remember what I did, but the point is that it was a crisis. It was a difficult situation. Another thing of equal import was trying to establish some pattern for discharge for girls, who were under much more pressure than the men were for family responsibilities. It was very interesting to us that - the mother dies, and the father insists that his daughter come home, where he would never dream of calling for his son, you see. Or the father dies and the mother must have help. We established a much more liberal policy of discharge...

Q: Compassionate...

Mrs. H.: Compassionate discharge. Simply because this was again a socially expected thing for girls which was not expected for boys. There were all the problems of - at first, there was the categoric problem - the statement that no woman could be married to a naval officer and be in the service because they weren't going to have this double problem. I think it was Tova Wiley who helped us break that down because she said, "All right, I'll leave the service, but I'm going to get married to Jim," and by that time...

Q: What was her maiden name?

Mrs. H.: Peterson. I think Admiral Jacobs had been out and had met her in California, and when I told him that this was the price we were paying for this severe regulation, he said, "Oh, we don't want to lose her, she's too good a girl," so they modified it, and they would not take - I think I'm right - all the way through, I think we didn't take the wife of a naval officer, who was already married, see, but we did let people get married in the service, but with the understanding that they would not be assigned with each other, that their assignment would have to be regulated by ordinary procedures. They could apply for it and if they could get it, they would. This kind of thing kept cropping up, to determine policy on things like this, and on that kind of issue, they really left it pretty much to us to decide what we'd like to have done about it. But untangling the administrative decisions - I think we probably tangled them more than untangled them, I suspect.

Q: Tell me, in this area of acceptability on the part of the

Mrs. Horton #2 - 81

regular Navy, this was a gradual thing, wasn't it?

Mrs. H.: Oh, very. Yes. There were some people who at the very beginning were glad to have women there and received them happily. There were some, I think, who until the bitter end were unenthusiastic about it. But again it's part of this business of accepting what is ours, that once we were there, we were first to be tolerated, and then to be accepted if qualified. I really think it was the effectiveness of the training of these girls so that they fitted into the military picture adequately, and their past experience out in society, which made them very acceptable sailors...

Q: In other words, there were a few disappointments, I suppose.

Mrs. H.: Oh, unquestionably. There were many disappointments, and we certainly had our discipline problems with the people that got in by mistake, weren't the kind of people we wanted to have around. But, by and large, it was an awfully good group of people and I used to be interested because there were a good many comments made to the effect that it wasn't quite nice for a nice girl to be in the Navy. I mean, you know, a girl in every port for a Navy sailor, and I used to make quite a point when I was talking to a recruiting groups that there was a kind of control over the girl in the Navy which she never had in a factory, for instance. If she was going to go into war work in a factory, she was really on her own, but there were standards of conduct and behavior which were watched for in

Mrs. Horton #2 - 82

the Navy and which she had clearly explained to her and expressed for her. I never had any feeling that a girl was going to be thrown with such bad characters that it was going to hurt her reputation, and I think this is really true that they weeded out the bad actors pretty quickly.

Q: As we agreed last night, I mean you yourself, as a person, and the kind of position you held, were a tremendous factor in establishing this credibility for service in the Navy.

Mrs. H.: Well, I have the feeling that I was a factor in establishing credibility, but that it was an unjustified factor. Really, I mean, it was so diffused through the whole service that with the wrong commanding officer you could get into trouble with any of these situations, but certainly the Navy supported me very thoroughly and consistently in my insistence that coming into the Navy was not going to stop these girls from being feminine and being nice girls, and we weren't going to cheapen the thing to attract numbers. And we never had to do that. We were never really down to the bottom of the barrel, because we never had so many people that we had to take anybody who came. This was a real problem in the Army, where they really wanted so many people so quickly that they were encouraging and recruiting people to get in a lot of people which was much harder to control, than when they came in a few at a time. I remember when the Army - Womens Army Auxiliary Corps was changed into being Women's Army Corps and they came into the full Army, I was present when Oveta Hobby was made a full colonel. She had had simulated

Mrs. Horton #2 - 83

rank - what do they call it - anyway, she acted like a colonel and she dressed like a colonel as an auxiliary, but when they came in - this was after the Navy started - she was made a colonel and I remember General Marshall saying to her on that occasion, "We can use 600,000 women any time you can get them for us." Well, that's an awful lot of women, and it sort of put the pressure on the Army to go out and get lots, and lots, and lots of people, which made a much harder problem for them than the one we had. Because it built up gradually for us and, as I say, I think all together we probably had about 150,000 women who were involved at one point or another - at one time or another - but never more than, I think, 6,000 at one time.

Q: That was the peak, yes. Did you have to get involved with the subject of appropriations, annual appropriations?

Mrs. H.: I remember the day that somebody from the Budget Office came up to me - this was in the first little office and I think I was probably there for two or three months after I went in...

Q: You mean in Arlington?

Mrs. H.: In Arlington, from the budget office in Arlington, and he came up and said, "I think we ought to talk about budget," and I said, "Well, I've been wondering all these days why nobody did talk to me about the budget. Nobody's ever told me anything about how much money there was to spend or what to do about this." and I said, "I suppose that because these women are replacing the men, you're just fitting them into the whole budget, but I have never had any information about the budget at all." At which they kind of threw up their hands and said, "Oh, well, I guess we'd better just handle it," and I never touched it. Never had anything to do with it.

Q: You never had to go before a congressional committee or anything?

Mrs. H.: No. I went before a legislative committee once or twice on some of these changes of regulations, but never on the budget. It was incredible. I mean the kind of question you're asking, you see, indicates a kind of influence which I just never had at all, and which was probably very good for the Navy that I didn't, because I didn't know anything about it. Indeed, I've always been touched by the history of the Navy which I think Samuel Morison wrote - I think he's the one who put somewhere discreetly in this manuscript, "it might have saved the Navy some confusion had the supervision of the admission of women been put in the hands of an experienced naval officer." I'm sure it would've. It's one of the things that makes me very happy that they are continuing a skeleton force because if ever they needed a large number again, there are plenty of women officers now who know what it's all about.

Q: Who've had the thorough indoctrination.

Mrs. H.: This is highly good for the good of the service. But I think it probably would cut out a little bit of the excitement *but* entertainment. I mean, it was interesting because we
and

Mrs. Horton #2 - 85

were all such novices and so stupid about things that it created lots of entertaining situations. We enjoyed it.

Q: Would you talk a little about that area, and the fact that there is an organization in being with regular personnel...

Mrs. H.: In the Navy, not just in...?

Q: Yes, and how you talk today in terms of volunteer services.

Mrs. H.: Yes. But the women officer in the Navy now are regular naval officers, not in reserve. They have all the rights and privileges, as I understand it, and are retired at the same time and same pension. You see, one thing the Navy did from the very beginning which we all appreciated very much was that we all had the same pay and allowances which the men had. I think we never had family allowances of the sort the men had because the presumption was that our husbands should take care of themselves, but the actual pay for the rank was always the same, and the present officers now are not limited even as to rank, I understand that the law has been changed so that there can be admirals in the Navy - women admirals.

Q: There can be?

Mrs. H.: There haven't been, but there can be. Indeed, I read somewhere in the paper the other day that there is some talk of getting a woman general, who would be a general for the Army women's corps. Of course, again, the fact that the women are not in combat and the fact that they are not a

Mrs. Horton #2 - 86

separate unit means that the present successor of the director, which of course is never a Navy term anyway, is now called Assistant Chief of Naval Personnel for Women. But it's hardly comparable to a general who - I mean to an Admiral - who must have some kind of sea duty and all these other things in order to qualify for that rank. So I don't know how long it will be before they break down and have some admirals. But at least it indicates a kind of acceptance which is gratifying to everybody and is, I think, a very good sign for the future if it needs to expand.

Q: Well, would - I mean, if some of these thoughts which are being expressed are ever put into effect, having a completely volunteer service and so forth, in contrast to the conscripted, drafted type...

Mrs. H.: You see, the Navy never did have conscripted people while we were there. It never drew on a draft. I think even for the men, in the actual war time. Isn't that true that they were able to fill their quotas with volunteers?

Q: That I'm not quite sure of. I thought that they levied their quotas on the draft boards...

Mrs. H.: No, they took very small quotas as compared to the Army, for instance, again because they needed fewer numbers, and for some time, at least, they took great satisfaction from the fact that they were - a volunteer service they thought the breath of the draft was driving many people to enlist, rather than be drafted, but that they were coming in voluntarily. Now, it may not even have been true then, but I think - of course, it isn't true now, I guess. But I don't think it would change the basic structure of the Navy if the people who came in were volunteers, because they'd have to have this structure, but just as the women had volunteered during the war, so the men would presumably volunteer and I think they'd still have the place for the women, who can certainly replace fighting manpower at a great many points, as was demonstrated in the war.

Q: Was there ~~ever~~ OVERT resentment at this replacement policy in your time?

Mrs. H.: In a few places the men didn't want to be replaced by women, but the fact of the matter was that the war psychology was such that most men preferred to be out where the action was, and since they were going to be sent anyway they were perfectly willing to let women take over, because they were going to be gone, and they were going to be out of it. I think there were many places where it disturbed them. I think on some of these training programs in the Air Force it was embarrassing to men to be trained by women for these masculine jobs. They tell a story of one flattop, I believe, where the men concealed for a long time the fact that they had had their training at Pensacola where the girls were training them in Link trainers, until it finally leaked out that enough of their good pilots and gunners had been trained, so that they - it reversed itself and they began to be a little select group and to brag about the fact that they'd been trained by these girls down there. But they waited until they were sure there

Mrs. Horton #2 - 88

good

wereplenty of them and that they had ~~the~~ records, then they - it got to be a good story.

Q: How do you account for that attitude prevailing in our culture, when most of the school teacher in the lower echelons are women and men are trained by women in that capacity?

Mrs. H.: Oh, but they were little boys then, and when they grow up they get out of this, I think. Furthermore, the fact of the matter is that it never had been done by women before. This was - it ran the risk of being sissy, if girls - you know how boys grow up. They think it's very sissy to let girls know more about what they're doing than they do themselves. This is par for the course, I think. When they finally accepted them as qualified people and proved that they could overcome this reputation of having been taught by women, then they were proud of it and made a good story out of it.

Q: Well, now, you were perfectly aware of this psychology prevailing. Was there extra effort and care then taken in the assignment of WAVE officers to these particular jobs where they would be training men?

Mrs. H.: Yes. I think the - most of them were people who had more or less won their spurs somewhere and then were picked up to do these things, and they found that they could hold *their own* ~~down~~ satisfactorily. They never, in my day, had command responsibility, so that it wasn't a case of putting them over the men. Well, that's not strictly true. Had it been a case of discipline, they couldn't have taken command, but when it was being the authority in charge of personnel, for instance, they would issue the orders, but the issue was never raised about whether this woman was able to force a man to do her bidding and so on. The command situation didn't develop...

Q: But teaching...

Mrs. H.: But teaching did in fairly widespread areas, but they were apt to be people who were known to the commanding officer, in one capacity or another or recommended by the procurement office because they had a reputation which established them as...

Q: Of proven judgment?

Mrs. H.: Proven judgment, yes. I don't recall episodes of the wrong people getting put into that kind of position, and that was fairly late in the day. Most of the first training was done for the training of the women, and then as they got to be good at it, they'd take on this other thing, or when they ran short of men in a thing like the Link training operation, and the commanding officer would say, "Well, get me some girls and I'll train them to do it," and then it became his project of seeing that it worked all right.

Q: I would think it would have been almost disastrous to have had a failure in a situation like that.

Mrs. H.: Oh, yes, but it would be a situation, you see, in which there, they were enlisted women and the commanding officer would have accepted them and wanted them or they wouldn't have been there. I think it was more the men at the top who helped to control the situation down below than anything consciously done by us to see that they were women who could manage men, that was NOT really in the picture with us and we let their skills speak for them.

Q: We spoke a little last night about the area of public relations, but could you say more about the development of the concept of public relations as it pertained to the WAVES and their acceptance by the nation at large? Was the process handled entirely by regular Navy people, or did the WAVES have their own public relations set-up?

Mrs. H.: I had Louise Wilde in the office who was, from the national point of view - in touch with the national program, and on many of the stations the girl who was the senior woman officer had people working under her. See, she had to supervise the barracks and she would help on the allocation of the WAVES - the assignment of WAVES - to jobs, and would be the person who would work with the local public relations man to publicize the things that WAVES did. And at many of the stations the WAVES published their own newspaper for internal public relations to give newsworthy stuff to the public relations men who might stick to the outside of it. There are a whole series of special issues - special magazines - with somebody editing that who would then be in touch with the public relations man. Now, this grew up again ~~kind of~~ spontaneously when it became evident that if they had large numbers of WAVES, this was a good way for them to identify with each other as people that would be concerned about the same things. And, I think, on every station the WAVE officer in charge managed to do something periodically which would identify the WAVES as a unit, though all within the whole unit. I think there was much more of this internal publicity, which then, through the regular channels, got out to the public, than there was direct publication of - I mean, news distribution from the WAVES themselves.

Q: Well, naturally, if they were publishing papers locally, this would get out. It was in print. But I suppose there was a wealth of talent in newspaper women who could do this kind of thing.

Mrs. H.: That's right. Exactly. And then they got put onto the staffs of the public relations officers in many of the districts, these women who had had experience with it.

Q: Were women used extensively for speaking engagements? Were they involved in the Navy E Program?

Mrs. H.: I think, though not wholesale, by any means, but very frequently when a public relations man discovered that he had somebody who was good in his area, he would call on them. We tried to keep the women really in the relationship of replacing men for a long time. I mean a one for one thing. The Congress was very insistent on this for several months and it established a pattern, really, that you don't put women in to do things which men would not be doing if there were men to do them. We had quite a little trouble, for instance, over the fact that several of the districts wanted to have women's bands and choruses and things, and many of them did it, but it was frowned upon nationally, because these girls hadn't come in to be showmen, they'd come in to do the work that the men would be doing. Men didn't have choruses, they had a band, but this was for military purposes, In New York, for instance, because there was a recruit school there, they had fine bands and marching teams and things, and expanded it because the girls were interested in it. It was a very popular kind of thing, but they were constantly being held in check through the placement officers - that this mustn't be full-time, this must be an auxiliary service, because they were there to carry on the work of the Navy. Well, this meant therefore that, except where there was a public relations project going and a woman could be assigned to that because there weren't enough men to do it, there wasn't much assignment of people to do the thing as women. It was just - there really were real replacements there. Now, this doesn't mean that there weren't a great many women's musical organizations, for instance, or - and, of course, the recruiters - we had a lot of women recruiters doing a lot of speaking around. They were assigned to the office procurement offices as I told you last night, which made a few complications, but they were used very widely and had a good deal of influence on the public relations, but I think it was more in specific connection

Mrs. Horton #2 - 93

with recruiting. The E Program, if I recall it correctly, was much more involved with industrial expansion.

Q: It was an accolade for living up to the contract or exceeding it.

Mrs. H.: That's right, and that wasn't the thing with which our women were directly involved to any great extent.

Q: A little footnote I'd like to add in the nature of a question: were the WAVES called upon to serve in some of the principal army bands?

Mrs. H.: I think you mean the Navy bands.

Q: I mean the N avy bands.

Mrs. H.: Not to my knowledge. I don't know of any instance where they actually played with the men. They had their own bands and they had...

Q: That would have been a development in keeping with the official attitude, wouldn't it?

Mrs. H.: Well, I think so, except that a Navy band is a pretty close-knit outfit I think, and so far as I know there was never any request for this kind of replacement. There may well have been on any one of the stations individual girls doing things individually I didn't know about, but I have no memory of any women in these special Navy outfits.

Mrs. Horton #2 - 94

Q: During our little break, my wife suggested that I ask you about the possible relationship between the WAVES and the lady Marines and the SPARS.

Mrs. H.: Yes. The WAVES got started first, and one of the people who were in this first early class was Dorothy Stratton, who was the dean of women at Purdue, and was trained at Northampton, then went out to be the senior officer in the training program out in Wisconsin, where the women were being trained in radio, and so on. When the Coast Guard decided that it was going to have some women in it, the commanding officer of the Coast Guard came to Admiral Jacobs and asked if we had anybody in the Navy whom he could tap to take over the beginning of that. And Admiral Jacobs asked if we had anybody, and we all agreed that Dorothy Stratton would be a fine person to head it up, and I was charged to go out to Wisconsin and persuade her to transfer from the Navy to the Coast Guard, which I did. We talked together, two former deans of women, and agreed that the women would not only wear the same uniform, they were going to do much the same kind of work and the sensible thing to do would be to train together, just do the whole business, and each of us talked to her commanding officer and they said that's a fine idea and we afterwards put it into effect, and this was one of the most interesting experiences in learning how these things function, because each of us had consent at the top for this venture and it got gummed up hopelessly, primarily because the Coast Guard couldn't pay allowances to people who were under the command of the Navy and not of the Coast Guard. They were **all at** Northampton and they were doing the same kind of things, but the diplomas had to be different, and their assignments had to be different, and after a very few months, or one or two classes as I remember, we simply had to disentangle this mess which two innocent people had gotten the services into without having gone up through the ladder, see. Each of us thought if the commanding officer said all right, that then that was all right to do, but we didn't realize then what we subsequently learned. And, of course, the head of the bureau supposed always, if an officer comes with a suggestion that it has been cleared down the line. We never dreamed of this and they didn't think we'd be that stupid, and so they gave consent without adequate groundwork, and this taught us a very good lesson. I mean, it doesn't pay to get an order at the top in the Navy any more than it does in any other enterprise, unless the thing has cooperation and understanding with people down the line. And the men who got the first orders for the uniforms for the Coast Guard women said, "We haven't seen any uniforms. We haven't anything to indicate that they've been ordered," because they were just women you see at Northampton and they could go about in the same uniform, but then they didn't have the right insignia. It just was complete chaos which everybody worked out very happily and agreeably without any real delay on things, but it was a good lesson about how you don't do things in the Navy. Then came along the Marines, and

Mrs. Horton #2 - 96

we thought this was a fine idea, we'd be glad to do the same kind of thing, lend a girl to the Marines, and I remember the long, long walk which I took from one end of the Arlington Annex way down to the Marine end to talk to the commanding general about this, and volunteered the services of the Navy, and I remember the complete and total gracious, polite rebuff of "the Navy would handle its own affairs, thank you," and they did, and they got-..

Q: The Marines would handle their own affairs -

Mrs. H.: The Marines would, yes. And they got - I don't know how - Mrs Ruth Streeter who was married to a booklover a bibliophile and she herself a magnificent club woman and a competent - She was born to be a Marine. She looked like a Marine in its most handsome uniform and was just the perfect person for them to find. Thereafter, we were all very friendly and amiable, but we had no official connections with each other.

Q: Rightly or wrongly, I think in the eyes of the general public, the lady Marine was of a lesser quality than the WAVE.

Mrs. H.: Of course, the lady Marines had what I think was a real disadvantage in the fact that their uniforms were so masculine, you know. It was just a regular good Marine outfit...

Q: But not making allowance for the female form.

Mrs. H.: Right. When a person like Ruth Streeter who has a

beautiful carriage and a magnificent bearing could carry it off in great style, but I think the fact that they came kind of late into the picture and were dressed more like Marines than like women may have created part of this impression, but the ones that I have known have been perfectly stunning people, lovely people, and one of their directors was in the same kind of activity that our were coming into from the academic world and so on, and were fine people. I always was very fond of them, but I think their enlisted women had a somewhat rougher time. The very fact of being trained in Marine training, which we all had stories about, made it rougher. I don't think they did the physical business of invading beaches and things, but the Navy, see, is a kind of <u>clean</u> service because it's out on a nice ship on the blue ocean, and you don't know what's going on behind the scenes. After the war war over and I had this trip to Japan on an education mission, we were housed on the way out in an army barracks which I think had been occupied by army officers - it had been closed for a while and was cheerless and cold out in California at that time, so that it's not a fair picture, but it confirmed the impression that I had that the army operates on a principle that you've got to keep your people hardened up for whatever emergency may exist, and therefore I'm sure you don't - I mean in their own barracks - you don't create much comfort for them - because you've got to be ready for the time of real discomfort. The Navy's principle which was also explained to me, was that on shipboard there is great congestion and very crowded quarters, imminent danger periodically, a lot of boredom, a lot of things that are uncomfortable, and that therefore when a man is back ashore, they compensate for this by trying to give him adequate elbow room and space. I got out to Guam, found that the army had to borrow, or scrounge paint from the Navy in order to paint up its buildings. It mattered to the Navy that its stations should be neat and trim, but it didn't matter to the army except that some army men wanted it to be this way, and they couldn't get requisitions for it - for beautifying the place, see. Well, this distinction and I really think the Marines par excellence are in the same category with the army on hardness, see, I think built up a reputation which certainly can be exaggerated if you generalize it too much, but there is a subtle distinction there I really think. So, from the point of view of the first women in the army, the idea they were going into the army and going to be hard-boiled about this was easier to build up than the principle in the Navy, where after all, they were going to go on being women and the Navy traditionally is gallant to the women and so on. And I think we all profited by that very much.

Q: Did the lady Marines soon get the duty of serving beyond the continental confines?

Mrs. H.: I think not before ours. We were all under the same law, the Navy, Coast Guard, and Marines were all together in wartime, and I don't think they got overseas any sooner than we did. Oh, I think if they'd done that I surely would have heard it because we would have been so mad about that. That was one of the things I had to work very hard on because the girls were simply infuriated about the fact that they were discriminated against by not being allowed to go overseas.

Q: And what was the stumbling block largely?

Mrs. H.: I shall always think it was the southern gentlemen in the naval affairs committee, and Senator Walsh was no help on it either, because they were protecting womanhood between them for various motives. But, as I said yesterday, the Navy really didn't want to be bothered with them. On shore you could control the situation, but in the actual fighting situation or on the front - or near the front - they preferred to keep this principle, the woman being a softening influence rather than adapting to a messy situation.

Q: But as it's worked out, I mean, there's no reason for regret, is there?

Mrs. H.: No, because now they do go. They can go to an interesting post anywhere they want.

Q: I mean they haven't disappointed anybody.

Mrs. H.: That's so. I think they've done very well in situations, and I think during the war it was more a case of disappointment because other women were going to these spots that were interesting and different, and they wanted to go, too. But when Hawaii opened up that helped a lot. We had fine times in Hawaii. And very shortly after the war they were allowed to go out to England and various places, and I believe now there are some actually on shipboard. There are some women on the transports I think, paymasters and things like that, and I'm sure hospital corpsmen doing some of that.

Q: This change didn't actually come about during your regime?

Mrs. H.: No.

Q: I suspect that maybe you had something to do with it. What I'm referring to now is the legislation in '46 - in the middle of '46 - which incorporated the WAVES as a part of the permanent Navy. Did you have anything to do with the discussions on that?

Mrs. H.: No, I really didn't.. I think it was for that reason that they asked me not to resign until '46, though I had been on inactive duty since the summer of '45, because they thought there might be reason for my taking part in the discussion, but there wasn't any, and I didn't go back to do anything about it. But I think we all of us talked for a long time about the fact that it would be a waste of motion not to maintain some nucleus of the service. And it was for some time a very small nucleus, I think, 5,000 enlisted women and 1,000 women officers, or something like that. We used to struggle to keep from equating, or balancing, officers and enlisted

Mrs. Horton #2 - 101

women because if we were going into the service individually, it didn't matter whether the officers were related to the number of enlisted women, and we didn't want to get the public thinking, or anybody else thinking, that it was only because we had enlisted women that we had women officers. We did use some of these officers and they were the only people who didn't replace men originally. People like myself and the woman officer who was in charge of barracks obviously were there because there were women there, and this was recognized as a necessary little administrative group, but normally the number of enlisted women didn't have anything to do with the use of the women on the station.

Q: Did you try to maintain a balance between - proportion - between the number of officers and the number of enlisted women?

Mrs. H.: No, that's just the point. We didn't try to because we wanted the women to be replacing the men in whatever job they could do...

Q: What did it work out to?

Mrs. H.: It worked usually to be about, I think it was about one to five, or something like that.

Q: How does that stack up with the Navy - the men?

Mrs. H.: I honestly don't know. I don't remember what it was during the war and I don't think it ever got higher than what the men's proportion would be simply because the men officers

Mrs. Horton #2 - 102

had the possibility of double duty at sea and on shore, which meant that there weren't many opportunities - there weren't as many opportunities for women to replace officers as there were for the enlisted women to replace boys, I think. I really don't know the answer to that question. You'd have to get that from some other source.

Q: When you had discussions on women sering beyond the continental confines of the United States, was there ever any suggestion that women serve on board ship?

Mrs. H.: Virtually none, because the tradition of the Navy that women were dangerous on ships. The only time that I got aboard was when the Missouri was being commissioned, on one of its trial runs, and the only reason I got aboard was that they invited the naval affairs committees and that included Manpower ~~Robert~~ Smith, and she was going to go there ought to be some other woman and I was the one to go, ~~and~~ I've always felt interested in the fact that we were at sea just two hours, as I recall it, but during that time there was a misfiring of one of the guns and one of the men was killed, which they were nice enough not to say was because we were aboard, but I mean, this kind of legend grows about how the dangers...

Q: Superstition.

Mrs. H.: Yes, superstition about women on board ship. That has - -as I say that has now been waived for certain appointments. I get a letter occasionally from the office of the director

– of the Assistant Chief of Naval Personnel – and they cite occasionally the interesting new appointments and things, and I'm quite sure that I read there that there were some women doing this. But I think they were on transport ships, rather than on battleships.

Q: Well, actually, you BROKE ~~brought~~ the tradition, didn't you?

Mrs. H.: Well, I don't know that I did this first, but – and there were every once in a while tours abroad which the girls could go on, but nobody was assigned to a ship. I think that was in the legislation, too. I should assume that this would be the last thing that would ever go on any kind of a battleship, and that seems to me wise. I don't see any particular reason for involving women in a situation where the tradition of "women first" and so on gets involved with the actual belligerence of the thing. I don't see any reason why women should be required to complicate the lives of men when fighting a battle if the men don't want them there, and I should think they wouldn't.

Q: If it had been possible, I imagine...

Mrs. H.: Oh, a lot of women would have been glad to go.

Q: ...the women would have been anxious to go.

Mrs. H.: Uh-huh, I'm sure. I'm very definitely of the opinion that the war experience demonstrated that there are a great many things in the military service which women can do, and tht it is unreasonable to draft men until you run out of manpower, and then begin to use women, that it would be much better as general policy, within the limits that are reasonable for the simplicity of operation of the service, to include women in the draft, and exclude the men who are involved in family responsibilities and a lot of the things that go along with them. I recall ex-President Hoover being quoted, whether accurately or not, I don't know, as saying that he favored the use of men until the supply ran out, and then it was appropriate to draft women. I think that's just a silly waste of power, because some of the women are more capable than the last man you could draft, and it seems to me it would be much smarter to draw from the power that's there for the girl who can sit in an office and do a job without complicating the civilian life. My first preference would be not to have the draft, but if you are going to have a draft, I think the women ought to be in it.

Q: Have you expressed this idea to the powers that be?

Mrs. H.: Yes. I not only expressed it to, I think, Secretary Forrestal, I remember speaking at a meeting in New York which was an alumnae meeting I think of Radcliffe, they asked me to speak and I made this comment, more or less parenthetically, and received the most scurrilous anonymous letters which I've every received from people, obviously women, I mean who identified themselves as women, who considered...these anonymous letters implied that, somehow, equating women with men in a military draft was to demean women past the point of no return, and that if I really had any respect for women I wouldn't want them to be doing this dirty work of war, which I don't want anybody to do. That was one of my basic principles all the way through - never to ask for the women things that wouldn't be good for the men to have, but we could get them for the women sometimes. As for instance, the barracks, I noticed, we built with a little more space and with laundry facilities, and when the women were through with them the men used them very happily. I mean, they were not inappropriate for the men but they were the kind of thing you couldn't do instantly for everybody, but if you could do them it would be an entering wedge. And, on this same principle, if somebody's going to be doing this dirty work, it might just as well be some of the women who can do it just as well as the men. Some of the women were simply, as I say, scurrilous in their insistence that it was inexcusable to suggest that women should be going into this kind of thing. My personal feeling is that the experience of women in the war, as I saw it in action, was that they could keep on being just as fine in the war as they were out of the war, and they were not subjected to the kind of ghastly thing which is involved in actual battle conditions.

Q: Is there any difference, any noticeable difference, in the type of WAVE personnel today - I was about to say in a time of peace - as contrasted with World War II, when they came in on a wave of patriotism?

Mrs. H.: I really am not closely enough in touch with that to know. Now Rita Lenihan was in both then and now and could tell you much more about that. I went down a few years ago

Mrs. Horton #2 - 106

to one of the graduations at Bainbridge ~~or some place like that~~ and got the impression that it was a little harder now to attract people, there wasn't the same impetus to get into the service, obviously, that there was, but that when they came in they responded in the same kind of fashion. That particular experience was awfully interesting, too, because they had the graduation, then they had parents there and the pride of the parents in these girls and, I think it's fair to say, the contrast between the girl who'd gone through this and the less sophisticated parent was a very interesting thing, because the Navy had grown the girl up to a sense of responsibility and so on, which was hardly to have been expected out of the simple backgrounds that were at least represented on that occasion. I think therefore that, while it may be harder to get girls in, that they're still maintaining a very real feeling of patriotic obligation. I think they're doing much more now about guaranteeing the training along particular lines than we could do during the war. People could express themselves as wanting something, but if there wasn't a vacancy there they couldn't get it. Now I think they're allowing people to apply and to come in if they can be trained, rather than being required to come in and take what they get. So that they're adapting their recruiting, as I understand it, to interesting the kind of people that they need to have.

Q: I suppose now, as you point out, the benefits and emoluments of the service ...

Mrs. H.: Yes, of course they're getting increasingly good

emoluments and benefits.

Q: You wouldn't expect now, in more or less normal times, that professional women - professionally trained - would want to...

Mrs. H.: They certainly wouldn't go in blind. They'd go in to render their professional services if needed to, but all that I have seen or heard is that they are continuing to maintain a very good standard of quality of the people, by which I really mean just good, responsible human beings who are willing to take on a job.

Q: Mrs. Horton, would you tell me about your relationships with the - Admiral Nimitz during the war?

Mrs. H.: During the war, they were really very slight. I mean he was fighting a war, you remember, and I was fighting the battle of Washington.

Q: Yes, he was out in the Pacific.

Mrs. H.: He was out in the Pacific, and there was no reason why he would pay much attention to what was going on in this little tiny part of the service. After the war was over and he was living in California, he was virtually a patron saint for the women out there on the West Coast in any of their celebrations or anything. One of the phenomena of this experience which will never cease to amaze me is the continuing activity of these WAVES. They had a 25th anniversary reunion last year in San Diego. To my great embarrassment, they invited me to come out and I said I couldn't come out but I would send them

Mrs. Horton #2 - 108

a message for the party. At about the same time there was a reunion - in Boston. I wrote to that group quickly. As soon as I sent the letter to Boston I sat down to draft a message to San Diego and found to my horror that the celebration was over before I got the message out. They had celebrated before the 31st of July, which was the date of the anniversary. But I had several reports from them. There were literally thousands of women who went back to this celebration, the 25th anniversary, and they had a very big time, with several after parties. Frances Rich had a whole group of them go out to her beautiful place out in California, and I heard great things about it. The point of this digression is that, without any official structure like an alumnae association, which you have in a college, these women had some experience in the course of their service which attracted them. I've been to two or three of the reunions tho' I missed the big one. There's a camaraderie about it which prevails wherever you run into somebody who'd been in the service. At these occasions in California Admiral Nimitz was always one of the most popular figures that was ever around. He had a kind of paternal - grandpaternal, almost - relationship to these girls. I was out in California I think on a fifth or tenth reunion, or something like that, and he came to the cocktail party, and he came to the dinner, and he was benign in his appreciation of services that he had never seen rendered. He wasn't around where they were being rendered, but he interpreted what he had heard in the most favorable and delightful fashion. I think once with Admiral Jacobs' consent, I maybe wrote to him to ask if we couldn't send WAVES overseas - out in the Pacific somewhere. My memory is of a reply which indicated that he really couldn't prevent this - but it was couched in gracious terms, instead of strict Navy-ese, you know. I used to use him a little bit as an illustration with enlisted WAVES, tell them that they had a responsibility for the Navy that even Admiral Nimitz didn't have, because whatever Admiral Nimitz did, people credited it to Admiral Nimitz, but if a WAVE misbehaved on the street or was slovenlyly dressed or anything, nobody knew who she was, but it was the Navy doing it when she did it, whereas Admiral Nimitz was himself. This was a little unfair to Admiral Nimitz, perhaps, but it made quite a good point because it is true that he was the Navy, but they were, too, and that helped them to feel quite impressed with themselves, I hope. Anyway, they did behave very well, most of them.

Q: You had a particular relationship with Randall Jacobs. Tell me about him.

Mrs. H.: Well, he was a Pennsylvania Dutchman, just as stubborn as they make them, and he was a perfectly delightful friend. I've always regretted the fact that I sent him a Christmas card a year ago and it came back "deceased." I

Mrs. Horton #2 - 110

think it was last Christmas - and that I didn't realize at the time that he was failing or in danger of dying. He had an 80th birthday down in Danville, Virginia, and they asked me if I would write something about the celebration, which the whole town, apparently, turned out to give to their star citizen. And I wrote - well, again, it got there late apparently - but anyway they sent me a copy of the paper in which they printed my letter because it came in too late for the celebration. In that letter, I said that the way he ran things was just absolutely incomprehensible and fantastic until I discovered that this was just the way the Navy did things, and that the Admiral was just a very good Navy man, but that he was a never-ending friend of the WAVES. He adopted us as a special project, in addition to having to get this vast increase in numbers in the service at the beginning of the war. He was a bluff kind of person. He liked to think of himself, I think, as quite a tough old sea dog, and if anything happened which he didn't like about something, he'd say, "I'm just going to give him the silent treatment, and he'll get the idea pretty soon." But he was extremely friendly. He was the kind of naval officer who was bluff and gruff and very firm and so on, and yet the first Christmas that I was in Washington he asked me to his home for Christmas dinner, and there he was just a delightful family man with his wife and daughter, and a sister who had been at Wellesley and we had a fine connection there. He suddenly revealed the friendly, amiable side of his nature which I think he tried to conceal in the office, so that he'd be the tough sea dog. The Navy was his life and his great passion. I used to think he was extremely slow on accomplishing things which I though he could do overnight if he just signed his name to something. Then I learned through this thing like the Coast Guard business that even an admiral can't do it if he hasn't paved the way for it. I became very fond of him. He finally got out to sea duty which he wanted very much. Then Admiral Denfeld took over and I had great respect for him too. He was a very fine person. I found him a little bit less frustrating because by that time I'd learned how you do things in the Navy, but in my frustration with Admiral Jacobs, I yet felt that he was always on our side and was trying to accomplish the thing that would be best for the welfare of the women as well as for the Navy. He supported us at every point. One of my more embarrassing moments I recall in connection with that big anniversary celebration at the Washington Monument: he had said and I had completely approved it that we'd save "Ruffles and Flourishes" for Secretary Knox, who was going to come. But when Admiral Jacobs came along I just thought he looked so friendly coming walking across the area and he had done so much for us that I turned to the bandmaster and I said, "Why don't you - let's give him "Ruffles," too." But he didn't get my signal and he thought it was the Secretary, so we gave him the Secretary's "Ruffles," which greatly embarrassed the Admiral, all because I thought he was so nice it was too bad not to recognize him.

Mrs. Horton #2 - 112

I gummed things up like this in the Navy periodically, but was always very grateful because they forgave me. I think I must tell you before I stop one of my nicer stories about Admiral King.

Q: Oh, yes, I want to ask about him.

Mrs. H.: With whom I had no dealings, really, but he was always very gracious and very nice. The first Christmas after we got under way, we then had about 500 WAVES in Washington and of course all the uniforms were spanking new and they were just all out of school and were just darling-looking young things. We decided we would have a brunch at the Statler Hotel and we dedicated - we opened - the Presidential Dining Room, or whatever it was, for this brunch, and we invited all the Commanding Officers to which any girl was assigned. I tell the story somewhat to the embarrassment, I think, of some of my good friends, but all the top brass accepted, and the boys down the line who were the immediate commanding officers were not so sure about this and didn't come. But we had literally the Chief of Naval Operations, the Secretary, I think was there, and admirals galore, and we got the captain whose daughter was in my office, who was in the CNO's office, too, to work out the protocol, how they would all be seated and so on, very proper and very nautical. We had a girl who had just been recruited and trained at Northampton who was to be the person who arranged the seating, and just about as we were ready begin, in came an admiral with five stripes. There was one - and only one - in the service. And Betty went up to him, fresh-caught from Northampton, and said, "Good morning, Sir. If you'll tell me your name, I'll tell you where to sit." He said, "The name is King." We told him where to sit. But I've always thought that typical. I think he might have chewed out a boy who did this, but Betty was so nice and so innocent and so polite. They always forgave us for little breaks.

Q: He was another who was apparently very gruff in the office, but had a personal side to him.

Mrs. H.: Yes. There was one occasion when the congress was going to have a joint session on the progress of the war, and General Marshall and Admiral King were going to speak. They telephoned over and asked if we'd supply some ushers, and I quickly evolved the idea that it would be wholly inappropriate just to send a lot of ushers over without somebody to supervise the ushers, and I would be there to supervise them, to see that they did well, which got me in, because I wanted to go and hear these two gentlemen. I was fascinated -- Admiral King spoke from notes, maybe even manuscript, said very little, made it very plain that he was telling them all that he could reasonably afford to tell because of the secrecy of the operation. General Marshall got up, with no manuscript, no notes, spoke as though every secret were being revealed, and didn't say a thing that Admiral King hadn't been saying, but created the impression "now, you're in my confidence, and I'll just tell you about these things." It was ~~simply~~ thrilling because these two men, each of them doing the same kind of thing and involved in the same kind of security problems and so on, used entirely different devices, and General Marshall ~~just got away with murder, because he~~ didn't reveal a single secret, but he involved everybody and made them feel generous about this. And Admiral King froze everybody out. He knew so many things he wasn't telling, you know. But it was a delightful experience to watch the two men in operation, and I had great respect for both of them, of course.

Q: Did you have a relationship with FDR?

Mrs. H.: Virtually none. There was one occasion when Mrs. Roosevelt invited the heads of the four services to come and have tea with him, and meet him, and talk with him, but my father had just died and I was down in North Carolina with my mother and I couldn't get off to do this. Compassionate leave, as we said, it was for me. So I missed that opportunity. I went to his fourth inaugural and was shocked by his...

Q: In the White House?

Mrs. H.: It was out on the lawn. We stood on the lawn and he was up on the balcony. Tragic. He was such a sick man then, but I had no direct contact with him at all. But he was, of course, the dominating figure in the whole picture, so that we were all conscious of him on all occasions, but Mrs. Roosevelt was very gracious to all of us. She summoned me one time to come over for tea, and she'd said just been over to England, as I knew she had, with Ovita Culp Hobby to see how they were running the things for women over there. And she said, "I think you ought to go to England and see what they're doing about the WRENS," and I said, "I think I ought to, too, Mrs. Roosevelt, but I am now a commissioned officer and I can't leave the country without orders, and the Congress has said that I may not be sent overseas. So, I'm frustrated. I can't get there." She said, "I think that's absurd." And I said, I did, too, but I couldn't very well say so. And she said, "Well, I can say so and I do." Very friendly and very nice.

Well now, I'm afraid that I really ought to start being domestic if you need to get off on that 12.30 hour. I wish you didn't have to go.

Q: You've been very gracious, very wonderful actually.

Mrs. H.: Well, I've been having a good time reminiscing.

Index to Interview with
MILDRED McAFEE

Advisory Committee, 30, 31, 32, 33, 54.

Amsden, Capt. William F., 48, 56-57.

Crandall, Elizabeth, 67.

Dacowits, 32.

Denfeld, Admiral Louis, 43-44, 47, 111.

Forrestal, Secretary James, 47.

Gildersleeve, Dean Virginia, 4, 7.

Hartenstein, Paul B., 4, 15, 22.

Hobby, Ovita Culp Col., 32-33, 82.

Hoffeneffer, Mrs. (Wellesley Trustee), 34-35.

Jacobs, Admiral Randall, 2, 8, 13-14, 17, 43-44, 47, 80, 94, 109-111.

King, Fleet Admiral E. J., 112-114.

Knox, Col. Frank, p. 34.

Lenihan, Rita, 105.

Marines, Lady, 95-98.

Marshall, Gen. George C. 113-114.

McAfee, Mildred (Mrs. Douglas Horton), Initial approach for Waves, 3, 6; Trustees raise question of rank, 7-8; Relations with Congress, 12-13; Permission given for leave from Wellesley, 17-18; Problems of Rank, 15.; Discussion of Authority she brought to situation, 15; Induction Ceremony, 20; Views on Women and the Draft, 104; Method of leadership, 29-30; Wellesley interim arrangements, 34-35; Experienced based theories applied, 41-42;

How she approached the task in the Waves, 50-53; Location of training schools, 59-62; rank discrimination, 70.

Navy Public Relations, 27, 90-91.

Nimitz, Fleet Admiral C. W., 11, 107-109.

Reynard, Elizabeth, 4, 55-58.

Rich, Miss Frances, 66,,69.

Roosevelt, President F. D., 45, 114-115.

Rosenberg, Anna (Mrs. Paul Hoffman), 32.

Sergeant, Chris, 44.

Smith, Senator Margaret Chase, 102.

Stratton, Dorothy, 94.

Streeter, Mrs. Ruth, 96.

Towers, Admiral Jack, 13, 14.

Underwood, Capt. Herbert W., USN (Ret.), 67.

Vinson, Carl, the Hon., 10.

Walsh, Senator D. I., 10, 13.

WAVES, Law authorizing, 10-11; black stockings, 2-3; origin of title, 18-19; procurement procedures, 21-23; incentive for enlistment, 24; racial matters, 44-49; uniforms, 51-52; training, Hunter College, 56-57; training at Smith College, 59, 63; First Anniversary in Washington, 66; morale vs work assignments, 71-75; Navy Regs, their application, 75; vocational tests, 76; acceptance by regular officers, 81-82, 87-90; budgetary problems, 83-84; Waves vs Spars, Marines, 94-99; Overseas discrimination, 99; permanent organization, 100-101; 25th anniversary, 108.

Wilde, Louise, 25, 48, 90.

Wiley, Tova (Peterson), 66, 80.

Women, Wartime Service, 35-37; value - postwar experience, 37-41.

WRENS, 2.

Yeomanettes, 2.

Recollections

of

Captain Jean Palmer

U.S.N.R. (Retired)

U. S. Naval Institute
Annapolis, Maryland
1971

Preface

This manuscript is the result of a tape recorded interview with Captain Jean Palmer, USNR (Ret.) at her home in New York City on May 19, 1969. The interview was conducted by John T. Mason, Jr., for the Oral History Office in the U. S. Naval Institute.

Only minor corrections and emendations have been made by Captain Palmer to the manuscript. The reader is asked to bear in mind, therefore, that he is reading a transcript of the spoken word rather than the written word.

DECLARATION OF TRUST

The undersigned does hereby appoint and designate as her Trustee herein, the Secretary-Treasurer and Publisher of the United States Naval Institute to perform and discharge the following duties, powers, and privileges in connection with the possession and use of a certain taped interview between the undersigned and the Oral History Department of the United States Naval Institute.

(1) As an Open transcript. It may be read (or the tape audited) by qualified researchers upon presentation of proper credentials as determined by the Trustee.

(2) It is expressly understood that in giving this authorization, I am in no way precluded from placing such restrictions as I may desire upon use of the interview at any time during my lifetime, nor does this authorization in any way affect my rights to the copyright of any literary expressions that may be contained in the interview.

Witness my hand and seal this 3rd day of July 1969:

[signature]

I hereby accept and consent to the foregoing Declaration of Trust and the powers therein conferred upon me as Trustee:

[signature]
Secretary-Treasurer and Publisher

Interview # 1

Jean Palmer, Captain, USNR
Director of the WAVES　　　　　　　　by John T. Mason, Jr.
New York City　　　　　　　　　　　　May 19, 1969

Mr. Mason: Miss Palmer, it's a delight to be with you this morning. I have looked forward to this with real interest. I wonder if you'd tell me something about your background.

Miss Palmer: I was born in Omaha, Nebraska. Actually I'm an honorary member of the Nebraskan navy, which I gather is a political appointment. I have a great big seal which was done for me by a navy man who - he and I raced in the navy for promotion. He couldn't bear to be beaten by a woman, and he was in the Jag's office. He's a very famous lawyer. When I was promoted to Captain he said, he wouldn't make Captain in the Jag's office and he reitred. But he's the one who got me this citation - I guess it's a political thing.

I was born in Omaha, Nebraska and went to public school there for the first eight grades. I had the distinction of being graduated a little too young because the school was blown down by a tornado at one instance, and it took them a half a year to rebuild it.

So both my brother and I happened to be in the upper half of the class and when the new school was ready they took the upper half of the class and promoted us. Which meant we both graduated a half a year ahead than when we should have been, and then the problem of what to do. I was sent to St. Timothy's School in Catonsville, Maryland.

Mr. Mason: Really?

Miss Palmer: Indeed. My mother wanted me very much to go to college and she canvassed all of the eastern girls' schools to see which prepared for college, and that was why she choose St. Timothy's. In order to graduate at that time you had to pass Bryn Mawr examinations. At that time the college boards were given in the summer. And if you live in Nebraska you don't want to hang around waiting for them. Whereas if you graduate from St. Timothy's you had to pass the Bryn Mawr examinations and they were given earlier. Bryn Mawr always has to be a little bit different. In any event I happened to go there, and I did go to Bryn Mawr afterwards.

Then from Bryn Mawr I went back to Omaha. I took a secretarial course which lasted a full year. It was the college course they give in business schools now.

My basic motivation was, I regret to state, that I've always been crazy about riding horses. I wanted a horse, and I won one on a bet.

This man that I knew, who was no relation, but my uncle's brother - that kind of thing - said that if I could ride his horse I could have it. My mother said you don't accept horses from men. So I had to pay him a dollar for the horse. But the box stall cost a hundred dollars a month.

So when I finished secretarial school I got a job in a bank and earned a hundred dollars a month, which went for the box stall. I used my brother's car to get there.

Mr. Mason: Just the upkeep of the horse.

Miss Palmer: Exactly. My motivation, I'm sure, is the highest in which I entered the business world.

Subsequent to that, this was before air conditioning - you see some time ago - it was very warm in Omaha in the summer, as much as $110°$ in the shade. I was in the municipal bond department of a bank with offices in the cellar, and I found it quite warm.

Having been to school and college in the east I had all these friends here. Finally I saw this advertisement in the Junior League Magazine, and I belonged to the Junior League at that time. They were looking for somebody to be business manager, and you had two months vacation in summer.

Well you see again my motivation again was of the highest. I didn't care to work in 110° in the shade, and I didn't know what it was in New York. I thought that this would be a better thing.

Mr. Mason: And this was New York?

Miss Palmer: Oh yes, it was in New York. This was in the Association of Junior Leagues of America, which at that time was opening a brand new office in the Barbizon Hotel, right down the street here. So I set forth and lived at the Bryn Mawr Club which was then right around the corner.

I had this job in the Association of Junior Leagues of America. One of my close Bryn Mawr friends was the executive secretary, and I became the business manager. I remained there, after they moved to the Waldorf Astoria and took on a couple of floors of bedrooms. As business manager I had to cope with the renting of the rooms, and the publishing of the magazine, and personnel problems, and practically everything. I remained there for fourteen years.

All along the way – I think one of the major influences in my life was through Bryn Mawr and my friends. One of the friends had this beautiful ranch in Wyoming. She asked her Bryn Mawr friends who liked to ride to come out there in the summer. She asked me for two weeks.

Mr. Mason: During that two months vacation?

Miss Palmer: Exactly. I was in New York at the time. She asked me for two weeks one summer, and I think I stayed two months. I subsequently spent at least seventeen summer vacations on that ranch. I've got pictures of it right out there in the kitchen.

It was at the ranch that I got to know a great many of the people who certainly have influenced my subsequent life. Because my friends - they're my motivation I guess as I look back on it.

Actually at this farewell party that Barnard is giving me one hundred and eighty people are coming. There are representatives coming from every walk of my life.

Mr. Mason: Sort of a review of your life.

Miss Palmer: It's like that old radio - T.V. program, THIS IS YOUR LIFE.

The oldest is ninety-three, he's a trustee of Robert College in Istanbul, Turkey, on which board I served. The youngest, of course, is a Barnard undergraduate.

The friends have played a very important part. While I was at the Association of the Junior Leagues, World War II started. I was doing volunteer work for the USO in the Pennsylvania Station.

This great friend of mine, Elizabeth Taylor from Little Rock, Arkansas - I had known her at Bryn Mawr, at the ranch, and she had been president of the Association of Junior Leagues of America - the Navy asked her, because she was a prominent citizen in her part of the world, to recommend people to join the WAVES. Of course they were not known as WAVES at that time. They were trying to take women into the Navy, and they asked for her suggestions. She suggested me, and then she wrote to me.

Mr. Mason: How much after the establishment of the office in Washington with Mildred McAfee was this?

Miss Palmer: This was long before it.

Mr. Mason: Long before that?

Miss Palmer: Yes indeed.

The WAVE bill was passed as I recall, and you probably know this, in I think it was August of '42, or the end of July.

My commission was August 14th. I was the first Senior Lieutenant commissioned in Com 3. As you know, the fact of my being a senior grade Lieutenant had to do with my age, nothing to do with anything else.

I got this unbelievable letter, because Elizabeth Taylor had recommended it. This letter came from the Chief of Personnel in BuPers. It made no sense at all, if you were in business because it was about four pages. And it said that they were going to have some women who would relieve men for sea duty, and they could not tell you possibly what rank you would hold, how long you would serve, where you would be stationed, or what your recompense might be. But if your were interested please go down and see your officer of procurement.

Mr. Mason: In other words, have a big act of faith.

Miss Palmer: Exactly. Because we don't know what we're doing, that's what it said.

I took the letter and went down and saw Jim Giddings, who was a Lieutenant then. He was the one - the poor feloow who had been assigned the job of recruiting the WAVES. He was an officer so it was officer procurement. The Navy names were very suitable for women - you know, confinement procurement.

In any event Jim was just a darling, and I showed him this letter. Before I could even see him - this was my introduction to the Navy - I had to have a physical exam. They handed me a chart with the picture of a naked man on it. I went running around and they put my measurements all across where the men's were only they didn't exactly coincide, but that was the first thing.

Then of course we had to have the urine test, and I remember running all over, I think it was 90 Church, with this little 'thing' in my hand. And of course in an angel robe, meeting all these men going the other way. I just was having a wonderful time. I got all through the physical. I still remember one thing they'd say ---

Mr. Mason: You were the lone woman in that, at this point?

Miss Palmer: A few others had been commissioned.

Mr. Mason: I mean for this examination.

Miss Palmer: Oh, yes, there were no other women there.

They asked me about all the other ailments I had had in my life. And I reported, among others, that I had broken my back when I fell off a horse once. The man looked at me in horror and said, "Oh, you can't possibly join the Navy." I said, "Why not? It's healed and I've never had any trouble." "Oh," he said, "when you're sixty-five you're going to have terrible arthritis and you'll sue the Navy." And I said, "What a wonderful idea," but it would never had occurred to me. I did persuade him finally. I'm sixty-five now, and I've never had any trouble with that since ever.

In any event I finally got through to Jim, having passed the physical.

Jim looked at the letter and he said, "I'm the officer who's in charge in New York City for Com 3, for handling the applications of all people who are joining the womans' naval reserve." He hadn't seen the letter, and he hadn't the fogiest notion what it meant. He, too, said he didn't know — you see the Officer Training School at Northampton hadn't been established yet, nothing had been set up — he guessed it would be just an act of faith.

So I signed all the application papers. All the men I had known, you see, had waited years practically — the officers, to get their orders.

So I put my affairs in order with the Junior League and went out to Wyoming to the ranch, because I figured I'd take a vacation. I'd been there two days — of course it's a party line out there way up in the mountains — and the phone rang. The girl that owned the ranch said, "Lieutenant Palmer, no he isn't here, but she is."

And that's how I heard that I'd got a commission in the Navy. So I called Jim Giddings long distance. I said, "Where is this BuPers I have to go to?"

Mr. Mason: BuPers?

Miss Palmer: Well you know I'd never heard of it.

He said, "Well, you're certainly a naval officer. You call long distance to find out what your orders mean." Because I didn't have any orders, this was a wire you see. So I set out and came right back to New York.

And the orders I still have, I take them out at times to get a good laugh. I had to fill in my orders of course to get paid, listing the hour I left New York - I drove in my own car - and the hour I arrived.

If you could see what I went through in computing time the Navy way. I think I left at 1500 and got in at 1900. I had traveled in Europe so I really know all about that kind of time, but everything about the Navy was so different that it didn't occur to me that ----

Mr. Mason: There was noboby to enlighten you.

Miss Palmer: No.

First when I was sworn in Commander Paul Hartenstein was the one in the Bureau of Personnel who had been given the task of coping with women.

Of course none of the men wanted the women to be in the Navy. They liked women all right, but they were very much opposed to having them in the service, particularly some who didn't care to be relieved to sea duty didn't care to have women come in.

Paul Hartenstein was in the Procurement office, Bureau of Personnel, and he was supposed to cope with us.

1 Palmer - 11

The point is that nobody ever told us anything about what we were supposed to do. We didn't have anyone other than Paul Hartenstein, and he was of course in the Office of Procurement.

We had a special office in the Bureau of Personnel. When I arrived Miss McAfee was out touring with Commander Hartenstein somewhere. I had met her, but she wasn't there. And there were three officers, three WAVES and myself, in the office.

Of course I had had a business background and I was looking around. Here was this stack of mail, and I began looking at it, and I said, "Well, who's answering this?" Well nobody knew. They had all been referred to the Women's Reserve because they were all questions about - how do I get in, where do I go --

I said, "I know the answers to these questions, and I'm going to answer this mail." I had nothing else to do. I sat down at a typewritter. I had answered about fifty letters --

Mr. Mason: Did you have official WAVE stationery by that time?

Miss Palmer: Of course not. I had Navy stationery, but I would say - just Dear Mr. Smith, you know. I wasn't doing all this fancy Navy lingo, I just gave them the answers. I knew the answers, and about fifty people got told in one day what they wanted to know. I don't think that's ever happened before or since.

Finally the head Civil Service person who had been assigned to Miss McAfee, who was simply excellent, came up and sort of very hesitantly said, "You know it isn't customary for a senior grade Lieutenant to type her own letters."

I said, "Well, who does do them?" And she said, "If you dictate them the Civil Service people do that." I said, "Fine, I'd be delighted to dictate." And she said, "There are other departments in the Bureau of Personnel who should be answering some of these letters." I said, "Fine, let's find them."

I sent one girl down to Officer Personnel, because she said they ought to have something to do with this. And that girl went, she was very pretty, she was an Ensign, and she never came back. They kept her down there. And that was fine, because we should have had a WAVE in Officer Personnel.

Mr. Mason: You had somebody planted over there.

Miss Palmer: It happened quite by chance, like Noah and the Ark, we sent her out and she never came back. Well she did come back often to speak —

We found out, by hit or miss, that there really was a system in the Bureau of Personnel. Of course a lot of the men didn't know the system either. But none of them knew what to do with us, and that was for sure.

The first task that we really had to do was to try to set up the Officers' Training School in Northampton. Then came the problem of whether - there were about fourteen of us I think - we should go to school. We never did get there.

Mr. Mason: You just by-passed the school.

Miss Palmer: We just kept setting it up, and then we had something else to do. I remember coming to New York with the WAVE officer that we had assigned to the training department in BuPers. Of course this was the one that set up the schools.

I came up representing Miss McAfee's office. I was her executive officer for awhile there. But I was much too abrupt in knowing what I wanted to do, and she was much wiser I think about things like that. I decided the thing to do was to find somebody who could replace me, and get a job where I could do the thing I thought I needed to do.

Mr. Mason: Write you own job sheet?

Miss Palmer: I got around quite a lot and was trying to find out the policies that affected the men. These were what we had to adapt to, the ladies. So I saw a great deal of the people in enlisted personnel where we were going to have quite a few WAVES. When we were beginning the WAVES were all officers, you see.

1 Palmer - 14

So I got to know the Director of Enlisted Personnel. Miss McAfee would send me down to find out what they did about this or that and the other. I detected there was quite a lot of feeling, particularly in enlisted personnel, about these women who came into the man's Navy.

The orders had been coming pretty much, I think, from Miss McAfee to the Admiral, then from the Admiral to the Director of Enlisted Personnel. You don't have to be in the Navy very long, or anywhere else, to know that if you want something to work you better start with the chief and sell him, and let the ground swell come up.

So I considered that my greatest service in my four years in the Navy - they asked for me to be the WAVE representative in the enlisted personnel office - down there I spent my time finding out what the policies were for men and getting them adapted to women.

For example, when we found quite by chance that the WAVES on the West Coast at one of the stations were being put through the same training course that the Marines had had for jungle warfare. They were being made to climb a twelve foot wall, they loved it, but it didn't make much sense when you were going to be in an office.

These things I'd find out. I had to find out who in this tremendous department of course of enlisted personnel was responsible for that. Then I'd go and have a talk.

The Chiefs, of course, resented the women almost more than anybody, and you can understand why. There was this old hard-boiled Chief, I had the biggest argument with him about parachute riggers. Because there wasn't any rating for parachute riggers at first, it was a civil service job. Then they didn't have enough civil service people to do it. What they were inclined to do, of course, was to order the WAVES to do what they couldn't hire civilians to do in order to get the job done.

Mr. Mason: You should be jack of all trades.

Miss Palmer: Exactly. And so I went to see this Chief. The male parachute riggers were required to make a jump after they had completely finished a parachute. This was a very intelligent thing, because you rig with care if you think that you might land in that parachute. I felt that the women who had joined the service were not expecting to jump from airplanes, balloons or anything else. This was a real public relations problem.

One of my jobs, of course, was talking to all kinds of people, telling them the kinds of things we did. This was all tied up with recruiting.

This hard-bitten Chief said, "Well the Russian women jump." And I said, "Yes indeed, but the Russian women don't volunteer. They're ordered into service. Our people are volunteering."

He said, "Well if they don't like it they don't have to volunteer." This is the way the thing went on.

Finally I said, "Now just tell me one thing - aren't the majority of parachute riggers civil service?" And he said, "Yes, hardly any of them are anything but civil service personnel." I said, "What rate of pay do they get?"

It was considerably more than the WAVES got. I said, "Do they jump?" "No, they're women." I said, "Well so are these WAVES." "Yes, but they volunteered to do the same job as a man."

Mr. Mason: They give them the dirty work.

Miss Palmer: In time I wore him down, and he said he guessed I had a point. Then I came back to Miss McAfee and said, "Now put through the directive that WAVE parachute riggers don't have to jump." She wrote the directive, sent it to the Admiral - that was Admiral Jacobs then - and he sent it down to Binford, who was the Captain was was the director of Enlisted Personnel.

I had an office right outside of his, so I waited. Pretty soon Captain Binford sent for somebody, it was his assistant director, and they had a talk. And then for somebody who did the assignments, there's another word for that in the Navy.

It went down the line from Captain to Commander to Lieutenant Commander to Lieutenant, all the way down the line.

Pretty soon my little Chief came, he winked at me, and I winked at him. After he had left the Captain asked me to come in.

He said, "You know it's been recommended that we not require these women to jump in order to get their rating. What do you think of that?" And I said, "Sir, I honestly think that if civilians don't have to it doesn't make much sense to make the WAVES do it. And it would be a very hard thing to explain to the public when we're trying to recruit more WAVES." "Thank you," he said, "that's just what I think."

That only took a week, and you see they got their rating without having to jump.

Many of the best jobs in the Navy were to be done by enlisted personnel. The best jobs for male officers were sea duty. By law WAVE officers, young Ensigns, couldn't get PT boats like men as they were not allowed to serve on sea duty.

They got that job of carrying confidential mail around and getting sore feet. Their great intelligence wasn't really tapped at all. We had a great deal of dissatisfaction with the young officers at first. Then a great many of them landed in communications.

Mr. Mason: Where they were especially skilled, weren't they?

1 Palmer - 18

Miss Palmer: Well they were able to do the job, but nobody bothered to tell them what they were doing. They were terribly bored and unhappy, you see. And the men were too, I think.

I remember going up to WAVE quarters D, which was where the communicators were housed there by the American University. They had something like 5,000 there. I don't know how I found this out, but one group was assigned long hours to sit in a row and just look at a screen. If they saw a "blip" they were to report it, where it was and what time it was. Well this gets sort of boring.

Mr. Mason: It certainly does.

Miss Palmer: None of them were told why. Of course I found out and I went in and just said, "You know if you see one of those, that's one of our ships that's been sunk. So it really makes sense that you should tell somebody right away, and that you keep your eye on it because your fiance may be on it." When they knew what it was about then they had the interest in doing it.

One of the reasons women did that job more easily than men is they knit. And it's something they can do other than just sit and look. That saved their sanity for quite awhile.

This whole business of trying to make the Navy make sense to women —

Mr. Mason: Was it largely a lack of communication there?

Miss Palmer: Yes, I think this was true with the men also. I think that many of the things that happened for the women were just as good for the men.

For example, we discovered that the libraries that were sent to the various ships, when we first got there, were largely murder stories, and they were directed to the high school graduate type of mentality.

Of course in the war many of the drafted people were well educated men and women. Now the women wanted different kinds of books, they even wanted poetry. We got them to change the selection. Everything that we got for the women, sometimes the men liked it better than the women.

For example, the women didn't care for Navy food. They didn't want beans and brown bread for breakfast, and they wanted lighter lunches.

We introdueced salads, on the stations this is. Of course the cafeterias in Washington had these things, but they did not have them on the air stations.

I think the majority of the WAVES were stationed on air stations. This was largely due to Joy Hancock, who was one of the directors that you probably knew, because she had been a Yeomanette and she was the top woman in BuAir. She personally did a lot for the whole WAVE operation.

When we got the salads in - you know who were eating them - the men. We had to double the number served.

Mr. Mason: And it's thought traditionally that men don't like salads.

Miss Palmer: I know, but you see some of them do.

In this process of adapting a man's world to women, or women to it — our biggest problem in the Womens Reserve office was to find out what did happen to the men so that we could do the adapting.

Now I personally was responsible for a terrible mistake. We started opening the enlisted schools after the officers schools. I think it was out in Norman, Oklahoma, or one of the ones out west, that was a yeomans school. The people all arrived, officers and enlisted people, and there weren't any blankets. Of course BuPers heard about this.

I'd eliminated the blankets. When Miss McAfee wasn't there they'd asked me the question, "Did the women want seabags?"

I said, "No, that wouldn't be suitable for women's uniforms, because their suits would get all mussed and you can't fold them just the way the men do and have the creases in the collars in the middies. They should have their own suitcases." In that decision I eliminated blankets.

Blankets come in the seabags, but nobody mentioned that. When I said, "No seabags," I just removed the blankets. It took them a little time to get them blankets.

This is the kind of thing that would sort of rise up and trick you when you least suspected it. It also made it terribly interesting.

1 Palmer - 21

Mr. Mason: You got more wary as you went along I imagine.

Miss Palmer: It wasn't that. I think the basic problem in our case was to find out who to ask. You see a lot of the men didn't know who to ask. Each one would know his business and his immediate superior's. If you asked someone in enlisted personnel what went on in officer personnel he didn't have the foggiest notion. You see we were in the Womens Reserve office trying to infiltrate in everything.

Mr. Mason: What's the overall explanation for this? Was it the sudden growth of the organization?

Miss Palmer: The fact that the war got going and the enemy never tells you in advance what he's going to do.

When they were trying to find out what schools to have, and how to train the women, they were trying to fill the requests from the various stations. We had many in the medical corps, and many in the air stations.

They would say they would want control tower operators. As you know in the Navy they order by rating not by individual name when it comes to enlisted personnel. The Commandant of Com 3 would send an order to BuPers that he wanted fifty yeomen. He didn't know that some of them might turn out to be female.

This we had to find out, and try to figure out where they were going to be living, because the women really don't care for gang showers or open latrines. I'm sure the men don't care for it, but they're used to it.

Then the problem of laundry - the women had to do their own pretty much. And their own ironing of the hat covers, and the shirt waists. This was all a different thing.

Women, also, were used to entertaining men where they lived, rather than going to where the men lived. So the whole barracks had to be built with a different type of framework.

All these things were what we were finding out.

Mr. Mason: After our experience today this wouldn't be necessarily true, would it?

Miss Palmer: Nothing would be so true today. It really is a crime we waited all this time.

I was thinking, one of the things I tried to do in looking out for what I choose to call the interests of the enlisted women - was not to have ridiculous rules that you couldn't enforce

I was one urging that they not have curfews. These were women who were all over eighteen, and it seemed to me that if you have a curfew they'll just break it if they don't agree with it. And I didn't want to have them all in the brig for breaking a curfew.

The women came themselves and said, "Please don't let them take away the curfew, because we have nothing else to say to these very attractive young men, except we have to be in because it's the rule. And we really want to go home at night and get sleep because we get tired."

It was at their request that I dropped the curfew fight, which I think is very entertaining.

Mr. Mason: Very interesting.

Miss Palmer: Miss McAfee was the one I think who made the first strike for a decent break for the black people in the Navy. As you know in the men's Navy they were almost always mess attendants. I think there was one black officer in the Bureau of Personnel when I was there, and we all knew who he was because there he was.

On our advisory committee of the WAVES we had Mrs. Bethune. Miss McAfee had know her for a long time, because she had had black people at Wellesley.

She and Secretary of the Navy James Forrestal had quite a debate, because he wanted to know why we didn't have more black WAVES. She said that she wouldn't have any black WAVES at all unless they could be on equal basis with all the other WAVES. She was not going to have any black WAVES with inferior jobs as she felt they had them in the mens' Navy. It was Forrestal who backed her up in that.

Our very first black WAVE officers, three of them as I recall, two of them were 'cum laude' from Smith. I remember when they arrived in the Bureau of Personnel we all took them down to lunch, and they were very attractive people. Then of course the problem of assignment was difficult too. I think they were mostly signed up here in New York where they could really have good jobs and good housing.

I remember one of the biggest problems I faced when I inherited the top job. I was only the head of the WAVES for the last six months, after Mildred McAfee got married and she went back to Wellesley. It was after V-J day and demobilization had set in.

I got a long distance frantic call from the Commanding Officer in the air station at Charleston, South Carolina. He had a WAVE ordered to his station and what was he to do, because they couldn't have any more bathrooms there - "heads," they were called of course. They had one for male enlisted, male officers, women officers, and they really didn't have room for women enlisted.

I said, "Is there any reason why the women couldn't use the same one?" He said, "What do you mean?" I said, "In the Bureau of Personnel there are over 5,000 people here, we all use the same one."

Mr. Mason: Officers and enlisted?

Miss Palmer: Yes, and civil service.

I said, "We haven't any of us gotten any awful diseases yet." You know I always talk this way.

Mr. Mason: Which is very disarming.

Miss Palmer: Then I began to check, because we had tried to guard against this in demobilization — to try not to have the women arrive some place where they had no quarters for them. We discovered that this woman had come from Charleston, South Carolina. The demobilization orders were to send them to the naval station nearest their home, and that's how she had gotten —

Mr. Mason: And she was black?

Miss Palmer: Yes, and the problem was what to do with her. I was sitting there trying to figure out how to cope with this, and I got another call — she'd gotten married and left. So I was saved that dilemma. Saved by the gong, so to speak.

I'm jumping around a great deal. I ought to get down to how I happened to get to Barnard. On this advisory committee was Virginia Gildersleeve.

Mr. Mason: Do tell me, before you make that point, about the role of the advisory committee. I'm curious about it. I don't really know who comprised this committee, who named them, and what did they do?

Miss Palmer: It was the Secretary of the Navy who named them.

Have you ever read Virginia Gildersleeve's book - MANY A GOOD CRUSADE?

Mr. Mason: Yes, I have.

Miss Palmer: Of course none of us who were in the Navy say there is any truth in our part of it, but I think that there is a certain amount of truth.

I know that Elizabeth Reynard was the one that invented the name of the WAVES, that I do know, Women Accepted for Volunteer Emergency Service.

The way many Navy men looked at it - women are very essential sometimes.

It was the Secretary of the Navy who asked the Advisory Committee to serve. He asked the heads of women's colleges primarily, throughout the country different types - one from the west coast, one from Sweet Briar, Meta Glass, Miss Gildersleeve, and of course he appointed Mildred McAfee. They were looking for the educated women.

Mr. Mason: But it wasn't confined entirely to that, was it? I saw some reference to the fact that Mrs. Tom Gates was on the committee.

Miss Palmer: Yes, she was on it. And so it must have been people who would help them with recruiting, people prominent in their locality.

Mr. Mason: The present head of the WAVES, Captain Lenihan, mentioned Mrs. Forrestal, but I wonder if she wasn't in error.

Miss Palmer: Oh, she was never on that committee at all.

I'll never forget the time I had with Mrs. Forrestal. She was regarding the WAVES the way that the Navy wives regarded enlisted men or officers. She regarded them as the servants of the men. She wanted a WAVE officer to run her house, to be her housekeeper.

I fought her on that. I tried to let her beat me at badminton, but I won. Because I said, "No WAVE was recruited with the idea of having this kind of Admiral's aide duty."

You couldn't expect her to understand that, because what she wanted was a good maid, and she couldn't hire one. And it's the same principle - they expected the people in the service to be ordered to do what they couldn't hire civilians to do. She was not alone in this.

Mr. Mason: And yet, why did she and others like her have this attitude when the WAVES were headed and organized by such a competent and recognized group of women educators?

Miss Palmer: I think she didn't wish to accept the role of the WAVES that Mildred McAfee and these other people had. She was never on the council.

The council — one of the things that they were so concerned about was who to get to head up the WAVES. They were the ones that suggested to the Secretary of the Navy that Mildred McAfee be the one.

Mr. Mason: Was Margaret Chase Smith on that committee?

Miss Palmer: No, she wasn't. She was on the House Naval Affairs Committee.

Mr. Mason: In the House?

Miss Palmer: Yes. I don't think she was on the advisory committee. I don't think any of the Congress people were on the advisory committee.

Mr. Mason: This is your chapter from BATTLE STATIONS, which is 1946, YOUR NAVY IN ACTION. What a glamorous photograph!

Miss Palmer: Well, my hair's doing nicely, isn't it?

This doesn't tell about that, but I'm sure that book of Miss Gildersleeve's would tell the membership of that committee.

(Supplement to page 28 - added later.)
See page 270 of MANY A GOOD CRUSADE.

Advisory Council for WAVES:

Virginia C. Gildersleeve, Dean of Barnard, Chairman.

President Meta Glass of Sweet Briar - 5th and 6th Naval Districts.

President Ada Comstock of Radcliffe for New England.

Mrs. Thomas Gates of the University of Pennsylvania.

Dean Elliott of the University of North Carolina,
   and when she resigned,

Dean Alice Baldwin of Duke University for the far south.

Dean Alice Lloyd of the University of Michigan for the middle west.

Mrs. Melborne Graham for the far west.

Recruiting was it's main function.

1 Palmer - 29

Mr. Mason: Well, it doesn't as a matter of fact. It doesn't set out to name the members of the board, it merely refers to various things that members of the board did. But one has the feeling that he doesn't know the total membership, this is why I ask. And also in discussion with Captain Lenihan she said, "Do ask Miss Palmer about the function of the advisory board, because it has always been rather fuzzy in our minds. We have never really understood its true function." And that's why I'm asking you.

Miss Palmer: There's one other person that I wish you would see, if she'll see you, that's Mary Josephine Shelly, who subsequently became the head of the women in the Air Force. She was the head of the training department. She was the WAVE representative in training in the Bureau of Personnel. She was there almost as soon as I was. She's very brilliant.

I don't have trouble talking, but wait 'til you hear her, you can't stop her. She, I think, having gone back and served as a Colonel as head of the women in the Air Force, may remember more of this business. She was down there longer.

Mr. Mason: Where is she to be found?

Miss Palmer: Right here in New York City. She's just moved to an apartment at 10 Mitchell Place, and I'll give you her phone number. (MU8-3259)

We WAVES have all stayed together. I live with one. Mary Jo Shelly has retired. I really think if you'd get her to see you - they're inclined to say that's all behind us.

They tried to get me to be head of the women in the Air Force, but I wouldn't do it, and recommended her. I thought she did a splendid job.

What they wanted at that time was to set up the whole training business, and she's the one who knew it. The very first thing was the training, and that was the thing that she did entirely for the WAVES.

Mr. Mason: And she had the experience of the WAVES to draw on. The fact that you had to sort of create this out of --

Miss Palmer: Out of nothing.

The trouble is you don't remember as much as you wish you did. I remember the funny things that happened, and a lot of them are connected with the difficulties of the early days.

I did a lot of flying around as the WAVE representative in the director of enlisted personnel's office.

Mr. Mason: This was publicity?

Miss Palmer: And I went to Hawaii.

They would send me out from enlisted personnel to inspect the places that had requested women, and to see whether they had suitable housing facilities, and whether they really had a job, or whether they just wanted women around.

This was a very interesting assignment. I enjoyed it very much. I got to many air stations here, and I flew out to Hawaii and saw those.

Mr. Mason: That was before the WAVES were permitted to go to Hawaii?

Miss Palmer: Exactly, yes. We had many problems to solve out there too.

This reminds me of today's educational problems, because when I was there I was stationed in the bachelor officers quarters. They were on one deck, and I was on the top deck with three other people - three women - with all the men below us.

At that time Dave Ingalls was the Commanding Officer. There was a great to-do - the Marine Captain, the Commanding Officer on a Marine station, had erected a stockade. They had a fence around the quarters where the women were, and they were having a lot of trouble because the men were climbing the stockade. So what Dave Ingalls did was to build a little picket fence, white, about two feet high, and he put it around the WAVE quarters. And he had no trouble at all.

Mr. Mason: This is a symbolic barricade?

Miss Palmer: Yes. In other words, the more you say no, the more excitement you arouse. Well that was another experience.

Mr. Mason: What requirements did you establish before WAVES could be sent to an assignment like Hawaii?

Miss Palmer: The WAVE officers all had fitness reports, just the way the men did. They had to have good fitness reports. The enlisted personnel particularly had to be in the ratings that were needed.

I started on that when the WAVES first came into being. The Secretary of the Navy and BuPers asked all Commanding Officers what kind of jobs they were short of that women could do to release men. So they got a list of the skills they were short of say on the first of September.

Then they set up the schools to train women on the basis of these shortages, but by the time they were trained somebody else had had to fill those shortages because the job needed to be done that day, and the enemy hadn't told us what he was going to do.

So out would come all these yeomen and all these storekeepers that had been carefully trained. In the meantime the jobs had been filled by seamen or somebody, so the storekeepers would probably end up doing mess detail. But in the period of four years this got itself pretty well straightened out.

About the time of V-J day, after which I left, I think that the women were pretty well placed, and the officers too. But there were many new positions.

For instance the control tower operators and the link trainer operators - all of those were jobs that hadn't existed. They didn't have any rating, and some of our very best people were trained for those jobs. They would be still seamen, third class seamen, first at least, but they couldn't get a specialist rating. So they would be earning less than a yeomen, and many of them had been stenographers before they joined the Navy. This is the kind of thing that I made it my job to try to correct.

I remember when I first came to Barnard I was Director of Admissions. I was visiting schools. I went to one in Buck's County, Pennsylvania and the headmaster there had been in the Navy. He had been stationed at Banana River, which I believe is what is now Cape Kennedy, isn't it?

Mr. Mason: I think so, yes.

Miss Palmer: I had been down there, and I was just horrified at seeing the wonderful jobs these women were doing training the men as link trainer operators, but they didn't have a rating. I fought, bled, and died, and I GOT them the raing of specialists.

So I happened to meet this man. He said he'd spent his whole time in the Navy trying to get a rating for these women who had been working under him. I looked at him and he looked at me. I was the one that got it for him in BuPers. And we just happened to meet in the area of education, which was where we were afterwards.

These were major problems. Actually we think of it so often now. In our day women and negroes were at the end of every train. They were the ones that were the big headaches to the top brass, and they always had to have special provisions. Now we still have to make special arrangements for the women. I think the negroes are no longer a problem as they are accepted on an equal basis with whites.

Mr. Mason: They're getting their places too.

Miss Palmer: I don't mean to imply any injustice there, because I think the women could get anywhere they want to. They have won the right to top jobs. Many of them don't want them because they really want to stay home with the children.

Mr. Mason: Would you talk a little about that as you saw this develop in the Navy? Because the attitude did change, didn't it, in the four years? I mean at first there was great resistance to the WAVES in the service, but then this changed. Would you talk about that?

Miss Palmer: Let me tell you a perfect story about that.

We had a WAVE representative with every Commandant. In San Francisco, which is in Com 13, Tovah Wiley was the representative. She got a call from somebody when she was in the Commandant's office, and he wanted thirteen yeomen assigned immediately. So she took the proper steps.

He called later and he said, "Are you the person I talked to yesterday? This is Captain so and so. I ordered thirteen yeomen, and I got women. I can't run my Navy with women."

And she said, "Captain, I think you had better learn how, because the women are going to replace the men who are going to sea." "What's the Navy coming to?" he said.

Four years later she was the assistant director of the WAVES with Miss McAfee in Washington, D. C. Somebody called from the Chief of Naval Operations, and he got Tovah just by chance. He was an Admiral and he said, "I don't know what this Navy's coming to. I ordered a yeoman and I got a MAN. They are no good, give me a WAVE." She said, "Admiral, do you remember me?"

Now isn't that wonderful? Complete 'volte face', you see. It's a perfect story.

When they were good, they were just so much better than many of the men, because these people were trying to do a job. Many of the men had just enlisted because they were drafted.

I mean the motivation was quite different with the women. I would say that the majority of them had fiances or relatives or husbands in the service. They were very highly motivated for that reason.

I'm sure that one of the reasons that I was interested in joining one of the services was because one of my close friends — whose brother I had known quite well. He was a Harvard man who was born in this country, but his mother and father were Polish. He had gone to military school in France, and he of course was in the Polish army, stationed at Gdynia when the Germans went in. This made me mad.

Most of us had some connection. Most of the WAVES had a closer one than that. I do think that their motivation was wonderful.

I remember one thing that Mary Jo Shelly said. She's very verbal in her use of words. She said, "You know when the women joined the Navy none of them knew what to expect, and we couldn't tell them, because we didn't know either. So some of them were in a sense trapped. They had been typing all their lives, and they joined the Navy to get something different, and they got typing."

Mr. Mason: They thought they were getting glamor.

Miss Palmer: Exactly.

And then there were those who had been waitresses. They thought that they would get to the Pacific, and they would see sights they had never seen. And they ended up doing mess duty, or something in Bainbridge, Maryland.

Mr. Mason: Weren't we all, as a people, conditioned by the slogan of the Navy which was all over the place — "Join the Navy, and see the world?"

Miss Palmer: Yes. And the song of the WAVES was, "We joined the Navy to see the sea, and what did we see, we saw D. C." The majority of them were stationed in Washington.

Anyway what happened was when they got in they were trapped. Here they were, they couldn't get out. They were just in a little prison, and they didn't know what to do.

She said there were those who were smart enough to find out that if they pretended to be psychiatric cases they'd get psychological discharges. There were those who really cracked up that ended in St. Elizabeth's, the Navy's Mental Hospital.

By far the majority just looked around their little cell, hung up their curtains, and made themselves at home. And had a wonderful time.

We had a wonderful time. I've never worked such hours, and I've never felt so much frustration, but you felt part of something, and you felt that you at least were trying to help.

Mr. Mason: Tell me how much independence the WAVES, from the top on down, had in terms of the regular Navy. How much independence (you've intimated this and you've talked about it on the fringes) did you have in the development of your own WAVE policy?

Miss Palmer: Well, I think we had complete independence. We first had to find out what we thought was right, and then we had to sell it to the people who had the authority. In our case it the last analysis it was always the Chief of the Bureau of Personnel. I felt that we never had any serious trouble in selling them anything that was really right. I think our basic problem was to find out what was going on, and then to figure out how we could make it better.

To give you an example - I trust that you won't use all my examples - one of our biggest problems was the people couldn't get out of the Navy, except there were certain ways that they could. And they tried to use them.

Mr. Mason: You mean to get a discharge?

Miss Palmer: Yes.

We wanted to prevent women having abortions. We had a policy that if you were preganant you couldn't be in the Navy, and there were some who wanted to stay in. If they became pregnant they would have to get out.

And so we tried to write this policy, and it was so hard to write. The first time it came around it said, "When it has been determined that a WAVE is pregnant by a Navy medical officer —." We decided it wasn't quite the way we better word that one.

Mr. Mason: That would be somewhat limited, wouldn't it, in it's application?

Miss Palmer: I was the one for enlisted personnel, and another friend of mine from officer personnel, and then Tovah Wiley for Miss McAfee's office - the three of us went to see the Chief of the Bureau of Medicine and Surgery, to find out what our policy should be about abortion in order that we didn't encourage it by our regulations. This was all we wanted in our simplicity.

There were all these Admirals I think the highest ranking of us was a Lieutenant Commander at this time. They were explaining to us, of course they were M.D.'s, how difficult it was to determine whether an abortion was natural or whether it had been caused by artificial means.

When we got out of there this one friend of mine looked at me and she said, "It's obvious that the policy of Medicine and Surgery is, "Glad to have you abort."

We all had a sense of humor, we did have a wonderful time.

There were policies that were very hard to make. That was perfectly reasonable. That put an awful pressure on the doctors to try to determine what was a natural abortion. I can't remember what we finally did do with it, but we kept the policy, I think.

Mr. Mason: What was the general attitude of the medicos about the WAVES?

Miss Palmer: We had WAVE doctors you know. They were stationed largely at Marine installations.

Oh, I think that they liked them very much.

The enlisted women who were in the Medical Corps — they thought they were going to be nurses — did the kind of work nurses aides do in our hospitals. The people in BuMed wanted them because they did all this work, and they couldn't get anyone else to do it. Certainly their men were on duty overseas. Many WAVES were badly needed to have them released for duty.

The doctors that we had, not too many, one of them is one of my closest friends now. We all go to Block Island together.

The kind of things that we talk about are the kind of things that would not normally appear in a history! There's the one about when we were in the womens reserve office early in the day. A little WAVE yeoman from the Chaplain's office came in and she said, "Chaplain's office is in a terrible state of affairs. They've lost Aunt Mary." We said, "What's the problem?"

The Chaplain's office takes care of burials. Navy personnel is entitled to be buried by the Navy.

It seemed that Aunt Mary's coffin had gotten lost, she was supposed to be buried in Chillicothe, Ohio. They had called long distance to say they had opened the coffin and there was an Admiral in it and, "Please, where was Aunt Mary?" They'd like to have her. He (the Admiral) was in full regalia of course, dress uniform. So the Chaplain just didn't know what to do.

They finally discovered that Aunt Mary had been buried in Arlington Cemetery with full military honors, and they decided to leave her there. That's where she is. The Admiral is out in Chillicothe.

You can see what fun we had! We had some of these problems to solve ourselves.

Mr. Mason: Tell me about some of the morale problems you had to deal with.

Miss Palmer: The one I was thinking of was primarily with the communications people who had swing shifts.

Mr. Mason: Just boredom.

Miss Palmer: In other words - terrible hours and boredom.

I think that they were the ones that had the lowest morale, certainly the officers did.

I think the enlisted women who were on air stations had a very good time, because they had more interesting jobs and there were plenty of men.

You had to be able to adapt. There were many interesting jobs, and I felt that at the end of the four year period the people who had the brains and the background found their way into those jobs. It was pretty tough at first, because you didn't know if you'd ever get out if you landed in one you didn't like.

Mr. Mason: What was your policy when you learned that so and so was unhappy in a particular billet?

Miss Palmer: That depended on the cause of the unhappiness.

I remember when I was director of the WAVES I got a lot of calls from Congressmen. I got a call - move this WAVE from Pensacola to San Diego, because she's in love with a boy in San Diego. I wouldn't do that.

Mr. Mason: She's in my constituency.

Miss Palmer: They wanted the Bureau to make an exception to the policy, so that this particular move could be made because of some constituent of the Congressman.

Mr. Mason: Yes, that's what I mean.

Miss Palmer: I remember one of the Chiefs who was in the outer office with me. He was a "mustang" - you know the kind that come up to being an officer through the ranks.

He said, "You've got to learn that sometimes the fate of one little WAVE is not as important to the Navy as one vote for an appropriation for a new battleship." And I said, "That's going to be very hard for me to learn. I can understand it but —"

(They don't move enlisted people by name. They move them by "ratings" by whatever they do.)

I said, "To pick up somebody and put her where she wants to be because she's in love with somebody is the silliest thing I ever heard, because by the time she gets there she's going to be in love with somebody else. You mustn't just spend everybody's time writing orders."

Mr. Mason: You've something of a cynic.

Miss Palmer: I just felt very strongly about this.

Of course you'd get equal pressure from the parents. There was a girl in Corpus Christi the parents felt was in love with a man who wasn't suitable, so they wanted me to see that she got moved to New York, because there she could see the beau they wanted her to see. I just said, "I'm very sorry. I didn't join the Navy to direct individual lives."

Mr. Mason: When you assumed an attitude of this sort what reaction did you get from the Congressman? And how did you deal with him?

Miss Palmer: That was one of the advantages of being a woman in a service that had never had women before. You never quite knew whether they would treat you like a lady or like an officer. This was always a cause of concern.

If I was the senior officer present and we were on a small boat going out to a battleship I should be the first one off. Occasionally the ranking male would say he would like the lady to leave first. This was very embarrassing to me, and I never knew quite what to do. I had not been to Navy indoctrination school. You have to salute all kinds of things when you're getting on and off the ship. Of course this is why he wanted to put me on the spot. Anyway you had fun like that. It seems to me there wasn't too much difficulty.

Mr. Mason: The fact that it was war time, I suppose, the congressional contingent might not be inclined to apply as much pressure.

Miss Palmer: Oh, yes, they did.

They would request and the Admiral would send it down to the Director of enlisted personnel. Then he would toss it to me and I would say, "Don't do it." And they didn't do it. I never would know the repercussions of it.

I suppose if they went to Secretary of the Navy Forrestal — I don't think Forrestal would have paid attention to a request like this. I think quite a lot of the congressional requests were a form. They could then say that they had asked for whatever it was that had been requested.

I'll never forget when I came to Barnard as director of admissions. I had been there about a week, and I got a request from a Congressman to admit a certain student to Barnard College who was not in the least bit qualified, and the pleasure I took in writing and telling him so. I never felt we could to that in the Navy.

We never wrote our own letters. We wrote letters for the signature of the Chief. I always tried to be polite.

The biggest battle I had, I was naughty about that too —

Mr. Mason: Do tell me about it.

Miss Palmer: That was because Mrs. Forrestal had wanted a maid. To go every place with her she wanted a WAVE aide.

Mr. Mason: This was after she was dissuaded from having one as a servant? Now she wanted one as an aide?

Miss Palmer: Admiral Jacobs was then the Chief of Naval Personnel. He had a very lovely WAVE who was in effect his aide. The Secretary of the Navy had sent Mrs. Forrestal's request to me, and I recommended her because she had had this kind of experience. I really had a case there.

Mr. Mason: Snatch her away from the Admiral to give her to ——

Miss Palmer: In no time at all she came up into the office in tears. And I said, "Now just relax. I'm playing a little game here which I hope to win. I don't think the Admiral will let you go, but he's in a better position than I am to tell the Secretary of the Navy why."

I don't know what he told him, but she didn't go. They got a man, which I think they should have asked for in the first place.

Mr. Mason: I suppose this is not relevant, but why did the Secretary's wife rank an aide?

Miss Palmer: She didn't, but he asked for it. And this becomes embarrassing.

Why does the president of a firm — why does his wife rank anything? That doesn't mean she isn't going to ask for it.

That's the kind of thing that we had fun doing - to try to get what we thought was right by using your wits and finding out channels. There were so many channels. I mean it's a terribly big outfit.

We would find again and again - we'd start out with a directive (we call them letters) to all the ships and shore stations. Whoever started it out would peddle it. We had to take it to every department in the Bureau of Personnel affected.

If it was an enlisted WAVE it would have to go to the Director of Enlisted Personnel, to the recruiting department, to the training department, and to all different departments. There'd sometimes be twelve signatures or initials to approve it.

You'd take it to number one and he'd say, "What does this mean?" And then you'd tell him. He'd say, "Well why don't you say it that way?"

So you'd take it back and write it up and then you'd go to the second man. He'd say, "What does this mean?" And you'd tell him what you had in the first place. He'd say, "I like it better that way." I'd say, "But the Captain doesn't."

Then he'd have to fight it out. There were so many people involved.

I think it's amazing - I know that we sank a lot of our own ships just by mistakes. In anything as big as that I don't know how you can avoid it.

Mr. Mason: Anything that grew so suddenly, and without adequate time for preparation.

Miss Palmer: Then, of course, there were the Commanding Officers who really used imagination.

NAVY REGS are very much like the BIBLE. If you look you can usually find an answer to almost anything. In NAVY REGS you can find about five answers, and they're not always the same.

I'll never forget how mad Miss McAfee was. We all had to take our test in NAVY REGS, that was our homework. She got marked by some little Chief in the training department. She didn't get 100, and she was furious.

She went down and saw the head of the training department and showed him the answers she'd put. There it was in NAVY REGS.

Of course the guy had expected to have another answer. If he didn't get the one he expected, you got marked 'wrong.'

She cared about that. The President of Wellesley doesn't accept an F.

Mr. Mason: Tell me a little about her as she functioned as head of the WAVES.

Miss Palmer: She is, I think, a very brilliant person. I don't know, it's hard to say because the Navy is so compartmented.

I think she made a wonderful impression on the people that needed to be impressed. She had a wonderful command of Navy language, and a very good sense of humor. She didn't have any dirty stories, and didn't even understand them, because I used to have to explain to her some of the things she was saying had a double meaning.

One of them was there was a slogan at the time about - "Join the Navy and ride the WAVES." She thought that was a lovely slogan and she kept saying it. I said, "You know there's a double meaning," and I tried to explain what it was. She said, "Oh, nobody but evil-minded people would take that interpretation." I said, "In my experience ninety percent of the public is evil-minded."

She is a wonderful person, and a very fine character. I think that she was impatient with things that were inefficient. It was her tendency to just go to the Admiral and say, "This is wrong, fix it."

We officers in the Bureau of Personnel had a coffee mess. There was one of us in each of the departments. Every morning at eleven o'clock we'd meet in Miss McAfee's office for coffee, and share our knowledge. I think we knew more about what was going on in the Bureau of Personnel than the Chief or anybody else, because we talked to one another. We all had our little ears to the ground in our respective departments.

#1 Palmer - 50

Mr. Mason: And out of that came composite thinking.

Miss Palmer: That's right.

We wouldn't let Miss McAfee go to the Admiral until we had taken it to whoever's outfit it was, and found out what were the pros and the cons. If it didn't make sense sometimes there was a reason why. We really tried to work things out on an intelligent basis.

None of us had any power complex. I mean nobody was trying to get ahead. If you got ahead it was because of your age.

It was interesting to me that at my Barnard farewell party, given by the Trustees for my friends, I'm going to have three ex-Commanders, and one Colonel, and the director of public relations who tried to cope with me when I was the Director of the WAVES.

She had big black eyes, and she would look at me in horror knowing I was going to say something that shouldn't be said to the Press. She was the only person who was able to shut me up, because I did think she had a point.

My fun in the Navy, and I had plenty of it, was in the office of Enlisted Personnel. Being the Director was to me - somebody had to do it - is a thankless kind of a job because you make so many public speeches. You don't get to see the real works. In enlisted personnel I was finding out what ought to be done and taking it to the right place. Now that's job satisfaction.

Mr. Mason: How many gals did you have?

1 Palmer - 51

Miss Palmer: When I left I had 78,000 enlisted and 8,000 officers. I know because I just read it.

Mr. Mason: Yes, that's quite an army of women.

Miss Palmer: Yes.

The last part of my service was doing the battle in Congress with Margaret Chase Smith. She was on our team. Our aim was to change the regulations so that you wouldn't have to pass a law in the event of an emergency to permit women to serve in the Navy. This seemed to me absolutely ridiculous.

Of course in another war you wouldn't have time. In World War II it took them six months to get the law through that siad that you could have women in the USNR.

That's where I spent most of my time as Director.

Mr. Mason: To establish them as a part of the regular Navy. Tell me a little about that battle. Or was it a battle?

Miss Palmer: I was very naive. Oh, yes it was a battle all right.

I was very naive about Congress, because it had never occurred to me how much bartering is necessary. In other words the Congressmen would vote for the WAVE bill if Margaret Chase Smith would vote for some other bill they were interested in, which had no connection whatsoever with the WAVE bill.

Mr. Mason: I think they call that log rolling, don't they?

Miss Palmer: I think this is common practice.

One of the things that I had not realized was that of course the Congressmen have to be concerned with the thinking of the people who elect them. I was naive enough to think that the Congressmen had a responsibility to inform the people at home.

There were many Congressmen who's constituents did not approve of having women in the service. In this case they were very loathe to vote for anything that would permit it, because they felt that this would lose them votes at home.

This always seemed very sad to me, because it seemed to me there ought to be more of a two-way stretch that would be possible.

Obviously they were more concerned with their being elected than this relatively minor cause that we were championing. Margaret Chase Smith was simply wonderful, and was always on the side of all the women's services.

As a matter of fact I was very pleased to stand up with her when she got her honorary degree at Columbia. They assigned me to be her escort. She was for all the women's services.

I do feel that, by and large, the women in the Navy had a better opportunity than the women in the Army, because they were assigned on a much more individual basis.

I think that they really did a superb job. I think a lot of it was due to their motivation, and to their selection. They required much higher educational background, and I.Q.s, and all of that, for the women than they did for the men. I think it showed.

INDEX
for
INTERVIEW
with
JEAN PALMER

Advisory Council for WAVES, 28

Background and early career, 1-5

Baldwin, Dean Alice, 28

Bethune, Mary McLeod, 22-23

Binford, Captain Thomas, 16

Comstock, Ada, 28

Elliott, Dean - of the University of North Carolina, 28

Forrestal, James, 23

Forrestal, Mrs. James, 26-27

Gates, Mrs. Thomas, 26, 28

Giddings, James, 7-9

Gildersleeve, Virginia C., 25-26, 28

Glass, Meta, 28

Graham, Mrs. Malbone, 28

Hancock, Joy, 19

Hartenstein, Commander Paul, 10

Ingalls, David, 31

Jacobs, Admiral Randall, 16

Lenihan, Captain Rita, 26, 28

Lloyd, Dean Alice, 28

McAfee, Mildred, 6, 10-13, 15, 19, 22-23, 26-27, 35, 38

Reynard, Elizabeth, 25-26

Shelly, Mary Joseph, 29-30, 35-36

Smith, Margaret Chase Smith, 27-28, 50-51

WAVES, 1-51

Wiley, Tovah, 34-35, 38

Recollections

of

Captain Joy Bright Hancock,

U. S. Navy (Retired)

U. S. Naval Institute
Annapolis, Maryland
1971

Preface

This manuscript is the result of a series of tape recorded interviews with Captain Joy Bright Hancock, USN (Ret.) at the U. S. Naval Institute in 1969 and 1970. These interviews were conducted by John T. Mason, Jr. for the Oral History Office in the U. S. Naval Institute.

Only minor corrections and emendations have been made by Captain Hancock to the manuscript. The reader is asked to bear in mind, therefore, that he is reading a transcript of the spoken word rather than the written word.

DECLARATION OF TRUST

The undersigned does hereby appoint and designate as his (her) Trustee herein, the Secretary-Treasurer and Publisher of the United States Naval Institute to perform and discharge the following duties, powers, and privileges in connection with the possession and use of a certain taped interview between the undersigned and the Oral History Department of the United States Naval Institute.

(1) As an <u>Open</u> transcript. It may be read (or the tape audited) by qualified researchers upon presentation of proper credentials as determined by the Trustee.

(2) It is expressly understood that in giving this authorization, I am in no way precluded from placing such restrictions as I may desire upon use of the interview at any time during my lifetime, nor does this authorization in any way affect my rights to the copyright of any literary expressions that may be contained in the interview.

Witness my hand and seal this 22nd day of May 1970

[signature]

I hereby accept and consent to the foregoing Declaration of Trust and the powers therein conferred upon me as Trustee:

[signature: R. E. Bowker Jr.]
Secretary-Treasurer and Publisher

Interview #1 with Capt. Joy Bright Hancock, USN (Ret.)
At Annapolis, Maryland   by John T. Mason, Jr.
Subject: WAVES   November 12, 1969

Mr. Mason: Well, I'm simply delighted, Captain Hancock, to have you here today and to hear your story of your career in the WAVES. Would you, by way of background, tell me just a little bit about your educational background before you enlisted with the Navy, not in the Navy but with the Navy in 1918?

Capt. Hancock: In 1918, I was nineteen years of age and had just finished high school and gone on to business school in Philadelphia, the Pierce School of Business Administration. As you know in those days, college was not something that was accepted as the normal. I had one sister that went on to college.

Before I finished at Pierce actually, enlistments were open for women in the Navy. So that was the thing to do as far as I was concerned. I enlisted in the Navy as a first class yeoman.

Mason: As I worded it and I got this from the amendment to the Reserve Act in '42, it said for the first time women were serving in the Navy and not with the Navy as they served in World War I.

Hancock #1 - 2

Hancock: Actually the women in the Navy were under the classification -- U. S. Naval Reserve Force, class five, and men were also in that. There was not a separate division for the women.

Q: Oh, it was not?

Hancock: No, it was not. It was a reserve set-up already in existence under which they enrolled the women and of course, as you know, we had no special legislation for women to come into the Navy so they had to have a classification under which they could bring them in.

It was Secretary Josephus Daniels who found out it wasn't necessary to have legislation. Someone way back in writing up the law had merely said "shall be a citizen" instead of "male citizen." Then he said, "Bring in the women." Hence, we did.

Q: And this eliminated the necessity for days and weeks of discussion on Capitol Hill, didn't it?

Hancock: Or years.

Q: Or years. Because it was a new, a new enterprise for women. Well, tell me what induced you to enlist.

Hancock: Well, actually, I think I was the only one really

Hancock #1 - 3

eligible in our family. There were six of us. My sister was in college, as I said, and my brothers were -- three brothers younger than I were too young, and my oldest sister was married, and my father was a dollar a year man. You're not old enough to remember back that far.

Q: Well, in World War II there were dollar a year men.

Hancock: Yes, in World War I they canvassed the states selling liberty bonds, and so forth. My mother was also very patriotic and very active in -- for instance a leader in the suffrage movement for women and when I came home for the weekend and said, "I want to enlist in the Navy," they were delighted because they wanted military representation, naturally, if they could have it. Capt. Elmer Wood, a retired Navy captain living in Cape May Court House, whom I had known, when my father was sheriff and we lived there, had been recalled to active duty for World War I and was in charge of the Branch Hydrographic Office in Philadelphia. So my father said, "Why don't you go see Capt. Wood and find out how to do it?"

So when I went back the next day to school in Philadelphia, I went down to see Capt. Wood and told him I wanted to enlist. He had a son in West Point at the time who was later killed in World War I. He said, "Fine. The personnel officer of the Fourth Naval District is Capt. George Cooper." And he

Hancock #1 - 4

took me practically by the hand and we got on the streetcar and rode to the Navy Yard in Philadelphia.

Q: He's not going to have you change your mind.

Hancock: And we went in to see Capt. Cooper and he said, "I have a young lady that I can vouch for who wants to join the Navy." And Capt. Cooper said, "Well, she'll have to take a test and pass a physical."

I said, "Well, I'm willing and hopeful I can pass both of them." So I took a test and on the basis of that I was enrolled as a first-class yeoman. Although I was attending business school -- I wasn't very good. But I think I did improve later. Then I was sent to appear the next day at what is now the Naval Home. I guess it was then, too, on Grey's Ferry Road in Philadelphia.

Q: It's exactly at the same place.

Hancock: It is?

And I reported there for a physical, and they hadn't had any women. They hadn't any set-up for examining women for the Navy, you see. It was quite early in the game. I remember vividly one incident that for me was rather unusual. While I was having this physical examination, I remember standing on the scales very scantily clad, with something like a towel

Hancock #1 - 5

around me. In this old building there were transoms and as I glanced up there were about four nice young male faces looking through the transom at me and I -- well, the doctor very quickly got rid of them but they were having a fine time seeing one of the first women entering the Navy, I'll tell you.

Q: They still have those old transoms. I was there two weeks ago.

Hancock: Really?

In connection with that Naval Home I remember in World War II, the war was over, and Admiral Randall Jacobs was retiring. He was to have this, well everyone knows, very plush job as the Governor of the Naval Home in Philadelphia, always a rewarding job for a retired admiral. There was a sort of farewell conference and I said, "Admiral Jacobs, I'm awfully glad you're going up there because," I said, "you know you'll have women knocking at the door as being eligible for the Naval Home."

He said, "What!" And I never have seen such an expression go over someone's face. And I said, "Yes." And he said, "Oh no. Oh no. That'll never happen." Or something like that and I was very amused here in 1969 to note where it has been opened to women and they have about twelve I believe, now.

Q: Yes, they do. I interviewed one of them who had been a

yeoman (F) in World War I. Yes, there are very few women who are completely accepted, I must say.

Hancock: Oh really? Well, I was wondering at the time I read about it in the newspapers, what Admiral Jacobs' reaction would have been, had he still been around.

Q: Well, so continue telling me about your enrollment and your assignment. You were taking your physical.

Hancock: Oh yes. I've forgotten how long it was between the time I finished the physical and was called to active duty. It wasn't long. I would say somewhere in a matter of a few weeks. I was ordered to duty in the office of the Naval Superintending Constructor of the New York Ship Building Corporation in Camden. I reported there.

When I received my orders I was told to report to the Navy Pier in Philadelphia for uniforms, which I did. Then they said you go and have a cape made for yourself that looks like a boat cloak. They had prescribed no overcoats and I remember going to Peter Thompson who was sort of a naval tailor and getting a cape made. Then I reported to duty. There was no indoctrination or anything of that sort.

Q: Were you pleased with the uniform?

Hancock #1 - 7

Hancock: Oh yes! I mean it was pretty smart. It was only about seven or eight inches from the floor. But at that period of time it was considered quite short. We generally wore high button or laced shoes, you know. This sounds funny now but looking back it wasn't funny in those days, it was very smart.

Q: What did your duties consist of?

Hancock: Well, at the office of the Naval Superintending Constructor was a Capt. Elliot Snow. I don't think he had quite adjusted or was pleased with the idea of having women in the Navy. He was Construction Corps, of course. He and Commander Ralph Hanson were the two top naval people at the shipyard. It was clerical work, mostly filing and stenographic work. That was it, actually, until later I was transferred to the cost accounting office of the Navy at the shipyard.

Toward the end of the war, the Navy started ordering people to activities nearer their homes. I was ordered to the Naval Air Station, Cap May, N. J., which was very near my home in Wildwood. Here I became the Captain's Writer.

Q: You became the captain's writer?

Hancock: Writer, yes. And to me it was much more thrilling than working in the clerical outfit up in New York Ship Corp although light moments and very entertaining ones there will always be remembered. One such instance was connected with USS Idaho, the largest ship under construction in the yard at that time. Plans had to be sent from the naval constructor's office to the ships -- to those in charge of the working crews on ship. This meant going through the Yard from the main gate to the ship concerned (the Navy Building was on the outside of the Yard). I was given that job of courier work which was called for about two trips a day, which I enjoyed. However, the job for me only lasted about ten days apparently because it was a little disrupting to have a woman walking through the Yard. The rivet throwers would fascinate me -- I'd stop and see the red hot rivets being caught in a bucket and so forth --

Q: And they'd stop work?

Hancock: They'd stop work and I became known to them as "Heavy Artillery." "Here comes 'Heavy artillery,'" they'd shout. Finally one of the yard's efficiency experts said, "Don't send her through the Yard anymore. We're losing dozens of dollars everytime she's sent through." With any woman, of course, it would have been the same thing. My boss had said, "She's in the Navy. Give her any job that needs doing." Which was fine but the men of the shipyard were just too friendly.

Hancock #1 - 9

Q: Men being men.

Hancock: Then, of course, when I went to Cape May, it was my entry into aviation so to speak.

Q: Describe the station there.

Hancock: Well, you know it's the -- today it's the Coast Guard Recruit Training Center and some of the old buildings are still there, although you wouldn't recognize them, and some of the old sea plane hangars are still standing from which they operated the blimps and sea planes of the station. Mostly there were one story buildings sprawled over, I would say, fifty or sixty acres at that time. Of course, there's much more there now. It's on Cold Spring Harbor near the very southern tip of New Jersey. Cape May Point is beyond and that is at the junction of Delaware Bay and the Atlantic Ocean. It meant commuting. Of course, no government quarters were furnished enlisted women in those days. You found your own quarters. I commuted from Wildwood until the winter weather came and then I moved into Cape May and shared an apartment with another girl.

Q: Wildwood's only fifteen, twenty miles, isn't it?

Hancock: It's a little less than that actually, by road.

But the roads were of dirt-rutted or muddy and car engines were most undependable; tires were not on detachable rims so there was always something happening on the road or on station where the blimps were operating. The sea planes were still carrying out patrols, and the old submarines, O type, were in there. That was their base. And I remember the first time I saw Admiral Reed was when he flew the NC-4 into Cape May after the completion of the first trans-Atlantic to Europe.

Q: Yes. Yes.

Hancock: He and his crew had been assigned to do a recruiting job up and down the Mississippi and other rivers and waterways of the U. S. and thus they came into Cape May. I'll always remember that the NC-4 was missing one pontoon on the right wing, and that temporarily, in its place, were some two-by-fours. And that's the way they flew in and landed successfully.

Q: Like a man with a wooden leg, isn't it?

Hancock: Yes. We had the most marvelous time, of course, going down and inspecting that sea plane at first hand.

Q: It must have been ideal for recruiting. I mean having made a spectacular flight like that.

Hancock #1 - 11

Hancock: Oh yes. And the whole crew was making speeches all over. I don't know how far inland they went but I know they went up and down the Mississippi River on the recruiting tour. This NC-4 visit further wetted my appetite for aviation, in which I was to be concerned one way or another during the rest of my life. It was at the Cape May Station that I met Lieutenant Charles Gray Little from Boston who was a naval reservist, who had had all his war duty in France and had just returned to the U. S. The day he reported aboard, -- no, it was the day I reported aboard -- I was assigned the starboard watch. Well, up in Camden in the offices of the shipyard you didn't get much real Navy, you know, and a gong sounded. A yeoman, male, said, "You're starboard watch, aren't you?" And I answered, "Yes." And he said, "Report to the hangar."

So I reported to the hangar and I was handed a broom and I swept down. I was the only woman aboard, you know, and I swept down with the rest of them. It took about four hours to sweep that hangar deck to lay out the envelope of the "O" airship, which we had purchased from Italy as an experimental type, and it had to have a clean deck so it wouldn't chafe the layed-out fabric, you know.

That was my first job. I've never forgotten it although it wasn't the only time I did it. About the third time I was on the watch to sweep down the hangar, I found out that

Lieutenant Little, who had reported in that day -- it was about two months after I had reported in -- was over at the hangar, observing the whole set-up there and noted this one woman out there in the gang sweeping and inquired who it was. They said, "Oh, that's Miss Bright, our yeoman." And of course we were called Miss Bright. And he's the man I later married. He was then the executive officer of the station.

Q: Well, I was going to ask you a question as to how the naval officers of that time received women who were assigned to their duties?

Hancock: Well, I was, you see --

Q: You gave me the answer.

Hancock: But in both cases we were few in number. I was the only one at the air station for several months and then three additional yeomen (F) reported. Everyone was perfectly grand, you know. There were a few sort of, you know, but you get it any walk of life. But generally the acceptance was good. Both up at the New York Ship and down at the Naval Air Station at Cape May, I enjoyed it thoroughly, every day. You felt as if you were doing something. There was work to be done and that's the main thing.

Q: And you were, indeed, representing your family in the service?

Hancock: Oh yes. And my father, when I'd go home for weekends in my uniform, would walk me up the street to church on Sunday. Of course I grew up in that town. I knew everyone, but father would stop everybody we'd meet, "Well, of course, you know my daughter, Joy? She's in the service, you know." We'd go over that time after time. He was so terribly proud. And so was Mother.

Q: What a delightful episode in your life. And you spent two years with --

Hancock: Well, I was given credit for two years of service. Actually, I wasn't enrolled until the Fall of 1918 -- I think it was -- I've forgotten now. After all that's an awful long time ago. My actual service was just about a year and a half. I was discharged 4 February 1920. But I was given credit for two years service so perhaps that's what you have in mind.

Q: Yes.

Hancock: When there was an overlap into the next year, they gave you credit for it.

Hancock #1 - 14

Q: That is precisely what I had in mind because that's the record, you see.

Hancock: While I actually didn't have the full two years in military service, I remained on at the station in a civil service capacity. I took civil service examinations for the first time and became one of the last perons to leave the station when it was decommissioned. The fact that I was still on board at the decommissioning of the station was helpful for I was the only person left who could remember where inventoried barrels of nails, airplane parts, boats, etc., could be located.

Q: Had you married Lieutenant Little?

Hancock: No. You see I stayed on because he was ordered to England in connection with the ZR-2. Its British designation was R-38.

Q: That was a Zeppelin?

Hancock: That was one of the rigid air ships that the U. S. had purchased. He went over for training on it and to fly it back. We were engaged at that time, and his training was supposed to be three months period. Well, when he got o-er there it turned out it was going to be another year so then after I finished my work at the air station, my mother, my sister Eloise, and I went to Europe and I was married in England at the commanding officer of the American detachment's home and I stayed in England for eight months. Then I returned to Lakehurst, where the ship was to come, and rented a house in Toms River. And, of course, I was only home about a month when the ship crashed and Lieutenant Little was killed.

Q: That was that tragic event over France, wasn't it?

Hancock. No, no. That was over Hull, England.

Q: Oh, over Hull, England, yes.

Hancock: Yes. The one over France near Beauvais was --

Q: That was a ZR-3, wasn't it?

Hancock: No, no. That was not an American airship. The Shenandoah was the U. S. ZR-1. The British R-38 was U. S. ZR-2. The Shenandoah was built in the United States at the naval aircraft factory in Philadelphia and taken in parts up to Lakehurst, N.J., and assembled. She was started before the U. S. purchased the ZR-2. That's why her number is first although she didn't start operating until after the ZR-2.

Q: Until after.

Hancock: And that's always been sort of confusing.

Q: What a tragedy to lose your husband so soon.

Hancock: Yes, it was, but we had a very, very interesting time actually living in England and so forth for those eight months. After his death I took a job in the Bureau of Aeronautics as a civilian.

Q: This was in the days of Admiral Moffatt, then?

Hancock: Yes. It was at the time of the creation of the Bureau, 1921, and Admiral Moffatt was the first Chief of Bureau and I wrote to him and said -- told him who I was and I knew he was interested in airships, and said that I would like a job and had had experience as a yeomanette and I would like to come and work in the Bureau. So I went down to Washington and Cdr. Kenneth Whiting, one of our early naval aviators on duty in the Bureau interceded in my behalf.

Q: Oh yes. I've been seeing his brother.

Hancock: Oh, is that so? He took me under his wing so to speak and I had never been -- yes, I had been to Washington with my graduating class in 1916, but that was all. I was sort of roaming around, a 'Peg of my heart' idea, you know, a little lonesome, and he met me in this building and interviewed me and so forth and he said well, he thought he could get me a job, they were just setting up the Bureau. And so I was taken on as a messenger, paid by the Bureau of Supplies and Accounts, because in setting up the new bureau they had no funds so each bureau was taking on --

Q: Contributing --

Hancock: Contributing by paying the salary of someone to set up the new bureau.

Q: You mean you couldn't get Congress to --

Hancock: No, Congress was dragging its feet, and after all this air business, that was something new, you know. You just don't jump into promoting airplanes and airships. So I was taken on until the bureau could get its funds appropriated. As a matter of fact, I think it was just a delay in getting appropriations. I was taken on at the fine salary of twelve hundred dollars a year, and in those days, of course, that meant a great deal more than it does now but at the same time, I'm telling you, it was slim pickings for quite a while. So that was my start in the Bureau of Aeronautics, when the

Hancock #1 - 18

bureau started, in 1921.

Q: Tell me something about Admiral Moffatt.

Hancock: Oh, he was --

Q: He was legendary in the Navy, of course.

Hancock: Well, he was -- he was one of the most picturesque people. His language at times was most -- described as most descriptive and forceful. He was energetic, alert, all the time. He was a vital person. I think that best describes him and he was -- well, he wouldn't have been in aviation if he hadn't been, you see? When the Bureau started up, Coleman, Plug, known as Plug Coleman was his number two, Plug Coleman, yes. I don't know his right name. He was known as Plug. Cdr. Albert Cushing Reed, "Putty" Reed, was the administrative officer.

Q: Gene Wilson was there too, wasn't he?

Hancock: I don't know if Gene was there at the time or not. But Capt. Henry Mustin was.

Q: Yes.

Hancock #1 - 19

Hancock: Henry Mustin and Earl Spencer. Admiral Radford came in about that time as a lieutenant. He was my boss.

When he was a lieutenant, he was in charge of personnel at the time. He relieved Win Spencer who, as you know, was married to Wallace Warfield. I think Spencer was my first boss. And we were setting up files and do you know how we did it? There were about a hundred naval aviators then. I made two trips a day over to, I think it was about the fifth wing in the Navy Department --that's on Constitution Avenue -- with a pencil and pad. I would hold it underneath the lip of the counter and ask to see their file on so-and-so -- let's say Ken Whiting. They would show me the file and I would take off data from that -- steal it, you know -- by writing it on this pad. I'd try a couple a day only and that's how we set up our files. We stole information from BuPers, then Bureau of Navigation, which would not cooperate in this new project.

Q: They wouldn't cooperate?

Hancock: Oh, no. Not as far as personnel was concerned, you see.

Q: Well, how on earth did it get started then?

Hancock #1 - 20

Hancock: Well, that's one of the methods used in setting up personnel files. Other Bureaus were very helpful.

Q: It was just the determination of Moffatt?

Hancock: Go get it. Go get it. Go steal it. So I was to go get it. Walk in a room and ask for a file and naturally they'd let me see the file. So I'd write down everything I could out of that file and come back and write it up, you see. That's how we started our files. But oh, it was fun. Everybody was in there pitching; everybody was enthusiastic.

Q: Really believed in it.

Hancock: Oh, they believed in it, yes.

Q: And yet the senior authorities of the Navy couldn't accept it.

Hancock: No. No. It had to be pushed down some of their throats actually. Well, I used to hear the expression thrown around a lot about the Navy being slow, you know, in taking on these new ideas and -- but by being that way and exploring deeply into things, they made fewer mistakes. Well, of course, that has merit, too, but it is somewhat of an excuse for long delays and we used to get so terribly impatient in aviation.

But the --

Q: Of course, aviation as a whole got quite a boost from General Billy Mitchell, didn't it? In this same period.

Hancock: Yes. Yes. That is the overall. The Navy was entirely on the opposite side of the picture as you know. But it did bring the issue more or less to the general public's attention which we needed, also, because their interest and desire to go ahead was necessary to push the Congress in order to appropriate and to help out or help bring to fruition the ideas and all that were expressed by Admiral Moffatt and all his people.

Q: Now there, Moffatt himself was a most useful individual. I understand his relations with the Congress were awfully good.

Hancock: Oh yes, yes. They were very good. And it was always -- it seemed to me he lived on a first name basis and, of course, he was a master showman. I mean, I don't know who headed up the Barnum and Bailey thing, whether it was Mr. Barnum or someone else, but I would say Admiral Moffatt could have run him a second any time. Just his association, for instance, with John Philip Sousa -- Sousa wrote and dedicated a Moffatt march and all that sort of thing. He would put on a show that would get to more people, and his speeches were the same thing. He could go directly to them, get them stirred up and thinking and agreeing. You always came away agreeing with him. Well, of course, you couldn't have had a better person, particularly to start off the program.

Q: He was the right man in the right place at the --

Hancock: At the right time.

Q: Psychological and all. Well, that was an exciting period. How long did you stay with the bureau?

Hancock: Well, you know I have a way of discarding an awful lot of dates. Purposely as I grow older because I need so much room for all the new things that keep happening.

Q: Well, that's all -- you don't have to remember a specific date, then. I mean some incident that would --

Hancock: I started in 1921 but I resigned and was re-instated in the Bureau of Aeronautics, I think, four or five times. And every time I went back I was given a raise so apparently they did like my services. But, of course, I --

Q: I have you as going into editorial work and public relations in 1925.

Hancock: It was in that period when I started the newsletter, the Bureau of Aeronautics newsletter. I was the first editor of that.

Q: Tell me about that. Was this your idea?

Hancock: No, actually there was already in the bureau a mimeographed sheet that came out -- oh, not at any stated interval. But on things that were happening, the different sections in the bureau would try to inform the pilots, let's say, what they were trying to do in the way of improvements and so forth. When I went into my job, I said, "I'd like to run that." It was very stereotyped at the time, and the idea of having the squadrons contribute items informally via a Weekly Newsletter soon changed the complexion of the "paper." And from those weekly newsletters I was able to pull out things that would interest other squadrons. East Coast and West Coast squadrons discussed their small problems. It sort of became the melting pot of all information that would interest everybody. And that's how --

Q: Which served a real purpose.

Hancock: Yes.

Hancock #1 - 24

Q: A cross fertilization sort of thing.

Hancock: That's right. And how Joe Blow solved his problem in squadron VF-3. And then the squadrons started to compete with other squadrons for getting in their ideas and so forth and it really started the ball rolling. And of course, in the beginning, I did the stencil cutting and I ran the mimeograph machine and everything else by hand in those days, you know. But we really got going. That was the -- I was interested not long ago in the fiftieth anniversary of the Naval Aviation News Magazine in which they published my picture as the first editor.

Q: Well, that's a fascinating facet of your career.

Hancock: I think so. As a matter of fact, it was all interesting. It really was. And then, of course, when I resigned and went up to Lakehurst, because they were building the ZR-1 (Shenandoah), I had been in the bureau about a year at that time, and I asked if I could be transferred to Lakehurst where they were building, starting to complete the ZR-1 which was a sister ship, of course, of the ZR-2. They transferred me up there, and so I was in on the building of the ZR-1 and it was there that I met Lieutenant Commander Hancock who was the executive officer on the ship. I worked there with Commander Weyerbacker who was the naval constructor in charge.

Hancock #1 - 25

He worked between the Naval Aircraft Factory and NAS Lakehurst in the assembly of the ship, and I worked in his office. Here I learned about the ship, really, from girder placing right straight on through to its completion. Also, I worked for several months in the office of Lt. Zero Wick, who was in charge of the helium plant. I resigned when I married Commander Hancock.

Q: You were truly interested in lighter than air craft.

Hancock: Yes.

Q: Did you know Ralph Barnaby in the --

Hancock: Oh yes. Yes indeed. I had a note from him quite recently. I saw where he was in New York at some Early Bird's dinner, I believe it was. I had a nice note from him from Philadelphia. Yes, I think I lived through some of Ralph's soaring experiments. He was quite a person. Is quite a person.

Q: Well, he told me that fabulous story where Moffatt put his finger on him and said, "Can it be done?" Can a glider be launched from a blimp, Zeppelin. And he said, "Now don't -- you don't have to tell me now. Think about it overnight and remember if you say it can be done, you're the man."

Hancock: He and Tex Settle carried out the -- Admiral Settle, -- carried out the glider launchings. They didn't hook on they just released as I remember. Then I think Lt. Frederick Trapnel and Lt. "Min" Miller did the plane work of hooking on and releasing from the ship. But that was not the Shenendoah group. That was the Akron and Macon ships that came later.

Q: Yes, the later ones.

Hancock: That came later. Yes. Before they got into the heavier than air experiments. A lot of this is coming back to me. I haven't thought of it for years, you know. I'm surprised at the sequence.

Q: Well, when you returned to Lakehurst married to Lieutenant Commander Hancock you stopped you active naval career.

Hancock: Oh yes. I resigned then again and married Commander Hancock and then after his death, I went back to Washington to the Bureau of Aeronautics.

Q: Was he killed in an accident, too?

Hancock: He was killed; he was the Exec of the Shenendoah. He was killed in the Shenandoah and I was married to him just over a year, you see, when he was killed. So I then came to

Washington and went to Crawford School, preparation for the State Department which I did not make. I made -- I passed the writtens twice, two years and I flunked my orals both times.

Q: What, in language?

Hancock: No. Plain English. Personality --

Q: You?

Hancock: Yes. Well, after all only one girl got in at that time.

Q: This was under Wilbur Carr, was it?

Hancock: Yes.

Q: Wilbur J. Carr. I remember --

Hancock: Wilbur J. Carr and oh, Johnson, wasn't there a Johnson who was later ambassador to Japan?

Q; China.

Hancock: China, yes. Well, he was a meany on my board.

Hancock #1 - 28

Q: I thought usually it was a person's ability with French or German or some modern language which was the bug-a-boo.

Hancock: Well, my French was terrible but I did pass it apparently. I passed my writtens twice with over eighty which qualifies you for your orals in those days. I don't know what it is now.

Q: You also had the added burden of being a woman.

Hancock: Oh yes. Well, one girl did get in. One. You see they just opened the State Department work, foreign service work, to women, the year I started school at Crawford's in Georgetown in preparation for it, and as I say, one got in in those two years that I was trying to get in. And then later, of course, there were more accepted. But gee, if you're a pioneer in something, you know, you get a lot of kicks along the way. But it was fun.

Q: Well, you told me that your mother was interested in the suffrage movement, so you understood the pioneer --

Hancock: Oh yes. That's where you get the challenges, you know.

Q: Charming. So having come back to Washington and having

Hancock #1 - 29

attempted to get into foreign service, what did you do?

Hancock: Well, of course, it was at that time while I was going to foreign service school that I took up aviation myself. I mean flying, at the old Henry Berliner School over across the river. He had a flying school and I got my private pilot's license period. I never went beyond that because the training plane was broken up, and then there was a hangar fire. I was abroad at the time. After I soloed, I went abroad, and was back and forth quite a bit, and when I came back on one occasion the hangar had had a fire and the school was discontinued, so I didn't pursue my training further. As a matter of fact, I didn't want to because I was scared to death of flying. I only took those darned flying lessons to see if I could overcome the fear.

Q: Why was your -- was your fear related to the fact that you'd lost two husbands in --

Hancock: Yes. And so many of my friends. Of course, I was really in the thick of naval aviation, and in the Bureau you'd see someone that you'd talk to one day, and the next day he was killed. It was all around you in those early days, and always very best friends. And I thought well, because I had no plans to fly planes for a living, this is silly. I expected only to go back to the Bureau of Aeronautics and ask them again for a job. I got out of the training what I wanted; I knew how to operate a plane. Frankly, I liked the ground course much better. I loved working with the engines.

Q: Pretty engines.

Hancock: Much better than flying.

Q: But you -- did you overcome your fear?

Hancock: Yes. When I found out what it was all about. I knew that the possibility was always there of being killed, by doing something stupid, but I could see the reason why the thing flew, and with intelligent operation you eliminated a lot of the hazards that you dreamed were so terrible. I'd gotten a talking background so when I again asked for a job in the Bureau, I got it. I had more background to offer. I could talk to reporters more intelligently because, gee, I had finished training and had flown a plane, you see.

Q: My, you were accumulating a terrific background for the Bureau of Aeronautics.

Hancock: Well, they were terribly kind to me, and patient. For my part, I always found it fascinating in that bureau. It was a place you'd want to be if you had any interest at all in aviation.

Q: What did you do when you went back then?

Hancock: I was placed in charge of the Editorial Research section.

Q: Again.

Hancock: I think that's when I headed it up, was made the head of it. It had been General Information section, that's right. And when I went back I think the last, one of the last times, they renamed it editorial research with me in charge, and this made me the press and public relations officer of the Bureau. In that capacity I worked directly with the Navy public relations as the BuAer representative, you see.

Q: Tell me a little about that. I would assume that maybe BuAer was much more cognizant of the relationship problems and the need for them than perhaps the general Navy. Am I wrong in that assumption?

Hancock: Oh, you're absolutely correct. They knew all along they had to get the word out if they were going to get anywhere at all, which the regular Navy, let's say, didn't see as necessary. Theirs was the conviction that they could administer without fan-fare.

Q: They were established and accepted.

Hancock: That's right. Yes. And it was, I think, for that reason, this difference in the viewpoints, that a feeling of antagonism grew up. Regular Navy, or what was known as the black shoe boys, looked at this new group as up-starts, let's say; or the younger brother who hadn't quite grown up. It really was a generation gap, let's face it, there it was. One group was all enthusiasm and the other was supposedly the calming influence. It didn't work that way. There was always strife, really, and sometimes it was rather bitter strife, between the two.

Q: Can you recall any of the problems that you had to deal with as a representative from BuAer?

Hancock: No, actually, because as far as I was concerned, the public relations part of the Navy had was a more cordial attitude toward aviation than there was in the other parts of the Navy Department. I think the main public relations section of the Navy was more up to date, and were more alert to what the newspapers wanted. This was in the days of special aviation columns in newspapers and the press were asking for news and special material. So my work was supplying aviation to the Navy Public Relations Office; Press and Public Relations, I think they called it. I could feed it in and it would always be gobbled up. Then shortly the reporters started coming directly to my office in BuAer, which procedure was finally approved.

Q: You were a source of information?

Hancock: So they naturally followed the releasing of aviation photographs. These photographs could be used with the information I could give directly to the reporters. Oh, it became quite a bee-hive, and there was never any question of the fact that I was a woman. All the special writers and reporters knew that I had a background of aviation. They knew that I had been married in the Navy; that since World War I, I'd been in aviation, so to speak, at least in contact with it. So there was no question of the authenticity of my releases. Many were the friendships formed. Aviation was a sort of fraternity. And then, of course, there was the editorial side of the job. All the magazines we had in those days specializing entirely in aviation created a steady demand for material. Writing articles or getting BuAer's gunnery department, for example, to write one was a continuing function. I could go to the experts in BuAer and request such material when the magazines themselves couldn't. That's how we started feeding out all this naval aviation information. Oh, it was really fascinating to be in the midst of it.

Hancock #1 - 34

Q: And I would surmise that you were the right personality for that kind --

Hancock: I don't know, but I liked it particularly because no one ever said "could you do so and so," or "could this be done?" Instead it was "This is what's needed." You'd practically pull your hair out to secure it. For instance, all of a sudden the Senate Naval Affairs Committee House which it was in those days, inquired if they could get a good aviation picture to put in their committee room. So they called Admiral Moffatt. He was the Chief of Bureau. I was told to go up and look at the room and see what BuAer could put in it that would constantly remind Committee members of naval aviation. Well, when we finished up, we had airplane models which we persuaded the aircraft companies to give us (you know they were terribly expensive things). We had a beautiful model of an airship Cdr. Fulten got through the Goodyear Company. In addition, there were four beautiful pictures which the aircraft companies donated. Our efforts were most successful. Then, of course, the House Committee saw what the Senate had received and asked the Admiral to trim their Naval Affairs Committee room with aviation also.

Q: Was that Carl Vinson? Was he there?

Hancock: I don't -- it wasn't Vinson at the time. I've forgotten

Hancock #1 - 35

who it was. I don't think it --

Q: Was it Fred Britten?

Hancock: Britten. I think -- I'm pretty sure it was Britten. And so we turned to, and by golly we set up models of the then existing naval aviation planes, and so forth, and fixed their room up. So right there we had a coverage, a constant reminder of naval aviation, that you couldn't have enticed those people to take if you had gone to them and said, "Look, can we put this in your room?" But when they come to you, it becomes a golden opportunity.

Q: Guess and --

Hancock: They were the little things that came up, you know, that you just loved doing.

Q: Yes, that was a publicity person's dream.

Hancock: And then, of course, my newspaper friends got tipped off. I don't know how, of course. And they went up to the Hill with request to photograph the new decorations in the room. Well, of course, right there again it was more publicity for naval aviation.

Hancock #1 - 36

Q: And then your problems with the more staid versions of the Navy grew, didn't they?

Hancock: We weren't always welcome in other parts in the Navy Department. But it was fun.

Q: Well, was it a help, was there a noticeable difference when you had some of the more senior men training at Pensacola, like Admiral King?

Hancock: Yes. I -- there was a little feeling within the service itself, within naval aviation itself, when the older men were brought in and qualified. But we needed some rank, and that was the basis for it, actually. I think there was temporarily quite a strong feeling among the young naval aviators that this wasn't fair to them, to bring in these older people with higher rank, and qualify them. But the selection of what the young aviators generally termed nine old men was a very wise plan all the way through. Admiral King, Halsey, Bristol, right straight down the line -- for there was great need for more rank in aviation, with its expansion in personnel, its desire to have naval aviators as the COs of the aircraft carriers, and the prestige of rank in Congressional and inter-departmental confrontations.

Q: Kelly Turner.

Hancock #1 - 37

Hancock: Yes. Kelly Turner and all those -- they all had, without exception, those I can think of off-hand, talent that helped naval aviation tremendously.

Q: I would think so. I mean they're --

Hancock: Yes, and they were able to go into jobs which otherwise would have been filled by Navy officers, without aviation qualifications. In order to have someone then put in with the pilot training course behind them was a great boon to the whole set-up; more understanding, and so forth. So it turned out, there was a little resentment at the time, but it quickly evaporated when it was realized what type of person wanted to come in and who was selected to do so.

Q: Well, as I understand it and as I heard it from one of the -- now a senior but in those days a young officer -- men like King went through the whole course without any holds barred. I mean, they said they wanted to experience the whole thing and prove their mettle.

Hancock: Oh yes. They took it. They wanted it. They believed in aviation and its role in the Navy which was not held, as we've said, by some of the others. And the very fact that they did -believe in it and took the training and stayed with it, well, that in itself showed the type of person they were, and

Hancock #1 - 38

what it would mean to naval aviation in building it up as a permanent and important part, and not a separate part, of the Navy, which is what they wanted it to be and which it became.

Q: Were you in the Bureau when King was head of the Bureau?

Hancock: Oh yes.

Q: Tell me about him.

Hancock: He was rather terrifying at times, you know. He was the toughest boss that I had in that job. As you know, his saying many times over about the silent service -- "Deeds, not words" that was his sort of a slogan.

Q: Deeds, not words.

Hancock: Deeds, not words. Well, to be the public relations officer for the bureau, the Chief of which said, "Deeds, not words" was a tough situation. To get him to say anything was awfully difficult. I had a daily morning conference with him which was fruitless for Press purposes. For my part, I was frankly scared; scared of making a mistake, rather than scared of the man, although he was very stern and very forbidding. I would always take my notebook in in the morning, and I'd generally have at the most, a five minute conference. And

I kept that procedure up regardless of his "I haven't anything to say," Whenever he did say anything I would write it down because he was such a -- well, overpowering individual, in every sense of the word. And I would be so taken with what he was saying that when I left the office I'd frequently say to myself, "What did he say?" I mean, he really took up the whole atmosphere. That is why I wrote everything down, and I would rush to my office while I could still understand my notes and write it out in full. Just a few words from him and I could start something going for the Press. But he was really very kind, and he realized more and more that he had to give something in order to keep naval aviation rolling, and I think he did appreciate more --

Q: He began to understand more of Moffatt's approach?

Hancock: Yes. You had to give something if you're going to have understanding. But he was perfectly grand. I wrote a couple of articles about him. One of them I called "Uncle Ernie Cominch." You know he was known, not always affectionately, as Uncle Ernie in the fleet. It was published in one of the aviation magazines, which had asked me to do it, and he --

Q: Do you recall where? When?

Hancock: I have it somewhere at home. I've forgotten which

Hancock #1 - 40

magazine it was in now. I told of several incidents concerning Uncle Ernie. One told about him stamping on his hat in a rage, and how it flew voerboard from the carrier bridge and how no one seemed to have a spare hat and he went ashore bareheaded, later. Well, anyway, he wrote me a note and he said he thought I'd -- he was then Commander in Chief -- Cominch, -- been kind to him in this article for which he thanked. He also said he still very well remembered the idfficult times that he used to give me when I was trying to do a job. A very nice note that he wrote me, but --

Q: He recognized it as trying to do your job and he wasn't cooperating.

Hancock: He did. And he called me over when I enrolled in the Navy --

Q: In '42?

Hancock: In '42. I had just gotten my uniform, as a matter of fact. You see, I didn't go to indoctrination school at all.

Q: I wouldn't think you'd have to.

Hancock: They thought that I had had enough Navy to compensate for an indoctrination course. I had this call from Admiral

King's aide. I've forgotten who the aide was who said, "The admiral wants to see you." When I used to get that call when he was my boss -- when he was Chief of Bureau of Aeronautics -- I would grab a pad and pencil and run, wondering what's going to happen now, you know. So I went over to his office and said, "The admiral's called for me to come over" and I went into his office. You know what he had done? He said to me, "Weren't you in World War I?" I said, "Yes, Admiral, I was." He said, "Well, why aren't you wearing your World War I ribbon?" And I said, "Well, I thought about it, Admiral, but there's no precedent. I think I'm the only woman who served in World War I." "Well," he said, "You should wear it." And he said, "I have one for you." And he had. It was the World War I ribbon bar.

He said, "Come here." And I walked over to his desk and he sort of looked my uniform over and discovered the little flap over the pocket. He said, "Well, I think that's as good a place as any." And he lifted up the little flap and pinned the ribbon on it and then leaned down and kissed me on both cheeks. Then we shook hands. It was just the nicest thing. I had thought of that, you know, but I wasn't going to say, "Can't I wear the World War I ribbon?". I mean you just pull back from that sort of thing.

Q: Naturally, you do.

Hancock: I practically wept, I was so touched with the thing. He said, "Well, you're doing a good job now. Go ahead." And so I left and walked out of the office. I was absolutely in a -- you know, sort of in a daze.

As I started down the hall I saw this officer coming along. He was quite elderly and I sort of registered that he was one of the men that had been recalled to active duty, because just a couple of days before I had been talking to Admiral Yarnell, whom I adored, who had been recalled to active duty. I saw that this man coming was short, had white hair, wore a broad and narrow. Just as I got right alongside of him he said, "Young lady." I remember so well stopping, although I knew lots of them but not when I was in uniform. It made a difference. Immediately I stopped, of course, and he added, "Are you a WAVE?" That was a natural question, for there were practically none around as yet. I replied, "Yes, I am, Admiral." "Well," he said, "there's one thing you WAVES are going to have to learn. You don't wear decorations unless you earn them." "But Admiral, this is mine," I replied. "I was in World War I, as a yeoman." And just to prove my right to wear the ribbon, I said, "And Admiral King has just pinned it on me." He looked at me quizzically and said, "Well, there are only a few of us left."

I've never quite gotten over it. On many occasions I told the story to my WAVES around the country, particularly when the question of age would come up, and I'd say, "Just

Hancock #1 - 42a

remember, the admiral and I are old enough to --"

Q: And who was this?

Hancock: I don't know. I've never -- and I used to look around the corridors in the old Navy building to see if I'd ever see him again, you know. I never did. Might have been Santa Claus for all I know.

Q: He came at the appropriate moment, didn't he? Can you remember anything more about Admiral King? I'm collecting information on him.

Hancock: Right off hand I would say I can't remember any particular instance although at the time I served him, there always seemed to be something happening, you know, and his personality was always felt in everything that happened there. It wasn't a jolly one. It wasn't that -- it was entirely different from Admiral Moffatt, for instance. There was a sternness about him that seemed to be rather unrelenting.

Q: But this was, I believe, a facade, wasn't it?

Hancock: I think it was to a great extent but he certainly maintained it. Yes, he was a remarkable, remarkable and very strong character. You respected the man all the way through.

A lot of people were fearful of him. Fearful of his stern treatment of their invited comments. Also he was possessed of a biting sarcasm on occasion, and quite intolerant of slow thinking. I think he sometimes mistook slower thinking for stupidity, which he did not tolerate.

Q: In contrast with Admiral Moffatt, he must have been, when he appeared before congressional committees; how did he conduct himself, there? How effective was he?

Hancock: He was effective. He never let down. I never was present at any of his hearings. I read his testimony and from that I could visualize, generally, his presentation. I've heard him make other less formal presentations. But, I think, there was no question about his acceptance by the committees before which he appeared, and that he was held in utmost respect by them. But there was no temporizing, there was no, there was never any compromise in his voice, so to speak. Now Admiral Moffatt it would be, "Now look, let's talk this over." sort of an idea. You didn't have that with Admiral King, although he had naturally a very fine mind and I think drew the utmost respect from the committees before which he appeared. But he was stern. Unrelenting.

Q: Give me also a picture of Admiral Towers, will you?

Hancock #1 - 44

Hancock: Admiral Towers was colorful in a very quiet way. To my way of thinking, he had a tremendous amount on the ball and of course, you know his background and his work in early aviation and some of his disappointments like the event when his plane was not able to carry through on the NC transatlantic flight. But he was a fine administrator, tremendous imagination. I remember one day in particular in the BuAer board room which we had just decorated. (I was ably assisted in that venture by young Douglas Fairbanks, Jr., who had just come on active duty and --)

Q: He was in our office for a while, too.

Hancock: Was he? Well, he came over to help me place pictures and ready the room for its first press conference. The war had just started as far as we were concerned. Admiral Towers was, at first, adverse to the press conference which I had set up. He liked the press and he knew the necessity of it but he personally was shy. He was a shy man.

Q: Admiral Towers was?

Hancock: And he did not like to appear, say in a press conference. I finally got him to say he would head up this press conference and invited the press, cameramen, special writers - and they all came. First time it was being used. In his very quiet but entirely positive and assured manner, he made a statement which was like the proverbial bolt out of the blue. It was entirely startling, and the press grabbed it and ran with it. It made headlines all over. He said, "The aircraft carrier will spearhead this war." Successful action in this war will be accomplished by naval aviation operating from aircraft carriers fighting as the number one naval strength. The battleship is no longer the spearhead. Well, there was a thick silence; I'll never forget it. A silence that fell like a thick blanket and I think it was John Norris, one of the reporters who spoke up and asked, "Will you repeat that Admiral?" And he replied, "The aircraft carrier will spearhead the action in this war."

Well, it hit the papers and from that time on there was a case as far as he was concerned for showing that his statement was absolutely true. Get aviation in there, was the daily word. Of course, we were a materiel bureau really, although it handled operations as well, but with Adm. Towers working with David Ingels who was then assistant Secretary of War and Artemus Gates -- the plane output really started to hum. Also, President Roosevelt saw the naval aviation need and its potential and also put the pressure on.

Q: Artemus Gates.

Hancock: Admiral Towers was affirmative. For instance, the

Hancock #1 - 46

operating personnel would say, "We need so many planes." His reply would be, "We'll turn them out." And he would turn Heaven and earth to get the materiel part of it going, and at the same time working out the operations to vindicate -- not vindicate, but prove his statement to the press that aviation would spearhead the whole t-ing. He had tremendous backing of all the active people in aviation. He was responsive to them, and to their ideas, and he'd listen with patience to them. And he was frank to say, "I don't think that's good." or "Go on farther with this and let's see if it's good" or something of that nature. They knew where they stood, and there was no fear in their make-up. He was awfully good for naval aviation. He had imagination and ability and he knew the ropes. He knew the score. He had been with it all along.

Q: Was Louis de Flores there?

Hancock: Oh yes. Oh, what a character.

Q: Tell me about him.

Hancock: Well, he got kicked around a lot when he first came in. Of course, Capt. Radford was instrumental in getting a lot of talent like Louis de Flores possessed, to come in to naval aviation. Steiken, world famous photographer, Louis de Flores and many others with different talents. Osborn, you know, the artist? -- was another.

Q: Yes.

Hancock: And oh, just innumerable people. Well, Louis de Flores was brought in. I had never known him before and ashamed to admit that I had never known of him. No one knew what to do with him when he reported in.

Q: He was a genius, wasn't he?

Hancock: Of course, but he had no job assigned when he reported to the Bureau. I think Capt. Radford was away at the time. De Flores came in and was all dressed up. I think he came in as a lieutenant commander or commander, I've forgotten which, and he had no place to go. One day I saw this man wandering around and he said, "What do you do?" I told him that I was Editorial Research and asked him where he was located. "Nowhere as yet," he replied. "I don't even have a desk." So I invited him to my office and he sat in my office at a desk for several weeks with nothing to do and nobody seemed to know he was there. It wasn't that they didn't want him, they didn't know what to do with him if they had him, you see, whether it was purchasing or whatever you have in the materiel setup. Then they put him, took him and put him in a desk down in the blue print room -- you know where they draw the blue-

Hancock #1 - 48

prints for experimental planes and parts. I sort of lost track of him for awhile until all of a sudden the idea of the new link trainer and many special devices, pushed enthusiastically by Capt. Radford became the Louis de Flores project, which of course is what he was brought in for in the beginning but no one had known, in Capt. Radford's absence, where to get him started. And from that he operated like a streak of lightning, securing separate building in several places, and as you know. He was a fantastic figure throughout, with his inventive mind and the creation of machines for the testing of pilots with punch buttons, and the multitude of other training aids. I came to know him very, very well, and I thought he was a most remarkable person. Here was a man who dreamed dreams and had weird ideas, but you were there and you saw them come true. I mean you often hear of people that say this is a good idea and let's do so-and-so and they just peter out.

Q: But he implemented these things.

Hancock: He implemented these things and he trained the people and he instilled the people that he trained with his brand of enthusiasm, and he made their minds work. Oh, he was just fantastic.

Q: I'm glad to have that picture of him. Was Gus Reed on tap?

Hancock: Yes. Yes.

Q: Tell me about that whole idea of the reserve officers.

Hancock: That was the AV-S Program (AVIA-specialists). Well, he -- I remember Gus Reed particularly for his set-up at the Quonset Naval Air Station, which was remarkable. I had two brothers go through there incidently, and then two nephews besides, and Gus Reed and Dick Ferrelly worked very closely in the Bureau. Now Gus was the leading spirit in that AV-S program at Quonset, R. I., and Dick Ferrelly who was an administrative officer in the Bureau at that time. I used to go to Gus Reed for conferences. For instance, after they (BuAer) sent me, as a civilian, to Canada to look over the set-up up there to see how the Canadian Wrens and the women in the Canadian Air Force were set-up and working. Admiral Cook was then Chief of Bureau.

Q: Saavy Cook?

Hancock: No, not Saavy. Arthur. Arthur B. Cook. Saavy was over with Admiral King. I'd go to Gus Reed and talk out these ideas. -- on how to organize them into groups for administrative purposes so that they would be the least disrupting to the Navy when they were brought in. This was before the WAVES started, you see, and before we could get any legislation started. We worked on the premise that they were coming in

Hancock #1 - 50

eventually, so let's get something down in the way of planning that would be workable immediately in the way of housing, and discipline, and utilization. This BuAer went ahead and worked on.

Q: And this is where it began? BuAer?

Hancock: Yes. Yes.

Q: I'm delighted to get this little bit of a story which I have not been able to arrive at before hand.

Hancock: Well, of course, Admiral Towers and Admiral Cook and others knew what the women in Britain were doing, for instance. Captain Ralph Ofstie was over there during the years immediately before 1942 as naval attache in London during the blitzes, and he too knew what the Wrens and all these people were doing. The opinions of many persons were studied while plans were formulated. And Admiral Radford wrote a letter to BuPers and asked what were their plans on including women? You know what his answer was. "We have no plans, and we have no intention of using them." And Capt. Radford said, "There we go again. No looking ahead by the black shoe boys." Then began the struggle to get legislation introduced under the counter, which we did. And that put BuPers on the spot. They were really forced to take affirmative action.

Hancock #1 - 51

Q: Yes.

Hancock: They had to do something about it. We got Representative Mel Maas and Mel Maas got Senator Willis to introduce simultaneous legislation in March 1942.

Q: Cutting?

Hancock: No. It was Willis. As a matter of fact I have it all in my book, this whole darned story as I saw it, and I was in on it. But it is a fact. It's factual as to how the legislation finally got under way. It was not until months later that legislation more to BuPers liking was introduced.

Q: Well, I have quizzed various people, including Mildred McAfee, and she did not know this. Of course, she came on from -- quite from the outside and was amazed at the lack of readiness for a women's organization.

Hancock: BuPers had nothing. Nothing.

Q: Jacobs and the rest of them didn't seem to --

Hancock: They weren't going to have them. They didn't need them. That was their attitude, until they were put on the spot.

Hancock #1 - 52

Q: I'm rather surprised that this was Admiral Nimitz's attitude, too.

Hancock: It was. Definitely. But he changed over and he admitted it. He went up to the hearings on the regular Navy and said, "Keep them in." He said, "I was a convert. At first, I didn't want them."

Q: His remark, as reported to me, was that he didn't want any of those women similar to what they had in World War I.

Hancock: I never heard that. Never heard that.

Q: And wondered why he had taken that attitude. That's why I asked you earlier, I mean how did the male officers receive you in World War I? There was only a total of 10,000 in World War I -- all primarily clerical -- telephone operators, finger printing and communications. They had, as far as I know, a splendid reputation.

Now we are all ready to resume with the story - the making of the request to the Congress.

Hancock: The big shock which generated some activity was asking BuPers for the 23,000 women. That naval aviation activities could use 23,000 women, broken down into the jobs that they could do was the big innovation. Of course, we had to just just visualize many of the jobs that they could do because they'd never been in the fields before, but we had plenty of faith in the ability of women when properly trained.

Q: And the jobs were mushrooming and the stations were mushrooming.

Hancock: That's right. And Admiral -- then Capt. -- Radford, the head of training, was so instrumental in making that part of our survey come true because he said, "We'll train them. We'll see if they can do this. We'll see if they can be aviation machinist mates, and metal smiths, and so forth. Right straight through. Try them at every rating with the exception of those beyond their physical capabilities and those that are purely of a shipboard nature -- they will not serve aboard ship." And that's exactly what we did. And the planes were serviced by the women, they were repaired by the women, they were aerologists, they were communicators, they were everything.

Q: Did they manage the link trainers?

Hancock: Oh, well, they ran that whole program. And the control towers. Celestial navigation. Here's something that always impressed me because it's a fact that we can all be proud of -- after the WAVE program got underway and the first training was completed in various trades, not one pilot went into action who hadn't received some of his training from a WAVE. Whether it was aircraft gunnery, navigation, or high altitude flying, they were the instructors. And we utilized the 23,000 women that we asked for originally. It came out that way, which I think is unusual, the figure having been on an original estimate basis.

Q: Well, tell me about the struggle to get the legislation. You worked through -- BuAer worked through Mel Maas, did they?

Hancock: Yes. We couldn't -- you see we couldn't -- I say we, I'm speaking of the Bureau of Aeronautics, Admiral Towers, Captain Radford --

Q: But you were the publicity agent at that --

Hancock: Yes, but at that time I was not only publicity but I was doing this WAVE program about which they said, "All right you want to get in, don't you?" I said, "Sure." "Well, then we've got to get these plans together." I was doing a lot of that work in addition to my public relations job. And BuAer couldn't really go in and say we want so-and-so legislation. I mean you don't do that. It was BuPers's prerogative and they weren't going to do it. So there was --

Q: That was Admiral Jacobs at that point?

Hancock: I'm not sure it was Admiral Jacobs at that time. I've forgotten. The first bill was really introduced by Representative Mel Maas and Senator Willis. Behind its introduction is quite a story. There was an organization known as the Sons of Mom Chung. Have you ever heard of it?

Q: No.

Hancock: Admiral Nimitz belonged. It was only for aviators in its beginning and then she opened it up to submariners. Dr. Chung was in San Francisco.

Q: Oh, I've heard of her. Yes, yes. Mom?

Hancock: Mom Chung. C-h-u-n-g, Dr. Margaret Chung.

Q: I think I heard of her through Miss Wilde.

Hancock: Yes, well, she's a marvelous character. Mel Maas was one of her Sons.

Q: He was?

Hancock: Yes. I mean "Sons." All the members were "Sons"

including now Admiral McQuiston, who was in the Reserve Section of the Bureau. Irving McQuiston. And Mom Chung came to town to see what she could do for the war effort. Aviation wanted the legislation to enroll women -- what would she do to help? It was decided that she would go up and see Mel Maas, one of her Sons and say, "Why don't you introduce a bill? I want to get in the Navy." She did want to come in as a doctor. That she didn't make it always sort of broke my heart. For she had done so much for us. Mom Chung went up to see Mel Maas and said, "Look, we need some legislation. There is need for women in the Navy. Aviation needs them."

Mel Maas, of course, was in Marine Corps aviation and he said, "All right, Mom." And without further ado he called Senator Willis, a friend of his, from the middle West, and they introduced simultaneous bills on March 18, 1942, in the House and in the Senate, stipulating, "This is the authority to enroll women . . ."

Q: This would be an amendment to the Reservist ACt, wouldn't it?

Hancock: Yes, to the Naval Reserve Act of 1938. "--into the reserve and introduced them." In the meantime the WAC legislation had been introduced by Edith Nourse Rogers and she called BuPers and asked if they had any legislation in and they said no, and they didn't intend to put any in. She said.

Hancock #1 - 57

"I understand that a bill was just introduced on the floor of the House for that purpose and what are you going to do about it?" And that was the start of the -- Of course, those two bills were still in committee. When BuPers got busy and requested a bill that they felt would be better coverage. This was introduced May 14, 1942 by Senator David Walsh as a "Women's Auxiliary Corps" bill. Final legislation was not enacted until July 1942.

Q: And BuPers was then actually activated by a kind of a back fire?

Hancock: Oh yes. And then the -- it's in the records in the archives and everywhere else that then they visualized at the most a total of 10,000 women.

Q: Headed by a lieutenant commander.

Hancock: Yes, one lieutenant commander. However, only a total of 10,000 women was visualized. That was the number that had been used in World War I. As it turned out they enrolled 100,000 instead of 10,000. As soon as that ball started rolling and they were framing legislation, BuAer sent over their 23,000 request and BuPers (I've a copy of the letter) said, "We had only visualized 10,000. We will now adjust our thinking and try to set up recruiting to get -- as soon as the

Hancock #1 - 58

bill passes -- to get the numbers you need."

Q: Well, BuAer had by that time become much more respectable.

Hancock: Oh yes. This was in '41.

Q: The fortunes of the WAVES rode on the respectability and credibility of BuAer.

Hancock: And desirability of their services. And at that same time, of course, BuAer said when they're taken in we want to train our own women, and we will do it in already existing schools so that there will be no additional expense. This was done. They were integrated into the overall Navy program.

Q: Is this a part of your planning, too?

Hancock: Yes. And that has held and is still holding. They go to the same schools and they compete in class standing with the men, so that when they go on the job, say for instance the aviation mechanic, the men they're working next to don't say, "Oh yeh, you don't know from nothing." For the men know they had had the same course, they had taken the same examinations.

Q: Well, I take it from what you've told me that you were

Hancock #1 - 59

pretty basic to the planning then.

Hancock: Well, actually, I was for naval aviation. Simply because I was drawn into the planning by the persons heading up aviation, Admiral Towers, Capt. Radford, and all the people I had known all my life. They knew I had a background in aviation, they knew I had World War I service, and I think they felt I was competent in going ahead with this work, and they really threw it to me. But certainly, all along the way, it was their direction, their help, and their imagination that did it. At times I felt somewhat like the peg in a game of quoits. But I was in a position to know the plans from the ground up. I think that's one of the reasons why Capt. McAfee later said in a letter to me re my history of the WAVES, "You write it. You were in before it started. And you know it from the ground up."

Q: Yes. And I think she's perfectly right because as she says frankly, she knew nothing about the Navy at all.

Hancock: Oh, she had such a tough year.

Q: She was brought in for administrative purposes --

Hancock: And prestige.

Hancock #1 - 60

Q: Yes, and prestige.

Hancock: And she brought that to us. I don't know anyone else who could have done it as well. I really don't. She was fine. And she had an awfully tough time of it, believe me.

Q: She told me about for four months or something, having an office by the reflecting pool or some place in one of those temporary buildings with virtually nothing to do. Nothing passed over her desk or nothing came her way.

Hancock: She knew nothing of the organization of the Navy and she wasn't helped and when she was finally put where she could have her finger in the various things that were going on, Admiral Jacobs made her directly responsible to him. Well, of course, that antagonized everybody else. Because she would go directly to him with what was probably a very good idea, and it would conflict with overall Navy planning in practically every activity. She had no way of knowing this for she was not included in overall conferences until much later. She was always behind the eight ball and it wasn't her fa-lt. I mean they couldn't have had a more capable person but, gee whiz, she had an awful tough row to hoe. I think I'm a little tired now.

Interview #2 with Capt. Joy Bright Hancock, USN (Ret.)
At the Naval Institute, Annapolis, Md., by John T. Mason, Jr.
Subject: WAVES   Nov. 13, 1969

Q: Capt. Hancock, yesterday you had told me something about the initial legislation which would have made the WAVES possible. You want to resume your story from that point.

Hancock: Yes, the legislation as introduced by Congressman Maas was later discarded but it was the opening wedge, actually, and in my opinion, it was the wedge which sort of shook Bureau of Personnel, then, of course, was Bureau of Navigation, into considering this matter over and above the negatives that they had been giving out when inquiries had been made.

Q: Do you know what their reaction was? I mean what they -- who was it, Nimitz then?

Hancock: No. Admiral Jacobs was --

Q: Admiral Jacobs was there, then.

Hancock: Yes, at that time.

Q: Do you know what the initial reaction was to this Maas legislation?

Hancock: Yes, I later found out what the reaction was. "Who did this?" was the reaction. Unbeknownst to them, and with no prior legislative conference between the Hill and the Bureau this thing had taken place. Certainly they wondered who could have done this sort of thing?

Q: Most unorthodox.

Hancock: Most unorthodox, and, I think, as I found out later that the Bureau of Aeronautics was highly suspect in that matter.

Q: Naturally.

Hancock: Well, they, BuPers, had, actually, had a letter from Admiral, then Capt., Radford, also inquiring what they were going to do about the use of women and the answer had been, "we're not going to do anything about it. Civil Service can fill any jobs that we need filled by women."

That was the end of the picture as far as the utilization of women's skills were concerned. And Capt. Radford took that letter, which I didn't find out until much later, to Mr. Vinson, who was then the chairman of the House Naval Affairs Committee, and asked Mr. Vinson if he would do a little prodding, which I understand he did and he did the prodding right back to Admiral Jacobs and, of course, Mrs. Rogers had already written Admiral Nimitz about it, who had also replied to her in the negative, I think after conference with the Bureau of Personnel, which did not see any need for using women in the service.

So that definitely, once any sort of legislation had been introduced it put them on the spot. And all the inquiries coming in about it and they started studying the matter and, of course, in the meantime, Bureau of Aeronautics had gone ahead and drew up what they figured were the jobs and numbers of women that they could use in naval aviation itself, which came to about 23,000 women. When a bill was finally introduced then by conference --

Q: How did the bill that was finally introduced differ from Maas's original bill?

Hancock: Only in that it was more explicit into how they should be brought into the service and it was called the Women's Reserve of the Naval Reserve. It was still keeping them sort of a corps unto themselves. That was introduced with the backing up of the Bureau of Personnel; that is, with their approval.

Q: This had the official sanction, then.

Hancock: A bill to authorize a Women's Army Corps was very definitely active in the Congress under Edith Nourse Rogers. The Navy had to have a strong reason for not utilizing women and stop dragging its feet because of the momentum which had been created by the WAC legislation.

Q: What about the SPARS?

Hancock: Well, now, the SPARS were later.

Q: They were later.

Hancock: They were later, yes. I don't think that the Marine Corps was in the original draft but very shortly they became an amendment. You see in the beginning the Marine Corps being part of the Navy, hadn't been thought necessary but then to be sure they were named specifically and also the SPARS, they were taken up later.

Q: What was the reaction in Congress to this sort of thing?

Hancock: Well, it was negative. Really. Senator David I. Walsh of Massachusetts --

Q: Chairman of the Naval Affairs Committee in the Senate?

Hancock #2 - 65

Hancock: Of the Senate, right. -- was the main stumbling block. Carl Vinson who was so helpful to the Navy in so many things didn't get excited over the legislation. I remember we always referred to him as Admiral Vinson when things were going well for the Navy, which he loved incidentally. David I. Walsh, well-known bachelor, put his objection to the legislation on the basis that the women of America -- the womanhood of our women must be protected. He objected to women taking part in war.

Well now, he was old enough to remember that they had served in World War I, but he chose not to remember that sort of thing, and he was -- always when action was stirred up such as assignment to committee, or committee hearings and so forth, he blocked everything. We couldn't get hearings, we couldn't get this, that, and the other -- it was frustrating and it was always on the basis that chivalry must be shown to the women of America. And then when finally the bill -- the war bill did pass -- he was instrumental in getting in the man restrictions he thought necessary such as no overseas duty, no service in airplanes, etc. All of which had later to be changed or stricken by amendments.

Q: They bore the initial brunt of the Congressional criticism.

Hancock: That is correct. That is correct.

Hancock #2 - 66

Q: Was Margaret Chase Smith of any help at this stage? I mean with the first bill? She was in the House then.

Hancock: Yes. I do not know the specifics of her help. I know she was working with Frances Perkins and Edith Nourse Rogers and together they contributed a great deal. It was the affirmative thing. They were all interested in letting the women prove that they could do a job. They did not exert direct pressure, which was needed, on the Navy. But their legislative effort anent the WAC did rouse the people within the Navy itself. Of course, later she was of great assistance in Navy legislation.

Q: Was there not in being then an advisory committee of women, prominent women?

Hancock: Yes. Right.

Q: How did that come into being?

Hancock: That came into being when legislation -- when there was no doubt that some sort of legislation was going to pass. The Bureau of Personnel did go ahead and appoint this committee of women advisors to recommend what should be done in way of administration, standards, etc. It consisted largely of women educators, headed up by Dean Virginia Gildersleeve.

Q: Gildersleeve, yes.

Hancock: And there were approximately, I think there were ten on the committee. They were the group that recommended Mildred McAfee, then president of Wellesley to be the first Director. Dean Gildersleeve had done a great deal of studying and observation abroad of the British methods of setting up the various military organizations of women. The members of this advisory committee made a fine contribution. None of them, actually, had any Navy background, so they weren't expected to set up a practical working program within the service. That had to be worked out with the men in the service, you see.

Q: Now, they continued, and perhaps we could pursue this a little bit on in, they continued as an advisory group through the years of the war.

Hancock: Yes, Through the war.

Q: And what was their specific role? I ask this because Rita Lenihan said to me, "We're never quite certain as to their exact role, their exact purpose, just what did they do?"

Hancock: No one actual or specific accomplishment can be pointed to.

Hancock #2 - 68

Q: What was your idea of their role and their accomplishments?

Hancock: Well, I think definitely their role after selecting Miss McAfee, which of course, was a marvelous choice, and after they went back to their respective colleges and areas, they, because of the prestige which each of these women enjoyed, were able by their statements that they were interested in seeing young women join the Navy, and the fact that they were advisors in this Navy program gave to the whole recruiting picture a fine substance. The mothers throughout the country, and their daughters who were in their colleges of these advisors received a feeling, well, that this program was a good thing; that it has been looked into; it wasn't some fly-by-night thing. Then with the selection of Capt. McAfee they had additional prestige and assurance. The committee met, after initially getting under way, oh, I would say, two or three times a year, during which meetings they would be brought up to date, given briefings, sort of like the SecDef briefings we have nowadays for important civilians. And they would go back into their communities where they were able to answer questions and to make speeches. In other words, they aided greatly in recruiting of people and so forth. I remember on one occasion the whole group, including some guests, Margaret Chase Smith was one of them, that we arranged to take the committee "on tour" to study WAVES at work. Admiral McKane was my chief then, and incidentally Admiral McKane swore me into the WAVES; he administered my oath. He supplied the air transportation.

Q: Oh, he did?

Hancock: Yes, he was a delightful man, and of course, I had served under each chief of Bureau at some past time. He arranged to let me have an airplane large enough to take the advisory group on a trip to see WAVES at work. Of course, I just exuded pride in my WAVES and the job they were doing.

We selected NAS Pensacola as the place. We took the whole group down and really showed them "WAVES at work." They were astounded because of the various fields in which the women were serving very efficiently and competently. We had three, four days at Pensacola and outlying fields. And there again, after that visit, they went back to their communities and said, "Look, this is what's happening." I mean, that was really their function. And their suggestions were, a lot of them, good, or at least they were suggestions that could be talked out and then their practicability subjected to the judgment of the planning divisions in the Navy itself.

Q: Yes, Yes. Taken over and given a Navy stamp.

Hancock: Actually, I think that once under way we probably could have progressed without the committee. But we gained so much more by retaining them and letting them report the

Hancock #2 - 70

civilian reactions to the WAVES, which was helpful in evaluating our own opinions on various problems. And of course, I was in on all these conferences because I was the liaison officer between Aero and Miss McAfee's office. I would therefore be called in on all of these conferences, and was able to keep in touch with what her office in the Bureau of Personnel was doing. After inspection trips, for instance, I would give a resume to her, and the officers like Jean Palmer who was in "Enlisted detail, and Virginia Carlin, who was in Officers Orders, and the other women officers in the housing and other pertinent divisions. I would report to them the things that I met up with that I thought could or should be changed, or even some small problem like a Commandant's request for a redheaded yeoman, or the inability of the Women's Representative on the Commandant's Staff to visit Naval Air Activities within her Naval District without special permission, so she could see what the air people were doing. There was still definite evidence of the BuAer-BuPers feud. Frequently I discovered the air station in refusing permission had stated, "Joy Hancock represents us."

Q: You were saying about the great advantage you enjoyed in that you knew all these commanding officers and they called you by first name and so forth.

Hancock: Yes, yes, and it was an advantage because there were no formal preliminaries to be gone through when you arrived at each place. I was generally met by the commanding officer, whom I'd known when he was a j.g. or when he had had a tour in BuAer and we could start immediately, if he had any problems, to discuss them or anything else that was on his mind or mine.

It was quite easy for me but it was not so easy for the women who were representatives -- let's say the CO of Mare Island, a purely naval function, without aviation. The women officers would have to make appointments to see the commanding officer, and it would be formal, sort of stylized, and sometimes they couldn't get in. So they were forced to work with the other women officers too much, you see, trying to solve the problems, and in consequence, the commanding officer wasn't knowing about the things that he should know. Unfortunately, there was a definite lack of communication.

On several occasions Capt. McAfee reached the point where she'd say, "Oh, Joy. We found so-and-so and we've had reports of so-and-so. Could you look into that while you're on your next trip?"

I never got into hot water simply because my aviation friends always had friends of the non-aviation COs. We could iron out a lot of things this way, generally by telephone. It was difficult from Capt. McAfee's side of the picture. The women officers serving at non-aviation bases because of their initial lack of a naval background, let's say, and the unwillingness, to a great extent, of the men for whom they worked, to accept them

Hancock #2 - 72

freely. Instead of saying, "Look, this is the problem," they seemed to set all the women aside as a corps, let's say, with the indication that, "Well, that's women. You look after that."

Q: How long did this unwillingness, in a general sense,

Hancock: Oh frankly, in most cases, until they were hard-pressed by a manpower shortage.

Q: Necessity, then?

Hancock: Yes. And then slowly, a realization that they had talent aboard that they could use and instead of saying to their Women's Representative, "Why don't you go down and look into the women's barracks or talk to the Chaplain," they found out they could actually put women in administrative jobs. They found they had engineers among the women. They found all these sort of things, which they had not been willing to look for or accept until the need arose, and then, by gosh, they took hold and became more than willing to cooperate. Then it started, "Send us more WAVES," which was Capt. McAfee's reward for doing all that ground work that she had had to do, and having to learn the Navy from the bottom up.

Q: Somebody commented that this attitude on the part of so

many of the male officers was in part due to the fact that as naval officers they had lived virtually in a man's world and the female part of the man's world was the Navy wife, the Navy hostess, the pretty gal in fluffy ruffles, maybe. But they hadn't known, as a group they hadn't known women in professional life.

Hancock: That's true.

Q: Is there validity to that, then?

Hancock: Oh yes. That is absolutely true, I think. I agree with it a great deal. Because the acceptance of women in civilian life and in civilian fields, let's say, hadn't been too great, they were still as individuals, trying to break into this, that, or the other. Their acceptance equally even today is not entire. They've got to prove themselves in order to be accepted and when they do, they are generally accepted.

In the Navy, if they couldn't be put on a job where they could prove themselves, it was doubly difficult. But once the need for them arose and they were put in the job and it was seen that they could do the job and some certain types of work better than the men, only then did they send us the WAVES. I remember Jean Palmer telling the story one time she was on Enlisted Detail and this unnamed Admiral called up and said he had to have a yeoman immediately. Of course, one got used to receiving individual calls, as you know, each trying to press his own case. And she said she'd look into it and would send one if it was in his allowance. It was and she sent him a WAVE. In this particular case the Admiral had outlined his specifications. He wanted her cute, red hair was preferred, well, sure he wanted a stenographer but he rarely dictated, but she had to know how to type, but he wanted her to be a stenographer, as well, and so forth.

So Jean Palmer would go muttering, "Another one of these." However, sending this WAVE was highly satisfactory, but shortly after volunteers for Hawaii were called and this WAVE volunteered. She wanted to go and she went. And this Admiral called up again, for a replacement. He got a man. So he called up Jean Palmer and raised the devil. He said, "Why you sent me a man!" Jean replied, "Yes, and he doesn't have red hair."

Q: Isn't that cute?

Hancock: You could hear Jean now coming right back at him. But that is an indication of the turn-over that did come, you see and the acceptance. Then once they had them they wanted it.

Q: Tell me -- let's focus on your assignment from '42 until '46 when you were dealing with the naval aviation part of things as it pertained to the WAVES. Tell me about that and about your trials and tribulations with that job.

Hancock: Well, actually, that's a pretty broad approach.

Q: Yes, I know. But that's the framework.

Hancock: But, yes. Well, actually I was assigned, continued to be in BuAer and was named as the women's reserve representative for naval aviation, to the chief of Bureau of Aeronautics. Then later when the office of Deputy Chief of Naval Operations (Air) was created I was concerned with all matters concerning the women in naval aviation. Policy was part of the job, assignment within the bureau of women personnel was also under my office. Oh, any other thing that came up concerning WAVES. Any discipline problems, and so forth.

Thus I interpreted and carried out policies as set forth by the bureau, and as framed by Capt. McAfee's office. So that when she wanted to know about conditions on all the/aviation bases "We'll get Joy Hancock over and she'll brief us."

And the housing within aviation, naturally I was in on that; the disciplinary set-up, the constant traveling to see that everything was working, that the supervision of the women was effective, and that other problems didn't arise, or if they did, what to do about them. In the early days it was making policy on the spot because BuPers was way behind in setting forth many of the policies. As a matter of fact, in BuAer we published a book on policies, incorporating what had come out in the way of letters from BuPers to the field and what we had found necessary to do in naval aviation, and we put that booklet into circulation. Admiral Fechteler was the chief of BuPers at that time.

Q: Bill Fechteler?

Hancock: And I was sure in hot water, because we sent the booklet out without BuPers' prior approval. It was my mistake. I made a lot of them. I guess we all did, especially in a new organization. I'm not saying that as an excuse but LCdr Jean Palmer called me from BuPers and said, "Are you the author of this Policies for WAVES in Naval Aviation?" And I said, "Yes." She said, "Well, it's raising the devil over here." And I said, "Why?" "Many of the libraries around the country are writing in requesting a copy of this booklet telling how the organization should be set up on air stations." First, we were told to recall it. Admiral Fechteler changed this order and said to notify all original addressees to put a confidential stamp on it and no public distribution was to be permitted. That was the best way to handle it and not raise a furor. So that darned booklet stood as the policy for the administration of WAVES in naval aviation until BuPers was able to publish the overall policies.

Q: Did you get called on the carpet?

Hancock: Not beyond that admonition. Capt. McAfee and I talked it over and she said, "I know, all we have are these various policy letters but we're trying to get them into a pamphlet form so we can distribute them."

I said, "Well, there's a crying need. On all my trips I'm asked what do you do in this case and what do you do in that? I had to put something out. My bosses told me I had to. So I went ahead and did it." Frankly, I did not clear it with BuPers, because I felt it concerned only naval aviation. But I should have told them, which I didn't, for I knew that the knowledge of this policy compilation would mean another great delay.

Q: And there again, the immediacy of the problem and the red tape.

Hancock: There was nothing counter to BuPers policies in the booklet.

Q: Yes, Yes.

Hancock: But my method was wrong. I just took the old naval

Hancock #2 - 78

aviation attitude, and said, "Come on, let's do it." I shouldn't have done that. I should have referred it to BuPers.

Q: It all came out all right in the end.

Hancock: It came out all right.

Q: Tell me, did you sit in on Miss McAfee's coffee klatches in the morning.

Hancock: Oh yes. I did when they were of any importance. If I were over in BuPers on some business, such as training, I would go in for coffee. I was welcomed at all times, as a matter of fact. However, I was on the road a great deal, and I was terribly busy in my own work. But any policy conference or anything of that sort, I was the BuAer representative. In each of the Bureaus, there was a WAVE officer who was advisor on women to the Chief of her Bureau. There were many informal morning conferences which were profitable for all hands.

Q: It seemed like a very brilliant idea to me. Once she understood the Navy's way of doing things, to have the various representatives in the bureaus, but you people developed ideas together and then took those ideas back to the respective bureau and made it seem that it had originated there. Which was an awfully clever way of doing things.

Hancock: Well, I think that any way that you could get things done and as smoothly as possible, particularly in war time, was warranted. Actually, that method might not follow the Navy's prescribed book of procedure, but it doesn't disrupt things, and so I think it was justified, don't you?

Q: Yes.

Interview #3 with Capt. Joy Bright Hancock, USN (Ret.)
At the Naval Institute, Annapolis, Md., by John T. Mason, Jr.
Subject: WAVES   March 11, 1970

Mr. Mason: Capt. Hancock, it's always a matter of great stimulation to be in your presence. I'm delighted to have you back at the Naval Institute again for this third interview. Last time when you broke off, you had begun to tell me about your duties and your problems during the period 1942 to 1946 when you were specifically assigned to BuAer. You had told me various things which I've enumerated to you off tape. Among other things you said that you did quite a bit of traveling during this period. I wonder if you could recall some of the things, some of the places you went and some of the things you had to do?

Hancock: Well, as you know, in the starting up of any program within the Navy or anywhere else, it's relatively an easy matter to sit in Washington, let's say, and formulate policies, and hope that they will be practical in the working out in the field. However, I felt, and certainly found out that bringing in large groups of women into a service, which hadn't known of such a thing since World War I, and most of those people who did know about it then, a relatively small number, either had forgotten that there had been women in the service, or just threw up their hands and said, "What, again?" However, the need to get out on the road as far as Aer was concerned, and at that time there was a great deal of difference in thinking between the Bureau of Aeronautics and the Bureau of Personnel, which was then the Bureau of Navigation, regarding, let's say, prerogatives. The aviators were of a new breed and had more or less surrounded themselves with independent thinking and action. They had, more or less set themselves up almost as a little separate entity, which, of course was resented and probably rightly so from the organizational point and administrative stand-point by the Bureau of Personnel. Well, the same thing held as far as the women were concerned.

Now BuAer had originally pushed very hard to get this legislation through so they could have the services of women, and had requested 23,000 of them to serve in aviation. BuPers practically threw their hands up at the request and said, "Well, any thinking we have done hasn't been in any such numbers as that, but we will attempt to get them."

BuAer again sort of held on to the training of them, the housing of them, that sort of thing, which necessitated that someone from Washington actually visit the air activities and see what could be done about answering some of the wild questions, and requests for help that came in from the commanding officers of these various air activities. No one was telling them anything but we were expecting an awful lot of them. So between my chief, who at that time was Admiral Towers, and my immediate boss, who was then Capt. Arthur Radford, I got the word. "All right, Joy, get on the road. Go out and help these people."

And in the early days that was really something because when you went to a station, you found that they depended on what you could tell them and what guidance you could give. And all you had to draw on was a bit of horse-sense. But knowing what efforts were being made back in Washington in the way of standards for housing and job set-ups, that sort of thing, was the basis of your dissertations. I had to keep a leash on my imagination for they took my word almost as the Bible because it was the nearest they could get to definite info in order to make decisions, which were, of course, up to them.

Q: And of course, by that time they had received copies, these confidential copies.

Hancock: Not at that time. No, that didn't come until quite a bit later.

Q: Oh, it didn't.

Hancock: At this time nothing had been published for their guidance.

Q: Nothing had been published?

Hancock #3 - 83

Hancock: Nothing. And since I was in on these early conferences I knew the trend of the things, and you just had to, sometimes, practically make up something right on the spot that you felt was logical. Luckily it turned out to be -- and it was because of all these various questions, unsolved as far as everyone was concerned, and still no policies published, that I wrote that booklet I told you about and because of which I got into trouble.

We tried to help them out. And, of course, those visits to the various activities continued right straight on through until I left BuAer and then they were carried on by my successor because we found that if someone was there to say "Yes, this is all right," or "This should be done," it just cleared the atmosphere and certainly cut down all the correspondence. And the commanding officers had a bit more time for other important things.

Q: How did you travel to these various --

Hancock: Generally by naval air and from one station to another they'd set up a small flight for me or something of that sort, you see, to the next station. And if I would go to one of the naval air training commands -- let's say at Jacksonville, that activity would fly me to all the out-lying stations under their command. The same would hold for primary training, technical training, I was sent all over the place. You see, if there was a flight scheduled, fine. There generally was, I'd go in the plane with others or else with just a pilot.

Q: Must have been mighty strenuous.

Hancock: It was. And I had quite a few experiences, rotten weather, ground looping, and that sort of thing, but I came through all right.

Q: Tell me about one or two of them, will you?

Hancock: Well, I remember one flight coming from Corpus Christie, Texas, and there were some naval scientists that were on the flight. There were four of us in I think it was a little Beechcraft. We got in a terrific storm and ended up lost somewhere over Mexico.

Q: Mexico?

Hancock. Yes. And we finally got back and landed. There isn't anything, really, to talk about except it was one of the most harrowing experiences I ever had. Of course, the pilot frankly said, "I don't know where we are right now. You see, my radio had gone out." It was certainly a terrific storm, and whenever I have to fly now, and I say have to fly because I don't particularly enjoy it, and we have any turbulence at all, I just sit and think of that terrific Texas-Mexico flight we had lasting several hours.

Q: That made an indelible impression, didn't it?

Hancock: It really did.

Q: Well, tell me about some of the knotty problems. I mean can you be specific about some of them?

Hancock: Well, they weren't sort of specific problems, they were overall problems, actually. About the -- well, for instance, the discipline question would be discussed. And one commanding officer, who was a fine old hard-boiled aviator, whom I had known all my life, said, "Joy, what do you do?" He says, "These women come up for mast and you stand there and you look at them and they burst into tears. What do you do?"

And I said, "Now, for instance, what offenses are you getting? What type?"

He said, "They're all such minor things." And he said, "I'd just give the men some extra duty for it, you know, for not showing their liberty card promptly when so requested by the marine guard at the gate, or something of that nature. Acting in a non-military manner, is another example."

"Well," I said, "why don't you give the women extra duty?"

He said, "Is that all right?" Questions of that sort now seem ridiculous, but on a 'first go-around' basis many commanding officers were at a loss with no printed policies to guide them.

Q: That would dry up the tears, wouldn't it?

Hancock: Yes. In the particular instance he was talking about, he had let two gals off scott free, with only a mild admonition not to do it again. I believe they had been reported by the Marine Guard for acting fresh.

I came back to this C.O. the next day and said, "I have something interesting to tell you. I've looked into the case we discussed and found these two gals you were talking about had after mast gone back to the barracks and said, 'Boy we pulled it over the old man again.'"

The C.O. rose and shouted, "What?"

And I replied, "That exactly happened." It opened his eyes. He told me later that at the next mast he spoke sternly about the silly things they do -- you know, like putting a hat on the back of the head on purpose to see if they'd be called on it. After that, and the assignment of the proper punishment, such action started to diminish. I pointed out that the WAVES were in the Navy, and if they didn't get the same treatment the men got, the whole structure could be ruined. He solved his problem from that time on. The men had to learn a lot about the proper handling of the women.

Q: They had to discard the rules of chivalry then and --

Hancock: Not quite. But in certain aspects they must be treated with firm regulations. And if they were not, the women soon found they were not part of the team. They really wanted to feel they were in the Navy. They were trying to do a man-sized job and they did not want to be treated like sissys. They used to say, "I can be treated that way in civilian life."

They really wanted to feel a part of the service. You could sense that. And when the commanding officers got the word and acted accordingly, it made all the difference in the world. It really did. Respect on both sides grew.

Q: I can see the point, yes.

Hancock: You asked for some specifics. I can think of one little thing that came up that could have been solved there but wasn't. We had trained aviation machinist mates. I went to one station and found they were all being used as yeomen in offices all over the base and this after the months of training at Memphis, Tennessee, and Norman, Oklahoma. They had trained with the men so they came out on the same basis, but they weren't being used as aviation machinists. "Why aren't they being used in their rating?" I practically demanded.

The gals were complaining bitterly, "I don't want to be a stenographer."

There were no toilet facilities for women in the hangars, so they weren't assigning the women there. So I said that I would look the facilities over. The toilet facilities proved to be adequate, and, of course, the women were supposed to relieve men which would not increase the numbers using the facilities. I talked to the leading chief and he said he didn't particularly want the women aviation machinist mates to come in. However, he had never worked with them. His was a part of that feeling in different degrees throughout the service, particularly on the part of the old-time chiefs, that women couldn't do the jobs properly.

I had found that once you could get those chiefs on your side, so to speak, you would have something. And it was true. I talked to the male leading chiefs and asked, "How are we going to solve this problem?"

And one of these chiefs came up to me and said, "Well, I guess we're going to have to have them. And here's what I'd do. Put a peg outside the door of the head, and when a man goes in, he hangs his hat on the peg and no women go in. When a WAVE goes in let her hang her hat on the peg, and the men will stay out." And that's how we solved the problem.

But it was something they wouldn't face up to without a push. I went back to that place later. They had installed additional toilet facilities for women as a sort of courtesy I think, for in war time even piping was difficult to get. If we had waited for this new plumbing, we would have lost all of that work from the women. Instead, being able to put your hat on a peg did the trick. And those same chiefs, for instance, once they had the women working there were delighted. I found they had trained helpful and willing workers.

It was little things like that for which you made trips. One problem solved gave ideas I could carry to the next base. They sound like very small things, and they were. But when a commanding officer is occupied with so many important things, these little details which came up in connection with women on the station for the first time could become real irritants and often seem almost insurmountable.

Q: And the natural prejudice still existed and had to be overcome.

Hancock: Yes.

Q: And it had to be overcome in a "show me" attitude. I mean, the Missouri type thing.

Hancock: I think, you know, in looking back, rather than prejudice it was more non-acceptance of qualifications. They just didn't believe that women could come in and do the job, for instance, as a mech or a metalsmith or many of the heretofore men's trades.

Q: Well, this is surely understandable.

Hancock: Yes, it is understandable, but at the same time, the people that didn't want the women to repair their planes, for instance on the stations, forgot the fact that those same airplanes were already being built by civilian women in the aircraft factories. The aircraft setups all over the U. S. were employing the women.

Q: Maybe they didn't forget this. Maybe they didn't realize this was happening.

Hancock: Perhaps they didn't.

Q: So it all gets back to the problem of publ-cizing.

Hancock: Selling. A selling job to being with and then maintenance of that knowledge as male personnel turnovers occurred.

Q: Well, you had a distinct advantage in that you were cognizant of selling techniques and so forth. And you were also cognizant of the problems on both sides.

Hancock #3 - 91

Hancock: Yes. And another thing, I think the greatest advantage I had, and I think I had it over and above any other woman officer who came into the WAVES, was the fact that I had worked for so many years in Bureau of Aeronautics, had been married in the Navy, and so had a substantial Navy background. I knew practically every commanding officer in naval aviation, and they knew me by my first name.

Many times, when my plane would come in at a station, the commanding officer would be down there to greet me, remarking that it was so nice to have the visit. That was an advantage in that I could talk sort of man to man. He and I had grown up in the same service. He knew I wasn't going to lead him down a path that wasn't practical. And I, without that background, would have had a much tougher job. As it was I always had, practically always, a hundred percent cooperation.

Q: My, how fortunate this was.

Hancock: Oh, it was fortunate.

Q: That you were in the right spot. You said in our conversation before that the WAVES who were under the aegis of Bureau of Aeronautics received a great deal more training than those who were under the general aegis of Bureau of Personnel. Do you want to talk about that?

Hancock: By more training I mean training in more skills. Bureau of Aeronautics was able to offer more diversified types of work, whereas under the Bureau of Personnel it was only the storekeeper, the yeoman, radioman, the mail man; that is, the general service rating. Where in aviation, they got in the electronics and other technical fields. They were trained for the control tower, as link trainer instructors, free gunnery instructors, navigation instructors, etc.

And, of course, the BuAer set all the training up in the existing schools. There was no question of any training separate from the men, which the Bureau of Personnel had started off with by leasing those various colleges and established the training of all the women, as separate from the men. This method was later abolished.

Q: One was the segregated attitude and the other was integrated.

Hancock: Was integrated, yes. And that was the attitude all the way through in BuAer. It was integration. The women would go into the same school. They would compete for class standing with the men. They would receive exactly the same training, so that when they graduated and went to work side by side with these men and until they relieved the men, they had to be able to stand on their own two feet and have the men know that they were trained exactly as they had been and could do the same sort of job of work, or they wouldn't have graduated. It was highly successful and it was economical to put them right in the same school. You didn't have to have any different staff or different accommodations and that sort of thing. And it was highly successful.

Q: Were there any sticky problems in terms of dormitories?

Hancock: Not for the women. There generally was in the initial stages, until the men were relived to go by the women who reported in, crowded conditions did exist and, unfortunately, in most cases the crowded conditions were imposed on the men. In order to have a barracks available, if we couldn't get one built in time, they would crowd the men in with other men. But the men rarely complained for they were the ones that were going to be relieved and a change of duty in the Navy is accepted.

Very shortly, as the building project got underway, barracks were built and that crowding problem was overcome. The barracks for women were the same, as far as the exterior building was concerned. Interiors, however, were somewhat different. And we had found, way back when, that the Bureau of Medicine and Surgery had recommended cubicles for men (this was long before they thought of women and was, I think, particularly in connection with respiratory diseases) instead of having the open bays in which they believed disease could spread to epidemic proportion.

Well, their plan was approved but it was never put into effect. It was Admiral Swanson, who was then Chief of Medicine and Surgery, who, when I talked to him about barracks for women, said there were some old plans somewhere that might be helpful. He found them and gave me a copy, which I took to my people in the Bureau of Aeronautics who were charged with the construction program. We went over these plans and the reaction to them was good for it gave privacy. And that is where the original cubicling of barracks started, doing away with the open bays.

And much later, of course, that was adopted for men. As the WAVE barracks were turned back to men after World War II, generally the chief petty officers grabbed them for they were a step up in accommodations. And slowly they were adopted in all the new barracks for men in the Pacific area. When I made my last trips out there in 1952, the new type was in being.

Q: This points up the fact that whatever the gender we all desire a bit of privacy.

Hancock: Right. Another example of their worthiness was demonstrated at NTC Bainbridge, Maryland. They had, in 1946, a flu epidemic which went right through the men's barracks. It did reach epidemic proportions. They didn't have one patient in the women's barracks at the same station. The women had cubicle barracks. The doctors at that time said it was the cubicles in the barracks that really made the difference.

Q: An interesting point.

Hancock: Yes, it is. How unfortunate that having been approved for the men, they had never received the benefits. I frequently found that you could dig in and find those people who wanted to do things, and who would get so far and then were stymied, either by lack of money or the negative attitude of some individual who hated change and who found it easier to keep on doing it the old way rather than try an improvement.

Q: I would judge that BuAer acted with great faith, and perhaps you instigated this faith, at the beginning when they said they could accommodate 23,000 women and that they were anticipating using these 23,000 women in all phases, in all these areas that you've been enumerating, these scientific efforst. They saw this from the beginning.

Hancock: Yes, they did. Their statement that they could use 23,000 women was based on jobs, not available accomodations. Although they knew that the women would replace men, there would eventually be space available. Nevertheless, there would have to be a certain amount of initial building. And that is where another disagreement came up between BuAer and BuPers -- a problem that took considerable to solve.

BuAer said, "Will you tell us how many we're going to get and where we can expect to have them so we can provide housing?" In other words, BuAer was ready to build for these initial groups if they could find out for how many and where.

BuPers would come back and say, "You tell us where you have housing and we'll tell you when you're going to get some women to put in them."

This went on for months, believe it or not. We couldn't start building until such building could be justified, on the fact that we were going to receive a certain number of women. Finally, we got a promise of approximately 300 of a group that was coming out of boot training. They would be sent to, I believe it was, Pensacola, and on the basis of that we started building. When the women came out of Hunter, they were to go to the schools that they were selected for, for training, after which they would go to, say, Pensacola and their outlying fields for service which would give us time to finish those barracks. When they were ready to come out of Hunter, the Chief of Naval Operations, then Cominch, took the entire group for Washington offices, and put them all in communications. He had been screaming for more personnel, so the initial group was diverted to that activity. Now that is the kind of problems you ran into.

Q: Yes.

Hancock: So I would run back and forth, back and forth, Bureau to stations, and I will say, looking back, I don't know why they had so much faith in me, because I almost, frankly almost, got to the point where I was lying about things, not only to myself, but to everyone else, saying, "Yes, we can do this," based on a hope. But everyone was doing the same thing at that time and you just sort of had to have an awful lot of confidence that things were going to turn out all right, and they did. It was challenging as the dickens.

Q: And this apparently was an element which BuPers was lacking in. In terms of women.

Hancock: Yes. But BuPers really did get on the ball, once the program got under way, and there was more understanding, frankly, between the bureaus and between the services when the women got together.

Working on matters of training, over at BuPers, the women would have conferences and once we'd get an agreement in a small group, the BuPers women would start selling their people (men) on the studies made. And when the lower echelon people were sold, then the higher echelons would come in.

Well, that process gradually disappeared as things worked out and problems were solved, and Capt. McAfee had a chance really to see things operating under the policies set up. Then things started moving smoothly. It was the initial, I would say, the initial year and a half that was very, very difficult.

Q: It was a pioneering time.

Hancock: It was a pioneering time, yes. And then there was a great deal more ready acceptance once that period was past. You could see what had been done, and how it was done, and that could be translated into other areas which were, let's say, in a little difficulty. For we then had successful trial areas to point to.

Q: What, in your estimation, would have been the most difficult job that the WAVES undertook under the aegis of BuAer?

Hancock: I don't know, I haven't the slightest idea. The job fields were all so different. Do you mean in the terms of a direct service rendered by women and for which they were trained? Enlisted or officers?

Q: Yes, I think probably. The really nitty-gritty things.

Hancock: Well, I think, actually, and this is from my own point of view, and I don't know if the women themselves would agree with it and from observation I would say one of the highly technical jobs, one which required a lot of skill that the women do not ordinarily use daily, was that of control tower operator. They had a terrific responsibility there, bringing in planes, working with planes in the air with damaged landing gear, instructing the pilots on landing, and so forth. And the noise conditions under which they worked in those towers, to me, were most nerve racking. Of course, they got used to it, apparently, and they could pick out the voices of their own charges from the jungle of eight, ten, twelve voices going at the same time, talking with their pilots, giving specific instructions regarding change of approach patterns and so forth. They did a spectacular job and I have yet to see how they could do it. I read now of the civilian air controllers that are working the crowded airports.

Q: Unhappy in their assignments.

Hancock: Yes, and of the terrific strain under -- I've just finished reading Airport. It gives you some idea of the strain of the job. My gals did it, and there weren't any breakdowns, to the best of my knowledge.

Q: Why isn't this thought of as a possible, partial solution at least to the present dilemma? The use of women.

Hancock: It should be.

Q: They're not used in this capacity, are they?

Hancock: No, and I don't know why not. There's still the battle of qualified women to secure jobs in fields jealously guarded by men. They're not taking the women on. These air controllers who are doing all this work say they need trained people to back them up. But no one has turned to the field of womenpower. The fact that they have already demonstrated their ability has been forgotten.

Q: Why shouldn't that suggestion be revived?

Hancock: It should.

Q: Could you not do it?

Hancock: Oh, every once in a while I get ambition and write little letters about different things women could do and sometimes I receive answers and sometimes I don't. It is not with the idea of pushing women, but rather asking if thought had been given of the angle of training women since women have done this sort of thing before. I've never written to anyone about the air control tower.

Q: Well, everytime I read about the dilemma, in the forefront is the fact that there aren't enough people involved and they're overworked.

Hancock: That's right. And we know that women can take the training and can do the job.

Q: Exactly.

Hancock: Now, for instance, in the ground control approach system (GCA), when that was started it was, I believe, in '45, '46. No, it was a little later than that. It was right after demobilization and we had no available men that they could put into the program. Colonel Day, of the Marine Corps, was in the Training Division of BuAer and he wanted to get this project underway and study it. "Have you any WAVES that we could bring in here?" he asked me.

"Certainly," I replied, "if you can use them, we can get them."

We ordered in about six or eight women in/for the training in a mobile truck out in a field at NAS Banana River, which is now Cape Canaveral -- Cape Kennedy. They didn't have any men to put in, so they put in women who ran the ground control approach experiments. On visits to NAS Banana River I'd visit that truck many times, and watch them bring in the pilots. I became somewhat familiar with the specialized jargon used while I watched the pilots follow the instructions of so many degrees right. You are on the beam. So many degrees left -- which brought the pilots in, while training them on this blind ground approach. That was years ago. Of course, now it's common. But the women in the Navy did that experimental job, enlisted women.

Bringing planes in when ports are closed in with fog is accepted practice now, but women are not being employed even though they pioneered the darned thing. And after these experiments by the Navy, Civil Aeronautics Authority was also in on the project, the findings became the basis of our ground control approach today. You can see why the job I had was interesting, and was another reason why I made these inspection trips. What are the women doing? Are they utilizing them properly? Or why not? Maybe, for instance, this program was ground control approach and they pulled them out of other jobs to put them in the program. All right. That's fine. But they are the things you had to keep aware of, and that necessitated my trips.

Q: And how much of this knowledge gleaned from these trips did you feed to the P.R. people?

Hancock: As much as they could use. I made written reports to my own bureau, for the people concerned such as training, housing, recreation, and I always gave Capt. McAfee a copy to keep her informed re WAVES in naval aviation. We had the closest cooperation on what was going on, and if she had anything special that would come to her attention that had missed me, she would tell me so that on my next trip I could look into that, for instance. Also, on all my trips I was invited to make radio appearances, speak at local clubs (men's and women's). The recruiting people always arranged a man killing schedule. There was very fine, very close cooperation with Capt. McAfee. Once, as she said later: "Once we got our bureaus to stop fighting, we really made progress."

Q: Let's see, what other aspect of that four year period needs to be developed?

Hancock: Well, I think I better leave that up to you and be guided by your questions, because I can ramble on and on, as you know. But specific questions do help. However, during that time, my activities were confined to the naval air part of it. The cooperation with Capt. McAfee and her office and the women officers assigned to the Training Division in BuPers, the Enlisted Detail, etc., became a close group and the conferences that Capt. McAfee always ran, so everyone could say what was coming up, what wasn't, what problems they were meeting and so forth, helped to work out a really good understanding, all the way across the board. The same thing, I think, took place between the services. I know that Capt. McAfee maintained close touch with Col. Hobby, WAC. I was very close later with Colonel Mary Helleran. We used to say

Hancock #3 - 104

that under Forrestal we had unification, but as far as the women were concerned, they were unified. We were on most friendly terms. We discussed the various angles of our programs in detail and reconciled many in service differences, while our male seniors were cutting each other's throats.

Q: Tell me about your cooperation with the Spars. I mean, they also got involved with aviation, didn't they?

Hancock: The Spars were a relatively small group and their original organizational set-up was accomplished in the early war years. I was not involved.

Q: 10,000, I think.

Hancock: Yes, I think that is correct. They were trained in some of the aviation and other ratings in the beginning, and, of course, as you know, their original group of officers came from WAVES trained at Northampton. Then they set up their own training as needed after those first groups, and that is the limit of my knowledge. Of course, I knew Capt. Stratton, we had various conferences, but there were never any closely allied subjects after they started training their own people. They had relatively few of their women trained in the aviation technical rating. Because the Coast Guard came under the Navy, actually, as soon as war was declared, certain facilities

Hancock #3 - 105

were made available to them in the way of aviation maintenance and repair.

Q: In the realm of public relations, I would think that the gals that were working with aviation would have been targets, I mean they would have been much more spectacular.

Hancock: They were.

Q: I believe that Bing Crosby made a movie, didn't he? Did you get involved in that?

Hancock: Oh, there were quite a few. Esther Williams made a movie, and so did Betty Hutton. They were all under BuPers, all those movie ventures. I think Bing Crosby was in on that one made on the West Coast. There were eight or nine, I believe, movies in which the Navy cooperated, but I had no part in those whatsoever. It was all handled by the Bureau of Personnel. Of course, I was in on, for instance, presenting a plaque to Esther Williams when I became the Director for one movie that she put out which was really a beautifully done thing for the WAVES but other than that I had no part in it whatsoever. Billie Wilde acted as technical advisor on one. I think it was the Betty Hutton picture, if I'm not mistaken.

Q: That was the Bing Crosby one?

Hancock #3 - 106

Hancock: Was it?

Q: In the war time period itself, did you find more of the WAVES coming into the service and asking for service with Aeronautics?

Hancock: Oh yes. But that came, you see, at the recruit training set up, in Hunter. And especially after we got our training aides in there, through Admiral de Flores, Louis de Flores, who recently died. He was a perfectly fabulous person. He was the one who made the Link trainer and other synthetic training devices available. He got all that material together and sent it to Hunter for visual aids to enable the selection staff to give the women they were screening an idea of the various ratings in aviation. You could no longer mention the opening of another aviation rating without having hundreds of requests pour in. Aviation had a lure. They all seemed to want aviation.

Q: That was the glamorous --

Hancock: That was the glamour. And so many of them who wanted to get into aviation had been secretaries or something, so they didn't want to be a yeoman. They wanted to do something different. They wanted to get their hands into something and a lot of them that I talked to said, "I could be a secretary on the outside. Why should I come in here and be a secretary? I want to do something to help the war effort." They couldn't translate the need of yeoman as great as that of fixing an airplane engine, or working on an airplane fuselage. We had no difficulty with filling quotas, they were always oversubscribed as fast as aviation ratings were opened.

Q: I remember one WAVE officer in our outfit who was, who was really quite disappointed and almost disgruntled at times. This was intelligence and she discovered that intelligence, as far as her assignment went, didn't have that much glamour either, and she was anxious to get out and get into aeronautics.

Hancock: But of course, with the officers, they were not technically trained by aviation until later on. They took certain courses but they reported in and actually found their niches after they were assigned to their duties in aviation. They reported in and were generally assigned to minor administrative jobs. They became War Bond officers, barrack supervisors, Mail Room supervisors. Later their qualifications for bigger and more responsible work were brought out. They started fitting into various other niches. But with the enlisted, it was a much more direct thing. You were assigned to an aviation school or trained on the job, and you were aviation. And I have yet to find one who wasn't happy that she got the aviation assignment. There was something about an air station and the daily life that was entirely different generally from what they had known when they were civilians.

Q: You, of all people, could put your finger on that something about an air station because you know.

Hancock: Yes. I can understand its great appeal. We never lacked for volunteers for any aviation program. We were over-subscribed, so to speak, The poor gal who was forced into becoming a mail clerk when she had wanted to be a control tower operator could be in the doldrums for a while or until she felt that she really was doing something directly for the war effort. Handling fleet mail always had a strong enough appeal to overcome her disappointment.

Q: What percentage, would you say, of the gals who volunteered for service in aviation, what percentage of them failed to measure up to, really, the stringent requirements some times? The rigors of the job?

Hancock: I don't know. I have no figures whatsoever or any knowledge of the women who might have been judged not qualified to hold the rating they achieved. I know of none. They went on up by examination in their ratings the same as the men. The thing was that they were very carefully screened.

The Bureau of Medicine and Surgery and the Aviation Training Division of BuAer set up the basic standards for selection, which was done at Hunter. Physical and mental standards had to be met. Everything was taken into consideration before they were qualified to attend the aviation school. It was quite interesting to attend a graduation of trainees in the mechanical ratings. For instance, at NAS Norman, Oklahoma with three or four hundred graduates at the one I'm thinking of -- there were eighteen, I think, Marine women still being trained by the Navy, and there were one hundred and sixty WAVES. The rest were men. They held the graduation ceremony in a huge auditorium. At that time, the commanding officer was "Squash" Griffin.

Q: Was who?

Hancock: Squash Griffin, Virgil Griffin, an old time naval aviator, he was really a toughie. Wow! He made a great to-do about these graduations and he didn't want -- he wasn't at first in favor of the women's program, but no one could have done more than he did once he knew he was to train them. At graduations he always presented what looked like a naval academy heavy gold ring to the number one student at graduation. And at this particular graduation, he got up and made his usual nice speech and said that he was now presenting the ring to the honor graduate. And then a 5'2" WAVE walked forward. He had put the ring on a ribbon and he hung it around her neck because it would have been more like a bracelet for her -- this big man's ring. And do you know what happened? God bless, that whole class stood up and cheered. The women did a perfectly beautiful job. I mean on maintaining class standards, they were embarrassingly in the top levels at graduation and psychologically they had been well tested, so there was no reason why they should have failed at their jobs. And they didn't.

Q: What about that initial examination for officers, which I've always heard was so terribly tough, and was geared to a man's experience and so forth, and a man's knowledge. You didn't have to take that, of course, but --

Hancock: No, I didn't have to take that.

Q: But so many of the officers with whom I've talked have said it was frightfully difficult and they didn't see how they passed it.

Hancock: Well, I think being geared from a different angle than they'd been used to was one of the big obstacles. I can't speak of that because, as you say, I didn't take it. They took me on blind faith, I think, rather than my test ability.

Q: They took you on the basis of experience.

Hancock: That may have been, but -- and I don't know the percentage of the women who failed at the procurement offices, for instance. And I don't know the percentage of the enlisted women who failed at that time, but I know that we had all the acceptable volunteers that we could handle as the program went along.

Q: Well, let's focus on the time when you took over the leadership of the WAVES.

Hancock: That was in July of '46.

Q: You succeeded Jean Palmer?

Hancock: That is correct. When I was released from the Bureau of Aeronautics to go to BuPers, it was on the basis of becoming the director of the WAVES. Otherwise the BuAer said that they would not release me. So I went to the Bureau of Personnel, having been nominated by Capt. McAfee as her successor, and took on the job of planning for regular, particularly for regular Navy, because that legislation was being introduced. I worked at that for the four and one half months that Jean Palmer served as Director.

Q: How did Jean happen to get sandwiched in between there?

Hancock: Well, she had been Capt. McAfee's number one, I mean she was a deputy director, let's say. I don't think that was the exact title but it may have been assistant director. Capt. McAfee, for some time before she finally left, had spent a great deal of time back at Wellesley and --

Q: She was a commuter, yes, between Wellesley and Washington.

Hancock: Yes, and so Jean had really been carrying on Capt. Mac's jobs during the demobilization period. Jean was very familiar with those demobilization procedures, being carried on by BuPers, and it was therefore quite a logical thing that she should carry on in that project. Therefore, I was ordered during that period as deputy director, to do the planning for regular Navy.

Q: Jean knew she was stepping down?

Hancock: Oh yes. And so that is actually what my job was until she left. It was in July 1946 that I became the Director.

Q: What were you confronted with as a major problem?

Hancock: Legislation.

Q: Legislation.

Hancock: For regular Navy.

Q: Tell me about that?

Hancock: Well, there was one bill, the initial bill had already come up but not been enacted. And here, I think, Bureau of Personnel made a very grave error. I'm rather good at pointing out errors, but at the time I also went on record as saying it was an error, so it's not hindsight that makes me say so. In that when the hearing started the women were told to carry the ball because it was legislation concerning women. Right there was the weakness. It was Navy legislation. So the women officers, headed by Jean Palmer, of the various offices in which they were working, were representing the Navy and attempting to answer all the questions but by the committee. Now Jean herself --

Q: May I interrupt for a moment? Does this indicate that underneath the gloss that was there because of war time urgency that the Navy really hadn't changed its attitude much?

Hancock: Right. That's true. There was no enthusiasm, you

Hancock #3 - 114

know on the Navy's part. The women officers were carrying out their orders, period. The attitude was, if it goes through, all right, but if it doesn't, all right. We don't need it in peace time. And the women who went up there to represent the Navy did not, and frankly so said, believe in a career for women in the Navy. They, themselves, were not going to stay, Jean Palmer was not going to stay. She was only going through the period of getting the women demobilized. She certainly was entirely cooperative, as far as I was concerned, and she knew that my job was plannning for the regular Navy, and she was delighted that someone did believe in it, and would carry the ball, so there was always the finest cooperation there. But I think the bill actually failed because it did not get official, on the spot, support or backing of the Navy. Sure they were on record that they supported it, but not any of the men of the Navy appeared to say so or that that was what the Navy wanted. This word is what the Congress needed to have rather than --

Q: Which they were accustomed to hear.

Hancock: Sure. And that's where it had to come from.

Q: Who was the sponsor of this bill that failed?

Hancock: Offhand I can't tell you who actually introduced it.

Q: Was it Margaret Chase Smith?

Hancock: I don't think Margaret Chase Smith introduced the legislation. I think it was Mr. Vinson. I think he was sponsor of the bill. It was introduced before the bill that finally passed which was a bill, combined bill covering women of the Armed SErvices. This first bill was a separate Navy bill.

Q: I see.

Hancock: You see --

Q: It was just a fragment of the whole picture.

Hancock: That's right. And then later, under Unification it was introduced as a bill for (Public Law 625) all women in the armed forces. That is Army, Navy, and Marine Corps. When the Air Force was formed, the WAF was tacked on at the end. Finally the Navy got into step. /Admiral Nimitz, Admiral Denfeld, Chiefs of Navy Bureaus, testified favorably.

Q: General Vandenburg.

Hancock: No, because you see the Air Force wasn't in being during the hearings, they got tacked on.

Q: I see. Yes.

Hancock: But on the second go around, when I was the Director, I was having very, very conclusive and almost disrupting talks and conferences with my boss, who was then Admiral T. A. L. Sprague. I said that if the Navy is asking or isn't asking for this legislation, I think they should say so. They don't want it. If they are requesting it, they've got to give it the same support they would give any other legislation that the Navy is asking for. And the men have to present this bill, not the women.

He said, "I'm not going to get up there . . ."

I said, "Well, we might as well sign off then, because if the Navy doesn't present it and ask for it, and fight for it, it's not going to go through. So why put forth any effort?"

And we finally came out, by golly, with the men of the Navy carrying the ball. Sure, I testified, but the men presented it. The Planning Division of BuPers with whom I worked did the legislative planning with rehearsals and visual aids, and I think that was the real reason why we finally had success. Admiral Sprague finally said, "All right. I'll appoint some one to run with the ball." And he called in --

Q: He was what?

Hancock: He was Chief of Bureau of Personnel. My boss. And he called in Capt. Darden, whose first name I do not know. D-a-r-d-e-n, who was head of Planning Division of Bureau of Personnel at the time. Of course, in my career in the Navy, I never called even my best friends by their first name. I always tried to set a good example of Naval etiquette.

And he said, "Well, I've got a smart officer in my outfit to run with the ball, so to speak, to work with Joy Hancock on getting together all the material for the hearing." He added, "I'm going to appoint Capt. Stickney."

Now Capt. Stickney, known as "Pete" Stickney, now retired, was a very personable person, a very forceful person, who had absolutely no time for women in the service. And I was with Capt. Darden, when we went back to the Planning Division that morning and he said, "Pete, I've got a job for you. The Chief just said I should appoint some one to run with the ball on the legislation for women in the Navy. You are that person. Get all the material ready for a presentation to the Congress."

And I saw the color start coming up out of his collar to his face and he said, "You must realize that I don't believe in it at all, as a part of the regular Navy."

Replied Capt. Darden, "The Navy is on record that they favor it and somebody must represent the Navy's view, and you're it."

And that's the last time I heard Capt. Stickney make a

negative remark. I knew he didn't believe in it, but when he testified at the hearings no one could have done a better job than that man did. If I ever saw an example of a Naval officer being given an order and carrying it out, that man did it. He would stay sometimes until ten, twelve o'clock at night in my office with us, getting all the materials together and propounding possible questions for discussion. He worked on the language of the legislation, the strength percentages that could be used. That man just gave his best and never once did he say, "Damn you women.," which I knew he felt at the time.

And you know at the end, he never said he was in favor of it. But he would say, "Well, that's good. That's a good feature. Now this will work for this reason." Every word and every attitude that he displayed, you had the feeling that he was behind it one hundred percent. And he certainly gave every appearance of being so. In other words, he did a job which was apparently not acceptable to him, at least in the beginning, and he did a marvelous job. The whole point, to me, is that it was a fine example of receiving an order and carrying it out, without question.

Q: Well, Capt. Darden remarked to him initially that there was a job to be done.

Hancock: Yes.

Q: And that the Navy had decided that they wanted the women as a part of the regular Navy, now who was reponsible for that decision, that they wanted the women?

Hancock: I would say Admiral Sprague, primarily. Of course, he had pressure and direction from other people -- SecDef, SecNav, CNO, etc. But he was the one, as Chief of BuPers, as I understand it and did at that time, who must initiate legislation on personnel matters. And their legal department is the one which works with the Bureau of the Budget, and everyone else, in getting legislation through. In other words, it was their baby.

Q: But even he demurred --

Hancock: Oh yes.

Q: From doing the job himself. I mean in making the appearance.

Hancock: Who?

Q: Sprague.

Hancock: Oh, he went.

Hancock #3 - 120

Q: He did finally go?

Hancock: Yes, he did and he made a fine presentation.

Q: But initially he said no, he wouldn't.

Hancock: Initially, yes. It was, "You women do it." And I said, "No, the men have got to do it." And before the Hearings started the whole male team was coached -- and Admiral Sprague headed up the team.

Q: Now at that point the CNO was Nimitz?

Hancock: In the beginning of wartime legislation Nimitz said no to Rep. Edith Nourse Rogers, who had introduced the WAC bill. You see, that's when the Army was initially seeking to set up the WAC. Nimitz had given evasive answers and actually said he was not in favor of the idea. He admitted that at the later hearings, on regular Navy status.

Q: He was not --

Hancock: Not for women in the service.

Q: He was not? At that point he was not?

Hancock: Yes. He sent a statement to the Congress during Hearings on Regular Navy status, in which he said, "I am a convert. I was against this idea in the beginning. I was shortsighted."

Q: This was when he was chief of the BuPers. I mean, when he was against it.

Hancock: Yes.

Q: At the outset of the war.

Hancock: At the outset of the war, he was against having women in the service.

Q: Yes. but when he became CNO, during the time of this legislation, he had been converted?

Hancock: Yes. The war service had definitely -- now let me see, was he CNO before? No, he was CNO after Commander in Chief Pacific, which was first.

Q: Afterward. Right afterward. Right after the Japanese --

Hancock: Yes. He was definitely converted because he was CinC Pacific when Jean Palmer and I went out to set up the housing for overseas service of women and, of course, we went to Honolulu where he had headquarters.

Q: And Pearl?

Hancock: Yes, and he was there then because he met us when we flew in. And this -- but he was definitely a convert. Now Gen. Eisenhower had always been for women in the service but Nimitz had to admit that he was a convert. When Edith Nourse Rogers had first called him before World War II, he was very -- he put her off. Some of her correspondence and some of his replies are in my history. I've forgotten exactly what the dates are.

Q: When she called him the first -- I mean this was in '42.

Hancock: Yes, what are you -- what's the Navy going to do about this? Well, the Navy will study --

Q: And he was ambivalent even at that?

Hancock: Legislation for regular Navy was helped when he did get on the ball and testify that they should be taken in on a career basis.

Q: Now tell me about the struggles through the Congress because Mrs. Smith was very important there, wasn't she?

Hancock #3 - 123

Hancock: Oh, she was. Very definitely. Now, I think the part where she was definitely important was a part played that absolutely stunned me at the time because I didn't understand her strategy. After these --

Q: Would you have to be on the inside to know the strategy?

Hancock: I think so. At this particular time, the hearings had been completed before the House Naval Affairs Committee, which it was at that time,/headed at that time by Mr. Vinson. Mrs. Smith was on that committee as a Representative, naturally, as she was in the House of Representatives at the time. Everything seemed to have gone very, very well in spite of some embarrassing questions that were raised by -- Dewey Short.

Q: Dear old Dewey from Missouri.

Hancock: Yes. He had some very embarrassing questions. One of which I shall not forget, because it was asked directly of me.

Q: He was a clergyman, by the way.

Hancock: He was? I'm told that he drank a lot.

Q: Yes.

Hancock: Well, I think that this day he had. But he sat leaning forward and he said to me, "Tell me how many pregnancies you've had with these women in the Navy."

And I thought, "Here it comes. What will I say now?" I answered, "I frankly haven't that information for you. You see, that is a medical question."

We had been on the question of discipline, and that was when he brought it in. And he said, "Well, isn't there any discipline connected with it when a woman has a baby?"

I said, "No. No more than there is for the man who fathered the child." And I said, "Why should there be any discipline attached to it? After all, no other woman is disciplined for having a child. All interest is whether her usefulness to the service has been . . ."

Q: Impaired?

Hancock: ". . . terminated because if she has a child our regulations state that a woman who has a child is not eligible for naval service and when she becomes pregnant, she goes out."

And as I paused and it suddenly dawned on me that that son-of-a-gun was trying to insinuate something unfavorable. He had been doing it in other hearings that I had read about, namely, the WAC. So I said, "Are you under the impression that these women who became pregnant weren't married?"

There was silence in the room. And Rep. Van Zandt, of

Pennsylvania, who had been in the Navy, jumped to his feet and said, "I think that the Captain should have an apology for that implication, if that's what you were implying."

It was a terrific occurrence but it was also terrifically interesting. You can imagine how those kinds of questions shook you when you were dealing with someone who was asking them in a snide manner.

Q: He was trying to undermine it.

Hancock: Undermine it, yes. Well, anyway, when the hearings were completed, and of course, I made what I found out later wasn't a bad mistake by addressing Mr. Vinson twice as admiral --

Q: You found it was not a bad mistake.

Hancock: Not then. I found out much later that he liked it. The Hearings finally completed, we appeared before the House Committee to hear the final decision. Admiral Sprague was sitting in #1 chair and I was next, Capt. Stickney, and all the rest of the Navy male team was on hand. Then Mr. Vinson announced that the committee had voted and discussed it and that they were in favor of the Reserve Section only. No regular.

Admiral Sprague turned to me and he said, "Good God! Did you know they were going to do that?"

Hancock #3 - 126

And I could only murmur, "No." Mrs. Smith's vote was against. She was apparently the only negative vote and this did something to the legislation at that point. They did not have full agreement on it and it had to be re-studied. She stymied the Reserve Section going to the floor, or whatever the next procedure was, which I didn't understand until much later.

Q: She was entitled to make a minority report, actually.

Hancock: Yes. And that was the thing that really stopped it. Then we had the adjournment of that session of Congress.

Q: She's still up to tricks like that, you know.

Hancock: Then the Congress went out of business, you see. But it wasn't the final session. It was availability of another session that saved us. So in the next session there was time for reconciliation, and a review of the whole procedure. The Senate was perfectly marvelous. They passed the legislation and then they got together with the House and reconciled the thing and saw that we came out with what had been requested. The combining of the Armed SErvices had then taken place and that had to be reconciled for women participation. Mr. Vinson's roiginal report which said no regular, but you can be in the reserve, was reevaluated and the Reserve and the Regular status prevailed.

Q: So there really was some politicking?

Hancock: Oh yes, and it dragged out, you see, for so long. It was in '48 before it finally passed. It was two years, and I'm telling you that was two years of suffering. For everybody.

Q: And by that time Mrs. Smith was in the Senate.

Hancock: Yes.

Q: And was helpful in the Senate, wasn't she?

Hancock: Oh yes. She was helpful all the way through. And, of course, Senator Saltonstall was one of the kindliest and most understanding, of men. He had a daughter in the WAVES who was an officer. She came in as an enlisted woman and she was in naval communications for her whole tour. And that was a difficult assignment, adjusting to the watches and so forth. She was on duty in Washington. There was never one gripe out of her. She did her watch standing!

Q: Was Senator Hart helpful?

Hancock #3 - 128

Hancock: Not to my knowledge, no

Q: He also had a daughter in the WAVES.

Hancock: Did he? I don't connect him at all with any of our difficulties or good times.

Q: Well, that was a major event in your term as director. What else came up that you had to wrestle with?

Hancock: Well, I'll tell you, in connection with that legislation, I want to right now say something about a man that I think also did not believe in the program for women in the Navy, and also was a most helpful person, and that's Capt. Ira Nunn, JAG adjutant general's office. Now when it came time for me to appear in connection with legislation as the Director, I went over to the JAG's office and said to him, "All right, now what was wrong in the last hearings that we can overcome? Will you tell me? Will you instruct me? Because I'm going to be asked questions. How shall I do it properly to help this legislation?"

And Ira Nunn was running the ball as far as JAG was concerned on the legislation. He said, "Will you do as I say?" And I answered: "I've come to you for instruction." And he instructed me, and pointed out some of the errors of the past presentation.

Q: Such as?

Hancock: Such as women trying to present this thing.

Q: Well, you knew this already.

Hancock: Yes. And some of the answers that were given. And he said, "This is what we've got to do." I worked very closely with him on all phases of the legislation, in the rehearsals on the presentation, and on research.

Q: Oh, you did rehearse the presentation?

Hancock: Oh gosh, we had set it up in the Bureau of Personnel. We prepared our answers to possible questions. We had our lectures on procedures. With all these men and myself were in on the preparations for these hearings.

Q: Is this a normal procedure?

Hancock: On legislation that BuPers backs, yes.

Q: It is? That there is a rehearsal?

Hancock: Yes. Their legal section sets it up and they get all their visual aids ready, and their charts, and statistics prepared.

Q: That's a revelation. I hadn't known.

Hancock: We carried the procedure out for the women, which was fine. In the midst of one of these very trying House Committee Hearings that I had on questions and answers, I thought, "I can't take this much longer." Things like those questions introduced by Dewey Short. And then I had this little note handed to me on a little piece of white paper from Capt. Nunn who was sitting down the line from me, and on it was facetiously written, "You done well." Boy, I needed it at that point. I was about to fly. It was all I needed. If Ira Nunn thought I'm doing all right, I could keep going. "You done well." I've never forgotten that. He had not been enthusiastic about the legislation. He had told me frankly he wasn't. But again, he had a job to do and he had certainly aided me in doing mine.

Q: On what basis?

Hancock: I think his own personal feeling that the Navy -- well, that it wasn't necessary for women to be in it. The Navy had always gotten along without them. In war time, fine, they really appreciated their services. It wasn't downgrading their contribution, but was it necessary in peace time? No.

Q: The Navy was still a man's province.

Hancock #3 - 131

Hancock: That's right. And I can understand that very well. I often, not often, but every once in a while, I find involuntarily the question will come up in my mind about men coming into what was heretofore a woman's field and so forth. And I think, well, it was perfectly fine. It's for both -- for instance, here's just one little example. Gynecologists and obstetricians are almost entirely male. Well, that used to be a mid-wife's field entirely. The male nurses coming into the field. And now in both services there are men commissioned as male nurses the same as they have women nurses. And you stop and think, well, that's perfectly all right. They need both. And yet, the question does arise. And I can see it on the part of the men in a field that had always been a man's field. Maybe it is a bit of insecurity on their part. But if there is a need for both, my feeling is, let's be open-minded about it.

Q: How do you think it has worked out?

Hancock: As far as I know, and from the information I've been able to glean, it's worked out pretty well. And I'm thinking of it more from the women's side of it, frankly, than from the man's side of it. I think had we not been able to offer the women a career field, we wouldn't even have held the nucleus, which is all women's strength amounts to. As a matter of fact, the women in service had to have that because the Reserve would not have held any substantial number of women who could carry on in case of amobilization of woman power. We've got something now which in itself, although it's small, is an important thing, I think, to the Navy.

Q: It's professional --

Hancock: It is a professional nucleus permanently set up, and we can get going on expansion -- not within a year, as it took before -- but within the time it takes to notify the recruiting offices or at the start of mobilization. In addition, the Navy now offers the women a dignified career, if they so desire.

Q: What about the caliber of the career people now in the WAVES as compared to the war time?

Hancock: Of course, the standards are still as high or higher than formerly. My understanding is that those accepted are of the finest calibre. I have not kept in close contact with what's going on day by day, so to speak, because I'm sort of like the Dean of Women of a college. I don't think the Dean of Women should ever settle in the college town in which she was Dean because she would be prone to look over her successor's shoulder.

Q: Amen.

Hancock: And I certainly would never do that, but the number of rejects, the percentage of rejects among the enlisted women applicants, for instance, is terrifically high. The Navy can afford to be very choosy, and they are being very choosy. It's difficult, in other words to get in, to make the grade, so --

Q: The culling process is still there.

Hancock: Oh, definitely. And more so than it naturally was in war time. And that has to be because war in itself is a motivation, and in peace time you must search farther for motivation. These new youngsters are smart, awfully smart, and I think their educational level is even higher at the present time opposed to the end of the war. We accepted then during the war two years of high school plus a certain number of years of business experience. Now they are required to meet full high school requirements. And some of these gals are realizing too the benefits that they receive from enlisting, in higher education benefits and so forth, the same as the men are doing. They are apparently not lacking for volunteers to enlist or for officer training. And, of course, with the number limited, we can afford to be highly selective. So it's -- I think it's been a pretty wise

Hancock #3 - 134

program all the way through. If I had to do it over again, I'd like to be again among those concerned with the early organization.

Q: No doubt. Well, now, your term as director continued how long?

Hancock: Seven years. Actually, when the legislation was enacted in '48, I asked to be transferred. And the answer was no.

Q: You mean you wanted to be transferred, what? Back to --

Hancock: So I would revert to commander. I wanted to set a precedent. I figured that later on it might be a little more -- there might be a different feeling about it, you see. Well, I could afford to revert to commander and set that precedent, so that the Director, having held the rank of captain, would feel no compunction about reverting to commander rank and going to another job. Of course, I'd always been in the women's program and I hadn't been on a regular Navy billet assignment job but Admiral Sprague refused.

Q: Where did you want to go?

Hancock: It didn't matter. Anywhere. Just so I would revert

to commander. After all, the normal tour was three to four years and I spent seven in the job, you see. But that was because of the transition period of Reserve to Regular and getting the new program under way, which the Admiral said I had to stay and do. And also, I found --

Q: In retrospect, you think he was right, don't you?

Hancock: Oh I -- well, yes, but I felt sort of selfish about the thing. There was still a terrific challenge there, and I was getting all the up-lift of the challenge, so to speak, but certainly there were other people around trained who could have taken over, I'm sure, in that period. And the regular -- Navy regular legislation had been passed, and that was really the big aim. I knew that once that was accomplished the other things would be taken care of. And he refused to do that. So I stayed on. And then found there was some sort of a quirk in the law in which -- you see, I had to retire at fifty-five. That was set in legislation.

Q: Oh, that was the --

Hancock: Oh yes. So I had to retire.

Q: A WAVE has to retire at fifty-five.

Hancock: Because you see, the highest permanent rank in the Navy held by women was that of commander, under the legislation. (It was November 1968, two years ago, that this was changed.) There was one captain, and that was temporary while serving as director of the WAVES. But the legislation also provided that on retirement, however, that person who had become a captain, would retire as a captain, with the pay of a captain, and credit for the number of years service. Well, I found out that in the legislation, commanders from fifty to fifty-five, you see. I found, because of some quirk in the law I couldn't get out until fifty-five, and that was when I asked for reassignment because I saw three years more ahead in which someone else, I thought, should be the director.

Q: Some commander could step up.

Hancock: Yes. And I could become a commander. And that was when the Admiral refused. So I stayed on in the job until I retired. I'll tell you one other peculiar thing that happened to me, you may want to cut this out of the tape.

When my time for retirement came up, I had a call from Admiral Russell, who was then the JAG and who had administered my oath into the regular Navy. There had always been a lot of repartee between his office and mine, because he thought the WAVES were fine and he put them on important jobs, etc. They were liaison to the Hill and they were this, that, and the other. He called me and he said, "Joy, what are you trying to pull over on us?"

And I said, "What do you mean?"

He said, "Aoubt this retirement of yours."

And I said, "Well, I have to retire."

He said, "I know you do. You'll be fifty-five years old."

And I said, "Right."

He said, "But this pay business?" And I said, "What pay--"

He said, "Seventy-five percent."

And I said, "What do you mean? I've passed my physicals. I'm perfectly okay. I came in with a physical waiver, but there's never been any -- I've never had one day sickness in connection with it. So I do not rate 75 percent because of physical."

Then he said, "Yes, but there's a law in which your law says that any laws not contained in this legislation that apply to men will also apply to women. You had service in World War I so you get seventy-five percent retirement."

I said, "What!" I hadn't had the slightest knowledge about that feature.

Q: Rather than fifty?

Hancock: Whatever percentage I would have received, which I presumed was fifty percent. But my service in World War I placed me in the seventy-five percent retirement plan, even though I had had only twelve years service. Oh, I was absolutely innocent. I had no part in the matter at all.

Q: Tell me about your retirement ceremony.

Hancock: That was at NTC Bainbridge, Maryland, actually. It was one of the most memorable and impressive ceremonies of my Navy life. Receiving the Legion of Merti, which Mr. Anderson, then Secretary of the Navy, presented me, was another memorable ceremony for me.

Q: Robert Anderson.

Hancock: Yes. And then there was also Admiral Holloway, when I was retiring --

Q: Jimmy?

Hancock: Gentleman Jim. He was then the chief, and he put on quite a show in accepting a portrait for the Navy Department, which was done by the same artist incidentally that did the one of me in the evening uniform. David Kamura.

Q: He did another lovely one of you in evening dress.

Hancock: Yes. If they want that one when I die.

Hancock #3 - 139

Q: You mean the Museum?

Hancock: Yes, if they want it, they can have it. But to return to the final review at Bainbridge, Captain Frederick Woolseifer set up this final review for me in which all the recruits, including the WAVE graduating class, were there. I was the reviewing officer. Capt. Woolseifer and I trooped the the lines. My family came down and it was a very, very beautiful ceremony and that was the end of my final go around, except for the outgoing receptions and the many WAVE parties that both the officers and my enlisted gals had for me.

Q: Really, it was a remarkable career you had in the Navy.

Hancock: Oh, definitely.

Q: And one which you obviously have enjoyed every moment.

Hancock: I think looking back, even at the sometimes tough going parts, I wouldn't trade one minute of that experience. It is marvelous to look back on. And so darned rewarding because I can see what has been accomplished, not just my own accomplishments but also being able to view so many things that were continuing to be accomplished. No, I'm very fortunate to have all those things. Most people don't, you know.
Does that do it?

Q: I think I've probably worn you out.

INDEX

for Interviews

with

Captain Joy Bright Hancock,

U. S. Navy (Retired)

AV-S Program, 49.

Barnaby, Capt. Ralph, 25.

Bureau of Aeronautics, 17; early setting up of files, 19-20; Newsletter, 23; editorial research, 31; public relations, 31-35.

Carr, Wilbur J., 27

Chung, Dr. Margaret (Mom Chung), 55; Sons of Mom Chung - organization, 56

Darden, Capt., 117

de Flores, RADM Louis, 46-47, 106

Fechteler, Admiral William, 76

Gildersleeve, Dean Virginia, 66-69

Griffin, Capt. Virgil C., 109

Hancock, Capt. Joy Bright (Mrs. Ralph Ofstie), Enlistment, WWI, 2-6; uniform, WWI, 6-7; work assignments, WWI, 7-8; impact of a woman in service, 8; work at Cape May, 11-14; marriage, 14-15; job with BUAIR, 16, 22-23; State Dept. exams, 27-28; marriage to Comdr. Hancock, 25; takes up flying, 29; enrollment in WAVES, 40-41; WWI ribbon bestowed by Adm. King, 41-42; her role in planning for WAVES, 54 ff.; liaison work, 69-71; WAVE rep. for naval aviation, 75 ff; travels, 80-83; background advantages for WAVE job, 91; P.R. chores, 102-103; becomes Director of the WAVES, 111-112; thoughts on success of WAVES, 131-134; retirement, 135-139

Hancock, Lt. Comdr., 24, 26

Holloway, Admiral James, 138

Jacobs, VADM Randall, 5, 61

Kamuri, David, 138

King, Admiral E. J., 37-40, 42a

Little, Lt. Charles Gray, 11

Maas, Congressman Melvin, 51, 54

McAfee, Capt. Mildred, 59-60, 77-78; 102-103, 111-112

Moffatt, RADM William A., 16, 18, 21, 25, 43

NC-4, 10-11

Naval Air Station, Cape May, 9

New York Shipbuilding Co., 7-8

Nimitz, Admiral Chester: attitude towards WAVES, 52; 120-121

Nunn, Captain Ira, 128

Ofstie, VADM Ralph A., 50

Palmer, Capt. Jean, 73-74, 76, 111-112, 113-114, 121

Policies for WAVES in Naval Aviation: book of regulations, 76-78, 83

Radford, Adm. Arthur, 19, 46, 48, 50, 53, 62, 81

Read, RADM Albert Cushing (Putty Read), 10, 18

Reed, RADM William A. (Gus), 49

Rogers, The Hon. Edith Nourse, 56

Russell, VADM George L., 136-137

Saltonstall, Senator Leveritt, 127

Shenandoah (2R-1), 15, 24, 26

Short, The Hon. Dewey, 123-125

Smith, Senator Margaret Chase, 66, 122-123, 126-127

Snow, Capt. Elliott, 7

SPARS, 104

Sprague, Admiral Thomas L., 116-117, 119, 125, 134

Stickney, Capt. 'Pete', 117-118, 125

Towers, Admiral John Henry, 44; press conference, 45-46, 81

Training for Aviation - older men, 36-38

2R-2, 14-15

U. S. Naval Home, 5

Vinson, The Hon. Carl, 62, 65, 126

Walsh, Senator David I., 64-65

WAVES: early efforts at legislation, 50; BUAIR request for, 52-58; 62-63; male attitude towards, 72-73; question of discipline, 85-87; aviation machinist mates, 87-89; non-acceptance of qualifications, 89; more training under BuAir, 91-93; barracks, 93-96; control tower operators, 98-101; movies made about, 105; discussion of appeal that naval aviation assignments had, 106-109; legislation for the WAVES as part of regular navy, 113 ff.

WAVES Advisory Committee, 66

Whiting, Capt. Kenneth, 16

Wilde, Capt. Billy, 105

Willis, Senator Raymond E., 56

Woolsiefer, Capt. Frederick, 139

An interview with

Lieutenant Commander Mary Josephine Shelly, USNR (Ret.)

on her service in World War II with the WAVES.

U. S. Naval Institute
Annapolis, Maryland
1970

Preface

This Manuscript is the result of a tape recorded interview with Lieutenant Commander Shelly, USNR (Ret.) in New York City on February 9, 1970. Subsequently Miss Shelly made only minor emendations and corrections to the manuscript. The reader is asked therefore to bear in mind the fact that he is reading a transcript of the spoken word rather than the written word.

DECLARATION OF TRUST

The undersigned does hereby appoint and designate as his (her) Trustee herein, the Secretary-Treasurer and Publisher of the United States Naval Institute to perform and discharge the following duties, powers, and privileges in connection with the possession and use of a certain taped interview between the undersigned and the Oral History Department of the United States Naval Institute.

(1) As an <u>Open</u> transcript. It may be read (or the tape audited) by qualified researchers upon presentation of proper credentials as determined by the Trustee.

(2) It is expressly understood that in giving this authorization, I am in no way precluded from placing such restrictions as I may desire upon use of the interview at any time during my lifetime, nor does this authorization in any way affect my rights to the copyright of any literary expressions that may be contained in the interview.

Witness my hand and seal this ___28th___ day of ___April___ 19_70_

Mary Jozephine Shelby

I hereby accept and consent to the foregoing Declaration of Trust and the powers therein conferred upon me as Trustee:

R. E. Bowker Jr.

Secretary-Treasurer and Publisher

Interview # 1

Miss Mary Jo Shelly
Mitchell Place
New York City
Subject: WAVES

by John T. Mason, Jr.
February 9, 1970

Mr. Mason: What a delight to meet you. I really have been looking forward to this story of yours about your service with the WAVES. I know that it's going to be quite an addition to the other stories which we have been collecting. You've demonstrated already a sense of humor and wit, which will give it a real push.

Miss Shelly: I hope. To begin at the beginning - I began in the same innocence as anyone else.

Q: Would you perhaps begin with a kind of a thumbnail sketch of your own background?

Shelly: I had been, up to that point, always in education but never a teacher. I was in educational administration. For a long time, I was at Bennington College in Vermont. That's where I was at this reading, in the role of assistant to the President.

1 Shelly - 2

Q: But specializing in personnel problems.

Shelly: Oh yes, dealing very much with the age girl of our enlisted women. When, before Bennington, I was assistant to the Dean of students at the University of Chicago, I dealt with all ages, including graduate students.

Q: It's a very tough problem.

Shelly: Some very tough problems, yes.

Q: What then induced you to seek service in the WAVES?

Shelly: I didn't seek service in the WAVES. The WAVES sought me. I was in this famous first twelve Lieutenants, I think perhaps the 7th or 8th commissioned.

Q: You were commissioned in September of '42?

Shelly: Yes, but I got a letter in July of '42, just before our legislation went through, saying that this legislation was in prospect of passing. The Navy was anxious to have a selected group, and they wanted among others someone from the field of educational personnel and administration. So I wrote back saying, "No, thank you." I felt that the colleges too were going to need people during the war.

Then, I can't tell you exactly how much later, after the legislation was passed, it must have been in August, I got a telegram signed by the Chief of Naval Personnel. I learned later what that meant. It was from a Lieutenant Commander Hartenstein who, though I didn't know it, was in charge of WAVE officer recruitment.

Q: Oh yes. Who knew about you, who had gotten on to you first?

Shelly: No. I suppose in a group of Deans of Women which was acting on an advisory committee to the Navy, there were people who knew me. Then there was Commander Gene Tunney who knew about me indirectly.

This was really quite funny. He had on his staff a young man I had encountered, whose name I don't recall, when I was doing graduate work at Columbia. We were good friends. Tunney had this great idea of physical fitness for everybody. The women must be physically fit. His conception of that was quite interesting. So my friend had put in my name.

Q: Barbells maybe?

Shelly: No, the thirty inch stride, please. All women must learn to do the 30 inch stride.

In any case, on the strength of this telegram I went to the President of my college. I said, "What do you think?" He said, "Jo, the women are going to be in this. You might as well go and find out what it's all about."

One went to Washington, of course, at one's own expense as a civilian, completely without knowing what the picture was. I there encountered Elizabeth Reynard who said to me, "Men are dying in the Pacific of fatigue, not just of bombs. The women must come." Elizabeth Reynard was a very dramatic person.

Mildred McAfee who had been asked to take on the top job was not in Washington at the moment.

Q: Maybe she was sitting over in that empty office in the temporary building.

Shelly: She may well have been.

I was impressed with the terrific necessity that "we must serve our country" but I went back to Bennington. Then I got another telegram asking me to report to 90 Church Street, or wherever it was we went at that time.

1 Shelly - 5

There I went through a physical examination. We were required to have a waiver for weight. I was 5 feet 7 1/2 and I weighed 120 pounds. But it appears that they were using the men's standards, and for that much height I should have weighed 25 pounds more. Therefore, solemnly written into my picture is a waiver for weight.

Q: That's indicative of those early requirements, isn't it? They were all predicated on the male.

Shelly: Strictly, absolutely. That would be an absurd weight for my build.

It was during the process of being interviewed that I met up with Commander Tunney. For some reason which I don't recall, we walked some place together. That was when he said, "Now you're going to have to learn the 30 inch stride."

Q: You knew him beforehand?

Shelly: No, I never saw him before in my life.

I reported to the Bureau of Naval Personnel on Labor Day in September 1942. There wasn't anybody there to speak of. Nobody could tell me anything to do. Fortunately, I had a very good friend whose husband was already overseas,

1 Shelly - 6

actually the mother of my godsons. She had a house and so I had a roof over my head. We officers all lived in civilian quarters in Washington.

I had nothing to do for about 24 hours. By this time I had met up with Virginia Carlin, Joy Grimm, and Jean Palmer.

Then I got a telephone call from Lt. Commander Hartenstein. He said, "Have you been commissioned?" I said, "I don't know, sir." I didn't know that you didn't call Lieutenant Commanders sir. He said, "I can't find any commission for you. Go over (wherever it was in the District) and get commissioned."

Q: Down at the navy yard I guess.

Shelly: No, it was the Officer Procurement Center. All WAVE procurement was through the Officer Procurement Centers, even enlisted women, which is why, I think, we avoided some of the trouble the Army got itself into. We didn't avoid them all, let no one ever tell you that we did.

I was the only woman in the group of men being put through the process, which was most confusing. There were no provisions for a physical examination for a woman. Finally some provision was made and I was rushed through a very cursory physical exam and declared fit for duty.

Q: But underweight again?

Shelly: Yes, but the waiver was already in the records that I had by that time. The waiver was duly entered all over again.

I was sworn in by a WAVE Ensign. A little male Navy clerk then handed me a copy of Navy Regs. I doubt if anyone else was given a complete copy of Navy Regs. He said, "Don't drop it, it'll break your toe."

I returned to the Bureau of Naval Personnel where we were stationed. By this time, Mildred McAfee had discovered that there was all kinds of confusion going on in the training situation. This matter of my having anything to do with Tunney and physical fitness went right out the window, quick.

I went into the Training Activity, as it was called, at which point every man in a big room got up and brought paper from his desk to mine. The papers proved to be letters from colleges and universities all over the country wanting a contingent of women, to help fill the gap, to help pay the bills. My task was to sit there and prepare the letters saying, "No." Many of these letters had Congressional pressure behind them.

The formula was, you thanked them for the letter in the first paragraph; in the second paragraph, you said "no, thank you" in very polite terms; then in the third paragraph, you said, "thank you," all over again. All this was in Navy form, and signed by the Director of Training.

Q: How long did it take you to learn Navyese?

Shelly: I learned it from the boys around me. We learned a lot from the boys around us. We never had anybody officially standing by to teach us.

I'll never forget one of my main tutors, who was very much a reserve officer indeed. He just hated this whole affair. Promptly at four o'clock in the afternoon, he couldn't stand it any longer. He used to stand up and pull a clothes brush out of his desk and brush himself all over. It was almost symbolic, as though he were brushing off the Navy.

Finally, it was decided there would be three WAVE enlisted schools - the University of Indiana for storekeepers, Oklahoma A & M for yeomen, and the University of Wisconsin for radiomen.

Q: Who had made this decision?

Shelly: I can't tell you. It must have been a long time in negotiation. I'm sure that Congressmen were in this picture.

Q: At that point, did they have any idea of the number of women they were going to have?

Shelly: They thought about 10,000. There was a definite legal limitation at first on rank. The top rank was Lieutenant Commander, and there were to be twelve Lieutenants of either senior or junior grade. I don't know whether they stipulated the number of Ensigns or not, I can't recall. It was some time before that limit was lifted.

All told we passed through recruitment and training, something over 100,000 women. We ended up with roughly 8500 officers and 85,000 enlisted. Those figures could be a little off, but thereabouts.

Q: The reason I raised that question, Joy Hancock had told me at the outset the Bureau of Personnel and the other authorities had anticipated only a few thousand.

Shelly: I'm sure they had.

Q: Joy said, the Bureau of Aeronautics said they would take 20,000.

Shelly: I think that each of the Bureaus and each of the Naval Districts were queried as to the numbers they could use. There were some very resistant responses and there were some very affirmative ones.

Joy Hancock's role, backed by the interest on the part of her branch of the service was simply extraordinary. It was miraculous. We would have remained storekeepers, yeomen, radiomen, supply officers and so on, in the most modest of roles, if it hadn't been for Joy Hancock. She cracked it wide open. We spread out into all sorts of ratings, as you know.

Q: How did she do this, simply because of the backing of her bureau?

Shelly: Yes. And then we began to prove ourselves.

But this matter of the first three enlisted schools envisaged no boot training. Because you were to get a stenographer to be a yeoman, she was ready-made. You were to get somebody who knew bookkeeping to be a storekeeper, ready-made. Just how you were going to get a ready-made radioman was not quite clear, unless it was that you knew touch typing. The result was a great many wrong people got to the right place.

Mildred McAfee had got wind of this. There was a class of women officers rushed into Smith College, into a dormitory lovingly dubbed the USS CAPON. It was a wooden unfireproof building.

This first class was made up of very distinguished professionals, many not as young, people like Dorothy Stratton, Dean of Women at Purdue, and who became head of the SPARS. She was recruited by Dean Gildersleeve, and had no more idea what had hit her than the man in the moon. Like the rest of us.

Mildred said to me, "Now I want you to go up to Northampton and help Captain Underwood assign that first class." I was already commissioned, although I didn't have any uniform; nobody had a uniform.

The last thing that Captain Underwood wanted was me. I may say, parenthetically, we eventually became very good friends. But that first encounter - he wanted no part of my assistance, thank you very much. I was a complete maverick.

Here I was a commissioned senior grade Lieutenant; the rest of these people were Midshipmen. They were in training, there wasn't anything to do with me except have me behave like a Midshipman. I had orders to be there, and I couldn't turn around and go away. So, I just went along with the rest.

I think perhaps one of the funniest stories at that period is about Elizabeth Crandall, who was in charge in some way. I guess she was Commander of Midshipmen in a sense, as you would be at Annapolis.

She had to march the whole crew down the hill to the Wiggins Tavern, where the mess was. The line of march crossed a main street. At that point, no provision had been made for dealing with the traffic.

Liz was marching the group to mess -- "One, two, three, four. Watch out for the cars ladies. Use your own judgment ladies --,". Never breaking rhythm, never breaking stride, but simply interjecting advice not to get knocked down by an automobile.

I was there at the closing parade for this class when they were commissioned. They were paraded out on a very bumpy side yard of the USS CAPON with a very thorny hedge alongside. The Midshipman commanding was so confused that she ordered them by the right flank, which would have led them straight into the bushes. And not a woman but turned left, which proved something.

Q: They were using their heads.

Shelly: I guess so.

There we got our first uniforms. Mine was one size too small. When I got back to the Bureau of Naval Personnel, I spent a good deal of time trying to keep my blue shirt from showing between the buttons. I looked like a Western Union Telegraph boy.

On my way back I picked up my car at Bennington and stopped in New York, all very blithely, and discovered that I had been AWOL because that was not in my orders at all. That's all I knew about it at that point. My car was nearby in Vermont, so I simply went and picked it up and drove it to Washington because I needed it.

Q: It took a while to get into the military straight jacket, didn't it?

Shelly: Oh, it surely did.

My next adventure was when Captain Mac, as we always called her (we called her Miss Mac, until she became Captain) called me in and said, "Never mind those letters. We've got these three schools and they're open. You go see what's happening. There's some place here where you go and get orders to go out there."

I know that you've been told the story of the officer who was sent down to the third deck to find out how you got orders and never came back.

Anyhow Miss Mac told Dorothy Foster, "Go down on the third floor (we didn't know enough to call it a deck). There's some place there where you get orders." The men on duty promptly seized on Dorothy Foster to start writing orders or just seeing that they got written. Later Virginia Carlin took over this job.

I got TAD orders to go to Oklahoma, Indiana, and Wisconsin. It seems to me it was pretty cold weather, it must have been mid-winter or at least late fall of '42.

There were men commanding each of these schools all the way down the line. Although there was also a woman officer shipped out from the first original rush class.

The prize gal was at the University of Indiana. The Navy had really taken very hard with her. I always remember they had just had a Captain's inspection and on cabin seven she had written a note - "Glove adrift on bunk." I can see it to this hour.

The mixup was so apparent. These youngsters were pretty young. Many bookkeepers hand't gotten to Indiana, or stenographers to Oklahoma, or radiomen to Wisconsin. At least there was enough mixup to make it clear that something had to happen.

So I, with backing, tried to make a case for a boot school for our enlisted women.

Q: This was your recommendation?

Shelly: It was mine, backed up, yes.

A school at Cedar Falls, Iowa was just being set up. It was going to be another yeoman's school with a capacity of a thousand. Instead, in the dead of winter, and I mean the dead of winter, in '42 a thousand civilian women were rushed in all at once for boot training. It was a mess, just a mess.

Captain Amsden, who became Commander of the USS HUNTER eventually, was sent out there to try to do something about this.

Then Elizabeth Reynard, who knew a lot about New York colleges, knew about the Bronx campus of Hunter. She got them interested in the possibility of our having the place for a boot school.

I can remember, I was then ordered to go up and go with her and the President of Hunter through the buildings. It was a very fine setup and they agreed to turn it over to us.

Q: What happened to the Cedar Falls school?

Shelly: As soon as they got Hunter, I don't know whether we let it go or whether we made it a yeoman's school. I think we made it a yeoman's school as originally planned.

From then on all boot training was at the USS HUNTER. My records are not complete, but apparently what happened was: a six weeks' training program for a total capacity of 6,000. We'd bring in 2,000 every two weeks and at the same time graduate 2,000.

It was a fabulous place. Captain Amsden was a natural showman. There never was a boot school before or since that bore any resemblance to it. The gals marched beautifully. The captain devised the idea of a singing platoon in each group. You never saw such beautiful parades as went on. They were simply stunning; they were absolutely perfect. These kids took to marching like ducks to water.

When the recruits arrived in New York, there were special subway trains run from Penn Station and Grand Central which rushed them way out to this remote USS HUNTER.

Captain Amsden, meanwhile, had contracted pneumonia out in Iowa. So his executive officer was running the place, and he didn't know from nothing. He was about as confused as it was possible to be. In the first place, he'd been in the Pacific Ocean a couple of times. I think he was recuperating and barely recuperating from really severe war experience.

We had to get some women up there to keep this thing going. We began trying to requisition from Northampton what we could get. We finally did get some women.

Then we sent a poor soul as senior officer who didn't want to go. We didn't know why at the time. We found out. She was in love with a naval officer in Washington, We sent her away from her beau, to be the woman assistant to Captain Amsden. Eventually some one else took over and she got to go back to Washington, and married the guy and left the Navy.

The training problem was that it had a very slow start. Once we got real boot training it helped a lot. For instance, we had an excellent classification system of aptitudes and skills and prior experience.

Q: Who was involved in setting all that up, the Captain?

Shelly: The Captain, the staff he brought in, and the women. There were 270 male personnel on board at the beginning. That was cut down to 196 and the rest were women. There were perfectly appropriate spots for men, although I think we could have manned pretty near the whole thing with women. Looking back now, I'd say we probably should have. But we were pretty green in any department you want to name, unless it involved civilian experience. When it came to things like classification, you could get hold of women officers who were positive experts even though, as it turned out, classification and assignment to duty bore little relation to one another.

Q: You were a part of a naval organization. In that, you lacked experience.

Shelly: We lacked control as well as experience. For instance - a big communications operation was opened in Washington, a highly classified center, talking to ships and stations everywhere. They comandeered the total enlisted output of at least three classes from HUNTER, regardless of classification, and rushed them in there. Which is understandable; this was war. But we didn't always understand that. We did gradually, but it seemed to me a terrible thing to do. Here we'd gone through this classification and many of these youngsters were ill suited to the communications task so that we had a higher discipline quotient than we should have had, because you had the wrong peg in the wrong hole.

Q: But lacking a Navy background, you couldn't appreciate what communications meant to the Navy.

Shelly: Perhaps not. But this was tough, monotonous duty. It was so highly classified that it was broken down into parts so that each operation was totally meaningless from any one other operation. It was an around the clock, 365 days a year, 24 hours a day job, done in eight hour shifts.

Q: So no one person would have a total picture.

Shelly: That's right. For a barracks, they took over a school across the street from operations. But that was in the duty area. That was really beyond my province.

Q: Just a footnote in that area: Did you have any problem with clearance of any of the gals who went there?

Shelly: Not that I knew of. You see I wouldn't have known,

because once they left HUNTER, they weren't my babies. They were Jean Palmer's babies. I don't know, but I remember no spectacular incident at all.

For instance, now that it's out loud that there was biological warfare research, we sent a contingent of highly selected girls to the naval installation, wherever it was, for this work. They knew they were going to a duty that was highly classified although they did not know what it was. They knew that they would be there for the duration, and that they would have limited leave, and still they volunteered.

By the way during the course of the HUNTER operation we took aboard, when their legislation passed, the SPARS and the Marine women. Where things were identical, they were part of the WAVE show. Where there was a separate area, they had their own program. For instance, the Marines had their own drill officers, wouldn't you know. Eventually the Marines went to Camp LeJeune and the SPARS to Palm Beach.

Also at HUNTER, in the classification process we discovered there were girls who did not need further schooling. They could be immediately assigned to duty in a number of ratings and that was done. Also at HUNTER we ran a Cooks and Bakers School.

Q: Was it a popular assignment?

Shelly: For certain of these girls. We didn't get all of the snobbish, effete elite. We had some pretty plain youngsters. Youngsters from the country, and some deprived to the extent that they saw no prospect of college. The only requirement was to have finished high school and have no young dependents. These girls were pretty young; the minimum age was 20. We ran awfully close to 21 1/2 or 22 as the average age of our enlisted women on through the war. We had every kind of girl, from debutantes to little peasants, some with an extraordinary motivation, some partly self-interested. But if you did the job you got on in the Navy, you got a better rating, and you got more pay.

My main battle, especially in relation to officers but also in relation to enlisted women, was that it was nonsense to have segregated training for women beyond boot, where a training facility for men already existed.

Q: Segregated from the male?

Shelly: Yes. Why shouldn't we simply go in. We only had to create separate housing.

I won my battle because of Captain Arthur Adams, who was an Annapolis graduate and a retired submariner who became administrative head of training.

We never had the same over-all director of training for 20 minutes in a row. But within the Training Activity was the administrative unit, which was where I lived. I mean, that's where my role was. So I worked for the administrative director.

I worked under a mustang first, who couldn't believe that there were women in this Navy. He just couldn't believe it.

One time - Joy Grimm, having read upside down the in-boxes that morning in Planning & Control called me up and said, "Jo, they shouldn't take over that hotel in Boston and change the plumbing all around. They're not going to need any more yeomen. They're going to phase them out and phase out the yeoman schools. They've got all the yeomen they need."

All day long I sat outside my mustang's door, waiting to try to persuade him not to put his John Henry on the orders to change the fixtures and put back the doors on the hotel in Boston and infuriate the public that was already too short of hotel space.

He knew I was sitting there, but rank counted with him and I was a lowly senior Lieutenant, just a woman with blue braid. So I sat. Finally at about 1900 hours I got in. I said, "Sir, I think perhaps, sir, we ought, sir --" You peppered it with 'sirs' when you wanted to get something

1 Shelly - 23

done, especially with mustangs. Anyhow we didn't take over the hotel.

Q: You persuaded him?

Shelly: I guess I persuaded him.

Eventually we were very successful with this business of the women going in with men as part of an existing class, especially with officers.

I remember two or three trying incidents. At Norman, Oklahoma we were training mechanics. They worked out on the flight line. It was very cold and the women's winter work clothes were designed for a very much warmer climate. In the Navy zoning, Norman, Oklahoma was in the temperate zone. So I had quite a fight to get foul weather clothing for these kids, who were working out of doors with all the props going on the planes, for a good many hours at a time checking instruments and so on. We got the foul weather clothing but often these things were late in happening.

Q: And the result of a battle.

Shelly: Oh yes, a carefully conducted battle.

Sometimes you picked up something very useful on our private WAVE grapevine. I remember it was Captain Adams who said to me, "How do you women know some of these things?" I said, "Sir, we have our own ways."

We would get information because we were scattered all through the Bureau. We were never out to gossip; it was not scuttlebutt for its own sake. It was scuttlebutt for the sake of 'let's make sense out of this thing as much as we can.' We also knew that we were in there to prove our case. And we were anxious to do it without being feminists; we just wanted to make sense.

Q: This underscores again the importance of this daily gathering to discuss things and develop strategies. You say carefully planned strategy in getting some of these things accomplished --

Shelly: Yes, for instance - at one point, then Secretary of the Navy Knox made a trip down the Potomac on his yacht and he came back about seven o'clock in the morning. He saw a WAVE enlisted woman and a sailor out on the dock holding hands.

He issued an order that all barracks for men and women were to be not closer than 200 yards to one another. The cost to the taxpayer of that move, as well as the improbable

1 Shelly - 25

efficacy of it, was something you couldn't stand still for. We all got into the act to stop the order because it affected all our areas.

One of the notable instances of my experience with our going into training with the men was a very specialized operation that took place to recruit outside of the normal recruitment standards of any kind, physical or otherwise, highly qualified young college women with great linguistic ability to learn Japanese in 14 months.

Q: For communications?

Shelly: Yes, this was for communications. This was done on such special dispensation that it had nothing to do with any other officer procurement that ever took place. Some one special went to the colleges. Some of the girls had just graduated; some were still undergraduates. All were indeed extremely highly qualified linguistically.

Q: They could come in with 2400 vision and be accepted?

Shelly: Absolutely, it didn't matter. They were put through no shakedown at Smith. They were commissioned as Ensigns and sent directly to the University of Colorado. There were several men's schools there. The arrival of this contingent of women greatly disturbed the commanding officer. He began sending out cries over the proximity of men and women.

I was dispatched by direct orders from Admiral Jacobs to get out there fast and sort this out.

When they were studying Japanese, a good deal of it was in their own rooms with special apparatus. You could see from one wing to the other. So I said, "Captain I will ask the women to pull down their shades." That seemed to settle that.

Another funny incident - it was suggested that Miss Mc-Afee and I go up to Bainbridge and see how the boot training was being done for men. We were red-carpeted beyond the name. We stayed at the Admiral's house.

Q: What you call a snow job.

Shelly: A real snow job. We had a wonderful time, except that we kept being toured around in the Admiral's car with his insignia on it so that everybody froze and saluted all the time. Captain Mac and I were sitting in the back and we had to keep saluting. When we left Bainbridge and got on the train she said to me, "Do you like to salute?" I said, "No, do you?" She said, "No."

One of the incidents that was a kickback on me -- We sent women officers to a meteorology school in California. One day I received the women's scores on running the combat obstacle course. They'd flunked, with which, I had to untangle that one.

Q: These things had to be accomplished piecemeal, I take it?

Shelly: Oh yes.

Q: Wasn't there ever an overall set of regulations covering the women?

Shelly: The Navy was very busy and very big and it had a great many things to do. But there was a special handbook which Tova Wiley wrote, which was sent out late in the game, awfully late in the game. And probably not bothered with everywhere, and why should it be.

There was a phrase in the book that must not go in the script, but I will put it in just for your edification.

The first draft contained the statement, "When a member of the Women's Naval Reserve shall be declared pregnant by a naval medical officer, she shall be released immediately from duty." That had to be rephrased.

Q: Mildred McAfee told me about that, and about the long conferences with all the doctors and so forth.

Shelly: One of my problems was with the parachute riggers at Lakehurst. The great question was, "Should they jump?" It was cited that the Russian women jumped. Our kids, it was agreed, would not jump to test the shoot that they had folded, but many of them managed to find ways to do it just the same.

Q: They wanted to.

Shelly: They wanted to.

At one point after the Marines were set up at LeJeune, there was a famous expedition. We all flew to LeJeune to see the show. We saw men receiving their guerrilla training; we saw flame throwers and so on. It was the only time that I saw the war, except in films. I used to see some of the uncut films.

I remember one Christmas Eve when the boys across the

hall invited me to see uncut films of the landing at Tarawa. Some Christmas Eve that was.

At another point, Dr. Mary DeWitt Pettit, who was attached to the Inspector General in BuMed, Virginia Carlin, who was in Officer Personnel, Margaret Dysart [Disert], who was then Commanding Northampton, and I were sent down to Annapolis to see how they did the officer deal. It was way late really for us but at least Annapolis explained to me why Captain Underwood had run Northampton the way he had.

Q: You understood him better?

Shelly: Yes, I understood him much better.

Q: You say, it was way late. How late?

Shelly: It would be '44.

I was traveling a great deal. As I recall the count we had 32 training units of one kind or another, some small and some large. Eventually practically all but boot training was integrated with the men's advanced training, both for enlisted and officers. I think we kept a few separate enlisted schools. I'm pretty sure we did.

Then the demand for us began tapering off. The shore billets were pretty well filled.

I have a note here, in October '44 I was out in California somewhere. I got a telegram from my pals saying, "Come home, you're a Lieutenant Commander."

One experience was when with some of the men from training I was sent to Williamsburg, to Camp Perry, which had been a Seabee training center but had been turned over now to all the illiterates the Navy had suddenly collected for itself. They never had any illiterates before but because they had come under the draft, they were now getting men who couldn't read or write.

They wanted to see whether our officers, many of whom were teachers, could help. We went down and we agreed on the spot that it was just not workable because the noncom who was handling the men as their instructor was also their platoon commander and their barracks officer. It simply would have been a very artificial thing to put women, at, say, the Williamsburg Inn, and trek them out to Camp Perry to teach because the men weren't being kept there very long, they were being given just enough to get them through - the essentials of understanding what their orders were.

There is an incident, which I perhaps should not record. It came over Miss McAfee, perhaps she told you this -- She called me and said, "Have we had any negro women?"

Q: Yes, this should be a part of the story.

Shelly: Did she tell you this?

Q: She told me something about this.

Shelly: There was an unspoken and certainly unwritten order or policy, how it traveled I will never know, but no negro women ever seemed to be recruited. Obviously they must have applied in quantity. Secretary Knox was strictly averse to this.

Q: You mean, to having them in the service?

Shelly: Oh yes, both men and women, certainly women. And he was very frank about it. I shouldn't say that he was against having men, I don't really know that.

I do know that he thought that it was improper for negro women to be WAVES. He had a very high standard for the WAVES. He wanted them to be absolutely Mainboucher uniformed, perfect, beautiful. I think it was just a misguided love of having us be excellent.

The exclusion of negroes offended a professional liberal like Mildred MacAfee. So when Forrestal became Secretary of the Navy, she sensed that the change might be there. She said to Admiral Jacobs, "I'd like to see the Secretary to find out about this question of having negroes." Admiral Jacobs, I think, himself couldn't possibly have been enthusiastic. He was a deep-dyed southerner. But he said, "Why, of course, Captain McAfee. I will go with you."

They went to Secretary Forrestal's office. Captain McAfee simply raised her question. Forrestal looked horrified and said, "Jacobs, you can tend to that, can't you?" Jacobs said, "Oh yes, Mr. Secretary."

I was frantic. The last class had gone into the USS CAPON. We were getting ready to start phasing out. We rushed two negro women into the last Midshipman class.

One of them was a 'summa cum laude' in history, brilliant woman. The other was a more modest sort of person, but a very fine one.

There was a tradition in the Midshipman class that the three ranking Midshipmen stood for the whole class to receive their commissions. They went up on the platform; the other commissions were handed out otherwise.

LIFE magazine was there, Mildred McAfee was there, and

Admiral Jacobs was there. And this gal was the head of the class having arrived at least a week late, if not longer. She was miles ahead of the rest of the class.

I should backtrack and say that one time when Miss McAfee and I went up there, we were both fighting for women to help take over the teaching role. We listened to a woman teaching from the book, SHIPS AND AIRCRAFT. When we walked out Captain McAfee said to me, "I feel as though the whole United States Navy just sank." It was so dull. They weren't all dull, however.

We began phasing out training in late '44. In March 1945, I was transferred to the Demobilization Activity, the planning division of it. There really wasn't anything but a planning division. There were three men and myself. We were stationed down on the bottom deck, above the cafeteria. We were quite a crew. We were completely ignored; nobody could have cared less.

Q: Had they begun to do this for the men also, plan for this?

Shelly: These three men were to do the men's job, and I was to do the women's.

1 Shelly - 34

Q: It was a combined thing.

Shelly: Yes.

The Army meanwhile, you recall, was running those little steel balls, dropping them in slots, developing a point system. It was pre-computer.

The Navy didn't diverge from that. They took the Army's findings - in other words, length of service, the weighing of combat, dependents, decorations, and so on. Obviously much of this was not going to apply to women, in whose service there were none of these special factors. So, I just sat still until the men got a formula and then deleted from the formula any points that were inapplicable to the women.

Q: Very smart move.

Shelly: There wasn't anything else to do. The Navy demobilization plan was duly written and submitted to CNO and it stayed there a long, long time.

Q: This was Admiral King?

Shelly: Admiral King.

We could smell V-J day coming; we could really smell it

coming. We were all called to duty not only the six days that we ordinarily worked, but Sundays. We quickly had the plan mimeographed. We all walked round and round the table - my three pals and I, some other officers that had helped, and a bunch of enlisted women - assembling this stuff and stapling it. It was quite fat.

V-J day came about 7 o'clock at night, when I was at home. I got to the Bureau pretty early the next morning. We received that morning for one of the chaps, I'm not sure he even had the rank of Lieutenant Commander, the working copy from CNO. But it had a face sheet marked "For study only, not for action"!

In the meantime, an All-Nav was being prepared. I wrote the paragraph that was to carry the WAVE point formula. So the All-Nav went out, but they left out the WAVE paragraph.

Q: Why?

Shelly: Just a mistake.

That settled me; I knew I had to watchdog this. We had a rough ride. We had a Captain Peterson, who was our boss, and he was wonderful. The Navy didn't quite know where everybody was. They weren't quite sure where some several hundred thousand men were going to come in, at which port of entry.

We had a press conference every afternoon at four. They weren't very interested in the women, but a little bit.

Back in my career, there had been one Captain James Holloway. He had been the boss of training. When he came aboard the Training Activity, he called us each in in order of rank. When I came in (I was a Lieutenant Commander), he said, "Miss Shelly, the Navy is a priesthood, and at times as crooked as a dog's hind leg. Now, I have a point of view about the Training Activity. It is to be dynamic, sanguine, and open-hearted. Am I clear, Miss Shelly?" And I said, "Yes, sir."

So all of a sudden after Captain Peterson and the rest of us had sweated out this demobilization operation and had it well underway, returned to command us, Admiral James Holloway. His office was way up front, full of leather furniture, pictures, and rugs. We were way back, still over the cafeteria. But we went along about our business.

I never will forget there came a point when they were handing out Secretarial Citations. They were handing them out like popcorn. My Captain Peterson never wore his, never. Because he had really done a nice job. He received it from the hands of Admiral Holloway, but he never put it on.

We had to reverse training and we had to debrief these kids. I had become so Navy that a floor would never again be anything but a deck, and a wall never anything but a bulkhead.

Mostly I spent my time fussing with that. Occasionally there was a little public relations to do about the women, but not much.

Q: In what sense?

Shelly: There was one thing. You could be held for 90 days on a military necessity clause. There was a tendency to hold our hospital corpsmen, our yeomen, our storekeepers to do the pick up work that had to be done. I didn't fight that too hard, but I tried to keep track of it. Captain Peterson was extremely sympathetic about this. Wherever there was a real situation where they were boxing them in, then I would move and try to see if we couldn't crack it out. For the most part, there was very little injustice done. There was some, in holding the women versus the men, although they held many a man also, enlisted men and some officers. That's understandable.

There came a day, it must have been early March or late February 1945, when the boys came to me and said that Admiral Holloway had to go up on the hill and defend Navy demobilization. Send home the men who aren't fathers, because they aren't. Send home the fathers, because they are. Send home the professionals for that reason and the non-professionals for that reason. The Congressional mail came literally by the truck-load.

Q: It was all encased in this great emotional wave for this thing.

Shelly: Yes. All these chaps were sitting there putting together stock paragraphs replying to this Congressional mail. It was a very difficult chore. These were mostly men who'd been in pretty tough combat, still were quite used up, and still could be held a little while.

Anyhow, my gang said, "Jo, you write his speech. You know him."

Q: Holloway's speech?

Shelly: Yes. So I wrote him a speech.

Q: For the committee?

Shelly: For the committee. I don't know what committee it was intended for, but somebody on the hill.

I put in "dynamic, sanguine, and openhearted," and a few of the things that had not quite burned themselves into my consciousness as deeply as those three unlikely words, and timed it all very carefully. Of course, you wrote under your BuPers number, you couldn't possibly be more anonymous.

The boys came back from the hill, and Captain Peterson's

executive officer kept avoiding me. We were very good friends. Finally I said, "Look, what's the matter?" He said, "He forgot his glasses. He muffed it. He absolutely fell flat on his face."

Q: Holloway did?

Shelly: Yes. He didn't have his facts, he didn't have the answers, he got crucified.

I said, "Okay, I'm going. I've had it." I had agreed when the All-Nav thing happened that I would stay until half these kids were out.

But then I applied for release from active duty and was released in March '45.

Q: I understand that the Navy demobilization plan was very methodical and very well done. But it was completely overwhelmed by this emotional wave.

Shelly: Yes, it was. It was a very fair, a very workmanlike job. Of the three men that worked with me, there was one chap who was a real brain. That thing was as much as anything the product of his thinking. It was clear, it was explicit. But it couldn't operate under the circumstances. It couldn't even operate in terms of the way it should. It was just bound to be too mechanical. There were all the things that came in to play, like transportation, weather, and so on. And the fact that they couldn't account for all their numbers or which port of entry they were coming in was perfectly understandable. We were spread over the Seven Seas; we were everywhere on this globe. To get the word way out and get everything moving was of herculean proportion.

One episode I did leave out. We did send women to Hawaii.

Q: Yes, I want to ask about overseas service.

Shelly: That's the only place we sent them. In order to find out how to do it Joy Grimm, from Planning and Control, and I were sent out to see how the Army was doing it.

Q: In Hawaii?

Shelly: No. We were sent with a woman Army transportation officer to California. This was considered part of training because these gals were to be selected and shipped. So that came within my function. It must have been in '44, in November.

Q: This was the result of special legislation, wasn't it?

Shelly: Yes, finally the Senate Armed Forces Committee had authorized WAVES in the American theater. Which meant we could have gone to Bermuda, Hawaii, and Alaska. The only place where we were really needed and where there were ready-made quarters was Hawaii.

We were preparing to send very highly qualified women, no one under 18 months of service, and with specialized qualifications - mostly yeomen, storekeepers, and a few air ratings. I don't remember the whole mix of people we sent, but we sent hand picked women.

My part of it was to go with Joy Grimm out to the Army port of embarkation at Shoemaker, outside of San Francisco. The Army was sending these women to the Pacific. Many of them had already been in the European theater. They ranged in age up through the late forties. There were top sergeants, many with grey hair coming out from underneath their helmets, all packing duffle bags.

We spent the night there and saw what they were doing, getting ready to go. We rode with them in the little ship that went down the Sacramento River. There was a wonderful young Army Lieutenant who was the escort officer. She had done this before.

It was an experience I shall never, never forget. It was raining, it was cold, and it was bleak. I still recall, as Joy and I went to the car to take us to the ship, sitting in the train on a hydrant was an old rag doll. The women were loaded aboard and we went down the Sacramento River.

Joy and I were invited to go up to the Wardroom and have coffee. There was a rap on the door and here was a little sergeant, she wasn't so young, with her hand over her mouth. She said, "Lieutenant, I have to see you." The Lieutenant said, "What's the matter?" She said, "I pulled out my front teeth." The officer said, "How did you do that?" The little sergeant opened her hand and she had a sticky piece of caramel, she said, "In a love nest." She was enroute to the Pacific. And where were you going to get these teeth put back in, if you could get them loose from the love nest? They were the two front teeth.

When we got down to the Embarcaderos, it was well into the evening. The troop ships were all lined up. The WAC were marched off, singing, "The WAC is a soldier too."

They stood in ranks under little electric light bulbs while the men in combat gear were put aboard. Then the women were marched up and were called from the roster. The sergeant would say, "Smith, Mary." "Here." "Jones, Leona." "Here." Then they were sent to their cabins, packed in. Joy and I went aboard to see them off.

Then we came back to the Bureau of Naval Personnel and

said, "This has nothing to do with the preparations of the WAVES for Hawaii." These women, for instance, had been required to go up a cargo net to a considerable height in full gear, gas masks, and whatnot and down the other side.

Q: Just as the men.

Shelly: Yes, many of them were going over the side of the ship into small boats at some of the Pacific islands. Don't tell me the WAC didn't go to war. I think they are the most misunderstood of all the military women. They stand as the symbol of all that went wrong. They went to war, and we never really did. We were a ladies war. It was a war of the heart and mind, but it was not war.

Q: Was this due to a different concept in the Army from the Navy?

Shelly: Sure. I met WAC officers afterward who went into the Philippines when it was still being bombed, and lived with a foxhole beside their bunks.

Q: They didn't resent this however, did they?

Shelly: No, they didn't resent it.

The WAVES, on the other hand, went to Hawaii in a Lurline ship in white gloves and had a ball. They were received by the sailors with leis thrown over their heads. It was very fine duty. I never could find an excuse to go to Hawaii because there wasn't any training going on.

Q: Why did it take the Navy so long to give this permission, to go to Hawaii and Bermuda and Alaska?

Shelly: We never did go to Bermuda and Alaska. The Chairman of the Senate Foreign Relations Committee . . .

Q: Was that David I. Walsh?

Shelly: Was he from Boston?

Q: Yes.

Shelly: He was it. He felt that this would endanger the morals of the women. The British were pleading with us to send women to England to help with our American chores there. The British women were doing the chores. I used to see the classified documents on the women in service, including the enemy, including the Japanese women. All were in combat areas.

Almost all the way through the record of every service there were two things which stuck out -- the women stayed with the repetitive jobs, where the man would gold brick. For instance in the Link Trainer job, WAVES took over the whole thing and did it magnificently; also the synthetic gunnery job -- where you said the same thing over and over and over to class after class after class -- that type of thing. The other trait was manual dexterity. This was true of women everywhere.

I really think it was Senator Walsh almost singlehanded who kept us from being shipped.

Q: He was very powerful, of course. He had a 19th century concept of women in the home I suppose.

Shelly: Strictly Victorian. I'm sure he didn't think we belonged in the Navy at all.

Q: Were you helped at all by Margaret Chase Smith?

Shelly: Yes, we were helped by Margaret Chase Smith. We were helped, I think, by the women in the Congress as a whole.

The men came around, because we began to be very useful and we had a minor percentage of discipline problems.

Q: You say, the men came around. You mean not only Capitol Hill, but Navy?

Shelly: I mean down at the working level, you couldn't miss. Of course, right through the war we still had WAVES being used as baby tenders for officers' wives and being used in the PX, where they shouldn't have been. This has nothing to do with training, except that I knew about it because it was part of everything that was happening. This was the silly side of our usefulness.

We did have a high nuisance side. Both in training and afterwards, we fought for accommodations for the women which eventually became the standard accommodations for the men -- a certain privacy, a certain respect for individuality, a certain room to move, have your own little trophies, and some feeling of being yourself.

Q: This is what you people who had been in college work brought to it -- a knowhow, and an understanding of what young women require.

Shelly: I think Mildred McAfee had the most remarkable supporting staff that one could have. It was a top drawer staff and it worked together with none of this female cattiness -- nobody cared who got promoted or not.

On the whole, I didn't have a terrible struggle. The men were having just as hard a time as I was. When I say that classification was often completely ignored, because there was space in the school or a need, sure, that's war. It would be absolutely unforgiveable to waste skills now, because it's wasting the person, it's not because it's wasting the task of classification.

But the gals were pretty smart. Many times I knew of youngsters who wrangled their way around and got themselves in the spot they belonged in, where their natural abilities and propensities put them.

Q: Is this inevitable? Male officers do this too.

Shelly: Why sure. They weren't just doing it for promotion. They found the job they wanted. And some of them were also the most remarkable malingerers that you can think of. I had a yeoman who was absolutely determined to get out of the Navy. She developed so many psychomatic symptons that finally the medical department discharged her.

1 Shelly - 48

Q: Was it very difficult for a WAVE to get out?

Shelly: Oh yes. We didn't realize what we were in for. I don't know whether Miss Mac told you this. She didn't have any idea she was not going back to Wellesley any day.

One night that first winter I went down late to take some papers to her office. She said to me, "What do we do?" I said, "We are here for the duration and six months. It took quite a while for me to get it through my head." This was a low point for all of us, that first winter.

Q: She was there for one year, she thought.

Shelly: Yes, I think they euchred her into it. They said, "Come and organize."

Jean Palmer and I were comparing notes about Miss Mac. I think we will never know a greater woman. She's a magnificent person, intellectually and with integrity beyond the name, and wit. Her public relations were something.

Have you ever heard the Navy Day story? Right in the middle of the war, there was a great Navy Day dinner held here in New York. She was invited, the only woman ever, and she could have five minutes. She wanted to make the point that it was not always remembered that women were in the service. So she prepared her speech. Louise Wilde, her public relations aide, went over it and said, "Mildred, you can't do this." The time was the Battle of the Bulge. The Army had taken one blanket from every bed in every stateside barracks. In order to make it more palatable, they had put out a poster -- a GI lying in a ditch, with his helmet half over his eyes and his M1 beside him, saying, "This man would be glad to be in your bed tonight." It went everywhere including to all the WAC barracks.

That was the story that Mildred used to cap her speech. The men rolled in the aisles. All the brass was there, both military and civilian. Her timing was so perfect, she made her point so subtly. She just threw in this little climax. For instance -- when Louise Wilde said, "You can't do this," she just said, "Um hum." And went on and did it to suit herself.

Again at the low point that first winter, she said, "It's time we were recognized. Let's have a birthday."

Q: For the first anniversary?

Shelly: For the first six months, or something.

The new Statler Hotel had just been built; it had a red, white, and blue ballroom. We threw a breakfast, all spit and polish, and everybody came. Admiral King came. He had no intention of staying any length of time at all and stayed to the end. We had a WAVE officer who was so far out of order that Mildred had her in her own office. She was impossible; she just never knew what day it was at any time. So Mildred kept her under wraps. It was she who was helping the gentlemen off with their coats at the breakfast.

As she was helping one gentleman with his coat she said, "May I have the name, please?" He said, "The name is King." Apparently she couldn't recognize him despite his stripes.

Mildred was toastmistress. She played on the business of our beingbabies in the Navy and the care they require. A baby is a delight, but -- It was a wonderful success. I can still see that room, with everybody in their most elegantly tailored uniforms, laughing.

Q: That's what you needed; the right kind of publicity.

Shelly: Yes, there were Senators and Congressmen, everybody. It was just right.

Q: It was a 'sell job' from the beginning, wasn't it?

1 Shelly - 51

Shelly: Yes, it was a 'sell job' and why not?

It's not part of this story, but I got shanghied into the Air Force.

Q: You did?

Shelly: You didn't know that?

Q: No. You tell me that, please.

Shelly: You don't need to transcribe this.

Q: Yes indeed. I want to have this; this is your story.

Shelly: I went back to Bennington in March '45. I was pursuing the even tenor of my way. I finally decided that I was long overdue a sabbatical.

My sister said she'd like to go to Europe, and my brother-in-law didn't want to go. So I said, "I'd like a sabbatical, please."

Q: Having just returned to Bennington.

Shelly: No, this is '51.

So we went to Europe. We got back, I was still in New York because I wasn't yet due back at college. The Korean thing was going full tilt. It was June 1951.

I got a telephone call from Jean Palmer. She said, "You are going to be called by the Secretary of the Air Force, Thomas Finletter." I said, "Look, Jean, I did it. I'm not going to do it again. Once is enough; I can't stand uniforms." She said, "You wait until you talk with the Secretary."

The next morning, he called me, having trailed me from Bennington. I said, "Mr. Secretary, I really don't want to do this." He said, "The way to figure that out is to come down to Washington."

So we flew down in his special plane. We drove in under the Pentagon and went up by special elevator. He dumped me in Anna Rosenberg's office. She was then Assistant Secretary of Defense. I was there about ten minutes, about five of which she was on the phone. Then I was rushed to a dining room with General Hoyt Vandenberg and Anna Rosenberg and Secretary Finletter, just the four of us. Anna pretty well took over.

The Air Force had become a newly independent department in '48, I guess. They had taken any women, but any, from the Army Air Corps mostly, with no screening whatsoever.

They were having every problem in the book.

To make a long story short, I said at this first meeting in the Pentagon, "When do I have to do this?" Anna Rosenberg said, what you'd think she'd say, "Yesterday." I said, "Mr. Secretary, I really don't want to do this. Isn't there some one, at least as well qualified, to just do an inspection job like this? Can't the Inspector General do it?"

He said, "Miss Shelly, none of us who is here wants to be here. There is a war on, and we do not know where it's going. We cannot afford this inefficiency."

At this stage, they were taking the women at 18 and you could leave for a marriage only. When I got in and saw the figures, I was utterly shocked at what it was costing, just simply alone on that basis. The women were coming in and they were only obligated to stay for the period equivalent to their training. Then they'd marry the nearest boy, and out they'd go. You didn't have to wait for pregnancy, legimate or otherwise. You just got married, and out. Too many had come to get the man. Also they were getting in very poor quality of women, recruited by ancient Army noncoms. The average age was very young, 19 1/2.

Furthermore, I got a study done at the Women's Bureau

of the Department of Labor that showed that at all times in a civilian pool there were millions of qualified women. We could just do what the British did, in World War II. Just go to the nearest Post Office and sign up, in a sweater and skirt.

I had to take a four year reserve commission. General Vandenberg said to me, "The day that you can file your recommendations and name a successor, you're out."

I flew in everything, except chopping bowls, I guess. I visited every major air command, with the disadvantage of a full Colonel's rank. It was a great disadvantage.

Anna was busy trying to get legislation to give us General and staff rank. I said to her, "You are making a mistake. The man looks at us, and he feels that we're occupying a spot that might be his. You're doing no service. It's a disadvantage simply to be a full Colonel. You have to disarm the men before you can possibly get down to the nitty gritty."

I found some pretty horrifying things; they weren't new, but they were existing in a proportion which were outrageous. The utilization of women was fantastically bad. Again, there was this business of excellent classification and total disregard of the findings in terms of assignments.

I happened to sit under a great, great guy, named Lawrence Kuter who was Deputy Chief of Staff for Personnel.

He was a magnificent person. Every day at four o'clock he held a meeting of his division directors, and I was just as free as anyone else to speak up. If there was no business to be done, the meeting lasted one minute. The rule was that you had to interest two-thirds of the people in the room, or keep your mouth shut.

Q: Wonderful rule.

Shelly: Wonderful, yes. The men had a terrible time; they had a worse time than I did.

It took me two years to be sure of what I wanted to say. Then I wrote a voluminous study.

Q: You were on the road all the time practically?

Shelly: I was on the road 90 per cent of the time.

I had tremendous experiences. I went to Cape Canaveral (now Cape Kennedy) when it was nothing; it was Patrick Air Force Base. Those boys begged for women. There was no one paying attention to them. They said, "Some day this will be the center of the world."

General Vandenberg retired and General Twining took over;

very fine, great guy, absolutely great. I'll never forget the day we had an officer call and he said, "I've got to go to the Joint Chiefs of Staff. Tommy White will be here. You'll all be all right. I don't want to go, but I've got to go for our sake." That's all he said, and put his cigar back in his mouth, and walked out.

One famous encounter was at SAC. LeMay said to me, "I'm not supposed to want to have WAF. That's not the point. I don't want a bunch of green kids here. You send me people who can run that switchboard out there and who can do the job ready made and I'll take any number of them. I don't care whether they're men, women, or children. I've just got a job to do here at SAC." I said, "I understand, sir. I don't have control over assignment. I'm not about to offer you any apologies; I at least will register the fact. SAC is prepared to take them, if we send the right people. I'm perfectly sympathetic with your position."

There was the great day when I was about to pick my successor. I went over the permanent Lieutenant Colonels, who didn't care for me, I might say. I was an outsider, I was a WAVE.

Q: You hadn't lost that identity for some?

Shelly: Not in their minds.

When I finally left for absolutely no reason, I was given a Legion of Merit with everybody standing around. I think it was an apology for some not too happy publicity at the beginning.

The report I had written was put in the files, and the drawer shut on it. They went right on taking too many women, anybody, having a big turnover for quite a long time. After a while, it tapered down. They came to their senses.

Now, from what I know, I think they're doing as fine utilization of women as any branch of the service. For instance, young women who are trained in mathematics or physics (this is true of the Navy also) are often going into the service because they are getting a real assignment superior to one they could get in industry, because they are women. They go right into research and get real jobs.

Q: That's an interesting point. That in the service now, they can really assume a proper place.

Shelly: After all, the shock has worn off. The use of women began in the forties. A sizable contingent of women have since gone into the regular service.

Q: But you had to earn your place from the very outset.

Shelly: Oh yes, sure at the very outset.

You know this - The first legislation written offered by some woman Congressman was for Army and Navy. The Navy got the Navy deleted from it. They had no intention of having us.

Q: Yes, I know this.

Shelly: But the Navy saw the handwriting on the bulkhead. So then they devised their own legislation and set their own standards.

As I said, our enlisted women all came in through Officer Procurement Centers with very good screening. Now, we got one of everything. You can't possibly win on even that number -- 100,000 women -- you're bound to have some problems.

By the way, these gals that went though the Japanese language school all got sent back to communications in Washington. 365 days a year, 24 hours a day, they were on duty translating Japanese documents. They were young brilliant gals. It's surprising that they held the discipline that they did. They made a few important discoveries -- one of them came upon a description of a plane that was brand new. It was like the British gal that discovered Penemunde. It wasn't quite of that magnitude but it was important.

Admiral Jacobs was very good to us. It was Mrs. Jacobs that kept us from having to wear black stockings. The nurses were wearing them. Oh, the nurses didn't like us, by the way, very well. We got more rank than they did, right away quick. They'd been there a long time. But I think the fact that we got the rank that we did helped to crack it. There was new legislation for them.

I don't think the Navy or Secretary Knox would ever have changed the legislation to make Mildred a Captain. But the Army jumped Mrs. Hobby up to Colonel, so they had to follow suit.

Q: I believe that this was the reason for the initial permission by the Navy to have WAVES, the fact that others were beginning to get women.

Shelly: They must have known that sooner or later there would be Congressional pressure for this.

Q: There was a bit of subterfuge too, I'm told. Joy told

me that they got Mel Maas to introduce a bill in the House. It threw the Navy into such consternation that they finally were . . .

Shelly: Joy Hancock would know more than Mildred McAfee would know, or almost anyone I can think of.

Q: She was on the inside.

Shelly: She was way on the inside. She understood the whole thing in a way that we, in a way, really never did.

I don't mean to sound as though my life was a miserable battle, it wasn't.

There is not one of us that you are interviewing who wouldn't say that this was one of the great chapters in our lives. As I said to you when I went over that jacket of mine, I was full of excitement and nostalgia.

I was very fortunate because of Arthur Adams. When he came aboard he called me in and said, "What do you want?" I said, "For one thing, and it's a simple thing, I want the mail that has anything to do with women either excerpted for me, that part of it, or sent to me and not to someone else. Sometimes there are things I could do that I don't even find out about." This was simply a mechanical oversight.

Q: Terribly important, however.

Shelly: It was very important because timing could sometimes be of the essence. When we got wind of the fact by our own grapevine, for instance, that in certain enlisted ratings we were not going to need anymore, time meant everything.

One night Joy Grimm and I went down and ran the adding machine after hours to see if we couldn't figure out (we called it 'hot bunks') how we could get these youngsters where they really ought to go. She had knowledge of the picture. We didn't know how to run the machine; it was very complicated. It began to give off nothing but asterisks. We didn't know how to stop it; so we just pulled the plug. I said, "Let's give it up. We're probably not going to hatch this fine scheme of ours anyhow. We better just play it as it comes."

There began to be more places where we were well used, where we were wanted, where the thing made more sense than not. I wouldn't want to draw the percentage, but I'm sure there was waste. Look at the waste with the men, it was inevitable.

Q: Because of the sudden influx. It couldn't be orderly.

1 Shelly - 62

Shelly: It couldn't be orderly.

Q: The precipitous attack on Pearl Harbor and all the rest.

Shelly: And the whole state of affairs.

Q: The thing that does amaze me about the setup of the WAVES is that at first so many of the decisions which really had to do with the essentials of the organization were attempted to be made by men rather than the women themselves. Why was this?

Shelly: Either it didn't occur to them that we had the sense to do it or -- they resented us, preferred we weren't there at least. Or -- often some decisions were made as in my area, for instance, about choice of school locations that were strictly political.

There's a school that shall remain unnamed where we sent yeomen, a very small college, by reason of the pressure of the then Chairman of the House Arms Services Committee. Straight out I said, "Why?" I went down to see the place.

Q: You mean Millidgeville?

1 Shelly - 63

Shelly: Millidgeville. I went down and I came back and I said, "Captain, this is absurd." The transportation in and out, the housing, the training facilities; you had to consider the recreational, the religious, the human side of the thing, because if that didn't go well, the military side of it wasn't going to go well. You knew that, if you knew anything.

That's why I think we often fought. On the human side of the thing, it seemed a little out of order.

Q: And those were special qualifications which some of you women had.

Shelly: But they were part of the whole picture. They helped the military thing to be efficient. But Millidgeville was a disgrace.

We had the offers of plenty of places that were ready-made.

Q: I was thinking of such ridiculous things. You mentioned the black stockings that you were saved from wearing and the type of uniform which Mildred McAfee told me about which she prevented, decisions like this being made by men seemed rather preposterous.

Shelly: Just on the score of the uniform, look where we came out. We came out with the best dressed military women that you could devise. We were better dressed than any number of civilians. They were beautiful uniforms. I paid more for my uniforms than I paid for civilian clothes by a longshot. We were meticulous about our appearance.

Q: You were indeed.

One other thing I'd like to ask about. If you could give me some kind of an estimate, I know there are no statistics on this. Some of you contributed so very much to the service, but you also acquired a great deal in the process. On the whole, did this mean more after service for the advancement of women in our country than most anything else?

Shelly: Distinctly, decidedly, definitely, yes. It was a real world compared, for instance in my case, to the academic world.

Q: It was a watershed then, was it?

Shelly: I think just the learning of skills, getting along with people, the sticking with it that took place was of a very high order and a very valuable kind of discipline. It was a very positive discipline, not negative at all, not conformity. It was a survival operation on the good side.

We were spared the horrors of war. We only heard the echoes of those but we were in the machinery.

I can tell you that I had insights that I have used a million times, subconsciously and otherwise.

The rate of learning that went on, how fast these enlisted youngsters would learn, the motivation to get on in this thing and to do it.

I don't know what the disciplinary record was. It must have been very minor.

Q: There were bound to be boy-girl things; this is inevitable.

Shelly: We seemed to play in great good luck. We seldom seemed to make the papers with some of the small things, the way the WAC did. The WAC got picked on for some reason.

I think the trouble came with them because when they changed from the Women's Army Auxiliary Corps to the Women's Army Corps they were under such pressure at that point, that they did not screen. The WAAC was so nearly civilian; they weren't under military discipline. They could come and go as they pleased. There was very little careful selection there. They should have done, if they could have, a tight selection when they changed over to a regular Women's Army Corps.

I say again speaking for a sister service, they deserve tremendous credit. Nobody's ever told their story. It's a tremendous story.

Q: Was it perhaps one reason why the WAVES escaped some of the things that happened to the sister service-publicity given them, was it because the initial group of women involved in the WAVES were of such high academic standing that this gave it a credence immediately?

Shelly: Yes, it did. In that special class of officers, many of them were distinguished professional women. I think the way we looked helped - the uniform, the grooming.

Q: It was feminine and yet it was military.

Shelly: It was feminine, but military.

One day at Northampton, Louise Wilde and I were to go over to Mt. Holyoke to the Communications School. It was raining. The uniform of the day, for the first time, was havelocks. It was about seven o'clock in the morning. We walked down almost deserted streets in Northampton. There were two policemen standing there. We of course never, but never, carried umbrellas. But we had on our raincoats and our havelocks. These two policemen -- it broke them up. They laughed and laughed. One of them said, "You know, that's a good idea. Pretty good idea, it really keeps the rain off."

Yes, to answer your question, I think we had all the breaks in terms of the superficial things that trigger opinion. Without people realizing, they are passing judgment. Somehow we looked credible.

Q: And along the line, you very quickly maintained this through your public relations, didn't you?

Shelly: We had very good public relations. The Navy was very smart about it.

Q: Now this raises a question. The Navy wasn't very smart about public relations in many areas. How did it happen to be with the WAVES?

Shelly: I don't know. There were women, for one thing.

There was a Louise Wilde, who was an extremely astute public relations person. There were several others scattered around. I think they knew how to see that the stories that went out were good stories.

It's a funny thing because in the WAC, they assigned a Colonel to sit right by Mrs. Hobby's right hand from the beginning, to give her the whole pitch.

Q: More like a commissar.

Shelly: Yes. Mildred McAfee didn't know any more 'fore from aft' than we did. She had to find it out the hard way too.

I still think, despite that, that they did not have the women with that much control at enough strategic points.

I think out at the naval stations they wanted a good picture. Maybe they didn't want the women there, but at least they didn't want a poor story about it.

I think we played in luck, and I think we earned some.

Q: I'm sure that should be underscored. You earned it.

Shelly: Let it be also said that we enjoyed it.

Q: Thank you very much, Miss Shelly. This has been wonderful.

Index to Interview with

MARY JO SHELLY

Adams, Capt. Arthur, 21, 24.

Air Force: recruiting programs, 53-54.

Amsden, Capt. William F., 16, 17.

Carlin, Miss Virginia, 14, 29.

Crandall, Miss Elizabeth, 12.

Finletter, Secretary Thomas, 52-53.

Forrestal, Secretary James, 32.

Foster, Miss Dorothy, 14.

Grimm, Joy, 22, 40, 41, 61.

Hancock, Joy Bright (Mrs. Ofstie), 9, 10, 60.

Hartenstein, Lt. Cdr. Paul B., 3, 6.

Holloway, Adm. James, 36-39.

Jacobs, Admiral Randall, 32, 33, 59.

Knox, Col. Frank, 24, 31, 59.

Kuter, Gen. Lawrence, 54-55.

LeJeune, Camp, 28.

LeMay, Gen. Curtis, 56.

McAfee, Mildred (Mrs. Horton), 4, 7, 11, 13, 26, 28, 30-31, 32-33, 48-49, 59, 68.

Naval communications, 18-19.

Navy illiterates, training of, 30.

Palmer, Miss Jean, 20, 48, 52.

Pettit, Dr. Mary DeWitt, 29.

Reynard, Prof. Elizabeth, 4, 15.

Rosenberg, Anna (Mrs. Paul Hoffman), 52-53.

Shelly, Mary Jo: Wave Commission, 2, 6; Lt. Commander, 30; Air Force Commission, 51, 52; Legion of Merit, 57.

Smith, Senator Margaret Chase, 45.

Stratton, Miss Dorothy, 11.

Tunney, Cdr. Gene, 3, 5.

Twining, Gen. Nathan, 55-56.

Underwood, Capt. Herbert W., USN (Ret.), 11, 29.

USS CAPON, 11, 12.

Vandenberg, Gen. Hoyt, 52-53.

Walsh, Senator David I., 44-45.

WAVE, Enlisted schools, 8, 10, 13; Cedar Falls, 15; Hunter College, 15, 16, 18, 20; Norman, Oklahoma, 23; Millidgeville, Ga., 63.

WAVES: Segregated training, 21; special training in Japanese language, 25-26, 58; Navy Regs for, 27-28; parachute training, 28; negro women in, 30-33; demobilization plans, 33-40; plans for Hawaii, 40-43; First birthday party, 49-50; advantages gained for women through wartime experience, 64-65.

Wilde, Louise, 49, 66-68.

Wiley, Tova (Peterson), 27.

Recollections

of

Captain Dorothy Stratton,
First Director of the SPARS
U. S. Coast Guard

U. S. Naval Institute
Annapolis, Maryland
1971

Preface

This manuscript is the result of a tape recorded interview with Captain Dorothy Stratton at her home in New York City on September 24, 1970. The interview was conducted by John T. Mason, Jr., for the Oral History Office in the U. S. Naval Institute.

Only minor corrections and emendations have been made by Captain Stratton to the manuscript. The reader is asked, therefore, to bear in mind that he is reading a transcript of the spoken word rather than the written word.

DECLARATION OF TRUST

The undersigned does hereby appoint and designate as his (her) Trustee herein, the Secretary-Treasurer and Publisher of the United States Naval Institute to perform and discharge the following duties, powers, and privileges in connection with the possession and use of a certain taped interview between the undersigned and the Oral History Department of the United States Naval Institute.

(1) As an Open transcript. It may be read (or the tape audited) by qualified researchers upon presentation of proper credentials as determined by the Trustee.

(2) It is expressly understood that in giving this authorization, I am in no way precluded from placing such restrictions as I may desire upon use of the interview at any time during my lifetime, nor does this authorization in any way affect my rights to the copyright of any literary expressions that may be contained in the interview.

Witness my hand and seal this 17th day of December 1970

Dorothy C. Stratton

I hereby accept and consent to the foregoing Declaration of Trust and the powers therein conferred upon me as Trustee:

R E Bowker Jr
Secretary-Treasurer and Publisher

Interview # 1

Dr. Dorothy Stratton
New York City, New York
Subject: SPARS

by John T. Mason, Jr.
September 24, 1970

Mr. Mason: Dr. Stratton was the first Director of the SPARS.

Dr. Stratton I thank you at the outset for being kind enough to give me this interview and to talk about your experiences in your days as Director of the SPARS.

Would you give me a little thumbnail background before you launch into your career with the Navy first, and then the SPARS? Where do you hail from?

Dr. Stratton: I was born in Missouri. My father was a Baptist minister, and so we moved around the country a good deal. As a youngster I lived all through Missouri, Kansas, and Kentucky. I went to school in Missouri and in Kansas.

My experience had been entirely in the field of education at the time I was sworn into the Women's Reserve of the Navy.

Mr. Mason: Where did you graduate actually, from what college?

Dr. Stratton: My B. A. - I graduated from a college called Ottawa University in Ottawa, Kansas.

1 Stratton - 2

Of course noboy in this part of the country ever heard of Ottawa University. They think it's in Canada. I've just given up on trying to correct that impression.

Mr. Mason: I happen to have known about it. And where did you get your doctorate?

Dr. Stratton: I got my Master's Degree from the University of Chicago and my Doctor's Degree at Columbia.

Mr. Mason: Tell me how you happened to get interested in the WAVES, because you did go into the WAVES first.

Dr. Stratton: Yes, I did.
 My first experience was with the Army, as a matter of fact. I helped to recommend for selection the first officer candidates for the WAAC, as it was then.

Mr. Mason: How did you happen to do that? Where were you at that point?

Dr. Stratton: I was Dean of Women at Purdue University at that time. I don't know how I happened to get the invitation, it just suddenly arrived, you know how things are. Mrs. Hobby was the Director of the WAAC.

1 Stratton - 3

After I had that experience I was talking with Dr. Lillian Gilbreth, who at that time was a member of the staff at Purdue University and was on the staff of the Dean of Women as a consultant in Careers for Women. She had been working with the Navy.

Mr. Mason: Was she on that special committee that they setup, an advisory committee?

Dr. Stratton: Yes, she worked with Dean Virginia Gildersleeve.

She talked to me about it. She thought that this was something that was important to do and urged me to see if I could qualify. So as I recall it, I went to Chicago for that delightful physical examination that one goes through.

Mr. Mason: She must have been pretty persuasive if she got you that far.

Dr. Stratton: Yes. Needless to say I was very much interested in the Women's Services and the fact that women were going to be given an opportunity to serve, and I felt pretty strongly that it was important that the United States should join the Allies and help to win the war. I know there's a good deal of talk at the present time about how this may not have been necessary, but

I still don't feel that way. I feel, to put it simply, that it was important that we should stop the Japanese and Hitler. So I thought that if there was any opportunity for me to do my little bit I wanted to do it.

Mr. Mason: How did your people at Purdue feel about your taking a leave of absence?

Dr. Stratton: Dr. Elliott, who was the President of Purdue, was very generous about it. He thought it was the right thing for me to do, and he raised no objections whatever. In fact I think he was glad I was going to do it. He always gave me wonderful support all through, not only during my years as Dean of Women at Purdue but while I was in the Service.

After I was commissioned as a Senior Lieutenant in the Women's Reserves —

Mr. Mason: That was a very high rank, wasn't it?

Dr. Stratton: I was pretty old. I was sent with the first class to Northampton when we had, as you already know, no pillows and hardly any blankets. We didn't have anything to work with or any uniforms. We didn't have anything, except the shots that we got, but we got along.

Mr. Mason: How did you react to that period of indoctrination?

1 Stratton - 5

Dr. Stratton: I thought I had made the worst mistake of my life.

Mr. Mason: It was in the winter time, was it not?

Dr. Stratton: No, it was in August and September. It was the 28th of August when I was called to duty.

I remember saying to Jo Shelly of the WAVES that this was the worse mistake I'd ever made in my life.

Mr. Mason: Did Jo feel the same way about it?

Dr. Stratton: She didn't go through this. Of all the Directors of the Servies, I was the only one who went through this period of training. I was glad that I did because I knew what the others, the officers, were going to go through in their periods of indoctrination.

Mr. Mason: You also learned how to march I expect.

Dr. Stratton: No, I didn't learn how to march because a Senior Lieutenant apparently doesn't march, or didn't at that time. So I had to do only one thing, which was lucky for me. I only had to say, "Platoon leaders take charge."

I think I must have known then what my future job after the war was going to be. Instead of saying, "Platoon leaders take charge," I said, "Patrol leaders take charge." And the Commander told me about it.

Mr. Mason: Who was in charge there then - Underwood?

Dr. Stratton: Yes, Captain Underwood.

After three weeks I was ordered to Washington. We'd just got our uniforms the night before.

Mr. Mason: There was quite a bit of talent represented by that first contingent, was there not?

Dr. Stratton: It was quite a class. You know who was in the class.

Three of us were ordered to Washington. We traveled by train in those days. As we walked through the train to go to the diner you could hear the whispers, "The WAVES, The WAVES, The WAVES."

We got to Washington, which was very crowded. I thought, "Dear Lord, preserve me from ever being ordered to duty in Washington during the war." I was ordered to Washington, and I hardly got out of it except for brief periods of travel during the next three-and-a-half years.

#1 Stratton - 7

Mr. Mason: Where did you land first?

Dr. Stratton: I was assigned to the University of Wisconsin radio operators' school, the first one for women. I was Assistant to the Commanding Officer there.

Mr. Mason: The Commanding Officer being a man?

Dr. Stratton: Yes, the Commanding Officer was a man, a Commander in the Navy, Commander Greene.

Madison had seen no WAVES before and there'd been no radio operators' schools for women before. We were all just stumbling along trying to find our way, but it was a wonderful group of enlisted women. I enjoyed it greatly.

Mr. Mason: Did you have any knowledge of the subject that they were being trained in?

Dr. Stratton: Nothing at all, nothing.

Mr. Mason: Did this cause consternation in your heart?

Dr. Stratton: No, not at all because I had nothing to do with the instruction. It was my responsibility to see that the women were looked after, and I had absolutely nothing to do with the technical aspect of it, so that was not a problem. But the housing, how we were going to get them fed, get them uniformed, and all that sort of thing were problems.

Mr. Mason: These were problems that as a Dean of Women you were somewhat familiar with.

Dr. Stratton: Yes, it wasn't too strange to me, that part of it.

But it was a little strange on Sunday. I remember the townspeople were very kind. They were going to come take the WAVES for a drive. This was the only time that enlisted women had for free time, so they didn't care to be taken for drives. They didn't fill up all the cars.

The townspeople came again the next Sunday, and the Commanding Officer ordered me to see that those cars were filled, which meant that the enlisted women who had free time were to be ordered to get in these cars and fill the cars up. We had quite a time I recall.

Mr. Mason: A difficult morale problem, wasn't it?

Dr. Stratton: But they were good sports and they helped out.

Mr. Mason: The center was actually in Madison?

1 Stratton - 9

Dr. Stratton: Yes, at the University of Wisconsin. Dr. Dykstra was President of the University at that time. He and Mrs. Dykstra were very kind to me and helped to make life pleasant, but I was there a very short time. I think I was there less than a month.

Mr. Mason: Your scholastic connections stood you in very good stead, didn't they?

Dr. Stratton: Yes, they did.

After I'd been there between three and four weeks I got a telegram from the Naval Office of Personnel telling me to report by the fastest transportation possible to Washington. The fastest transportation I could get was a train.

So I reported to the Personnel Office at the Navy and I was promptly taken to the Coast Guard over on 1300 E Street. There I was taken into a room full of Admirals. I think that I probably had never seen an Admiral before in my life and here was a roomfull of them. Then I was asked a good many questions.

Mr. Mason: These were Coast Guard Admirals?

Dr. Stratton: These were Coast Guard Admirals. Admiral Russell Waesche was Commandant, a wonderful man by the way.

I thought - six weeks from next Wednesday maybe I'll hear one way or the other.

1 Stratton - 10

Mr. Mason: They told you what they wanted at that time?

Dr. Stratton: Yes. They told me what they wanted and why I was there, but I didn't expect to hear anything for some time, being accustomed to the delays in civilian life on such important matter, but I heard almost immediately.

So the Navy lent me to the Coast Guard then. There was no legislation as yet.

Mr. Mason: Who was back of this move? Who sent you over there? Was it Admiral Jacobs?

Dr. Stratton: I can only guess - I think it was Miss McAfee.

Mr. Mason: I think it probably was too.

Dr. Stratton: Because Admiral Jacobs wouldn't have known me from the next one.

I was sure you would ask me that question and I can honestly say I don't know, but I think it must have been Miss McAfee.

Mr. Mason: This was her forte, finding the right person for the right job, wasn't it?

Dr. Stratton: I had known her while she was at Oberlin, although I didn't know her well. I think that's how I happened to be recommended to the Coast Guard, but that's a conjecture.

Then I went back to Madison and finished up just as quickly as I could and went to Washington. I had to find a place to live and there wasn't any place to live.

Mason: Were you eager for this new job that was being offered?

Dr. Stratton: I knew nothing about the Coast Guard, nothing. I had never seen a Coast Guard officer. I didn't know anything. I think I felt if that was the place were I could work, that was fine with me. In other words I only cared about being where I could feel I was doing something useful, and I thought this would be useful.

I got to Washington and, as I say, I was on loan from the Navy to the Coast Guard.

Mr. Mason: Did you have a conversation with Mildred McAfee at that point?

Dr. Stratton: I don't think I did, no. I didn't see her, as I recall it, but she was extremely helpful in getting the SPARS underway.

After we got the legislation on the 23rd of November I was sworn in on the 24th. I asked Miss McAfee if it would be possible to get a nucleus of the WAVE officers to start us off because it would save such an enormous amount of time. She said as far as she was concerned, "Yes," and the Navy said, "Yes."

So I went back then to Northampton and made a plea to women who were there in training and got twelve of the WAVES who were getting their indoctrination to come to the Coast Guard and help us get started.

Mr. Mason: Were they volunteers or did you select them?

Dr. Stratton: They were volunteers. Unless they wished to come I couldn't have got them. But there were some who thought, "Here's a new Service and it's a chance to help get this on it's way." By getting the twelve officers, who were tremendously helpful, it saved us a lot of time.

Mr. Mason: I'm sure it did.

Would you mind going back, and telling me what happened, what you did in the interim between your selection by the Coast Guard Admirals and the passage of the legislation?

Dr. Stratton: I'd be glad to tell you.

First of all I had to find a place to live and there wasn't any place to live in Washington. So finally at the American Association of University Women, which was then at 1634 I street, I got a sort of enlarged closet which had a couch in it. It had nothing else, but it was all there was. I said, "I'm not going to be here much anyway. I'll take anything." So I got this little room, which had a window opening on the shaft. You never could tell whether the sun was shining or it was raining or what.

Mr. Mason: About that time you probably thought, " Oh why can't I be back at Purdue."

Dr. Stratton: I was glad to get it.

Then came the question - what were we going to call this unit of the Women's Reserve of the Coast Guard? The WAACS had a name and the WAVES had a name, so what were we going to call the Women's Reserve of the Coast Guard?

There wasn't anyone else except me to think about this. Everybody else had his mind on more important things.

So I tossed on that hard bed many nights trying to think what we'd call this organization. Some times when you just absolutely have to do something you do it. Suddenly it came to me from the Motto of the Coast Guard - "<u>S</u>emper <u>P</u>aratus - <u>A</u>lways <u>R</u>eady - SPAR."

1 Stratton - 14

I proposed it to the Commandant and his Assistants. They accepted it and that was it. So that was one thing that I did.

Mr. Mason: Where did you have your desk at that point?

Dr. Stratton: I had a desk at the Coast Guard Headquarters. A Commander Carroll, who was in charge of procurement there, got me a desk and fixed me up.

Of course the Coast Guard wasn't air conditioned and we had wool uniforms. We not only had them that summer, we had them the next summer too. They never did have any air conditioning in my experience there, but that was not very important in the total scheme of things.

What else did I do? We had to decide what the women were going to wear. The WAVES already had a very good looking uniform designed by Mainbocher, as you know. Somebody in the Coast Guard had also designed a uniform for the SPARS, some man I think had designed the uniform. So which one was going to be chosen?

With great solemnity a whole room full of Admirals sat around and decided which uniform was the one to be worn. They finally decided on the WAVE uniform, with the Coast Guard insignia, which was a good idea because it was very useful and a very good looking uniform.

Mr. Mason: Did they let you have a voice in this?

Dr. Stratton: As I recall it this was one of my more amusing experiences - watching the Admirals go through this process of decideing what the women were going to wear. I think I probably put in my nickel's worth, but I wouldn't say that it was the deciding voice.

Mr. Mason: Did they also decide on the color of stockings and so forth?

Dr. Stratton: There wasn't much choice in those days, there weren't any nylons or anything like that. There was no silk and there was no nylon. We wore lisle stockings.

Mr. Mason: The reason I quiz you on this is because I remember what Mildred McAfee said. Everything was almost a'fait accompli' as far as uniforms were concerned. She was advised that the next day they were to be on display and did she care to come and see. She said, "Indeed I do." Of course she came and vetoed various things and got something of what she wanted. She said that originally they had thought in terms of a uniform that would have red, white, and blue on it in various places.

Dr. Stratton: This I didn't know.

I remember distincly one thing she said to me though, I'll never forget it.

She said, "I thought it was very important for me to keep the reins in my own hands until I discovered that there were no reins."

I think there was a great deal of truth in that.

Mr. Mason: I see a parallel.

Dr. Stratton: The Coast Guard didn't really want women any more than the Navy did.

Mr. Mason: How did they arrive at the need for them then?

Dr. Stratton: Admiral Waesche, who was the Commandant, was a very far-seeing man. It was a little hard to hold out after the Army and the Navy had accepted women. The Coast Guard did have of course a great many jobs that could be done by women, but the resistance in the Coast Guard was I'm sure just as strong as it was in the Navy.

I would say that my biggest job at the beginning was to get some kind of acceptance. My first job, personally, was to convince the Coast Guard if possible that the Navy hadn't foisted off the worst they had on them, because the Coast Guard was pretty sure that the Navy would give them the bottom of the barrel. So I had to live down the fact that I had been in the WAVES.

Mr. Mason: You also, on the other hand, brought prestige to the job coming as a Dean of Women of a large university.

Dr. Stratton: I think that part of it was probably all right, except that the Coast Guard didn't want to project the teacher image. Naturally since I had been in the field of education, and one naturally attracts the people one knows, a good many teachers and college professors did come into the SPARS.

Mr. Mason: Which in the long run was awfully good, wasn't it?

Dr. Stratton: It was, yes, because we were able to use them pretty well. That was one of the problems. You could get people that were too high-powered, because many of the jobs that were open didn't require too high-powered intellectual ability, and we didn't have too many openings for commissions. Practically every officer candidate was commissioned, after the first class, as an Ensign.

I think Miss Schleman, who became my Executive Officer, was commissioned as a Senior Lieutenant, but she was one of very few.

Mr. Mason: As you assumed the office of Director what rank did you get?

Dr. Stratton: I was a Lieutenant Commander.

1 Stratton - 18

Mr. Mason: As you were borrowed from the WAVES you were a Senior Lieutenant, and then you became a Lieutenant Commander which put you on a par with Mildred McAfee.

Dr. Stratton: That's right.

I always wondered whether this was the right thing or not because of course the SPARS were much smaller in numbers. We had all the same problems that the WAVES had, but we didn't have them in such numbers.

All the Directors of the four Women's Services eventually had the same rank. I think Mrs. Hobby was made Colonel first, and then Mildred McAfee was promoted to Captain, then I was, and then Mrs. Streeter, Director of the Women's Marines became a Colonel. Of course we didn't attain these ranks overnight.

Mr. Mason: In this interim period did you help draw up some pretty detailed plans as to the kind of organization you were going to set up and the numbers involved and all of that?

Dr. Stratton: The interim period was pretty short. I don't remember the exact day on which I went to the Coast Guard, but it must have been around early November.. So we only had until the 23rd of November before we actually had the legislation.

Mr. Mason: Was there any problem with the legislation?

Dr. Stratton: Not that I know of, no, there was no problem. The Coast Guard, I suppose, rode through on what had been done for the other Services.

We knew we were going to use the enlisted women as yeomen, which is like our civilian stenographers, and as storekeepers, which was in the field of finance, nothing at all like what the name implies. We were going to use them to man their own barracks. We were going to use enlisted women in galleys for the SPARS. But we couldn't foresee how much could be opened up, because that depended so much on how much the Coast Guard was willing to accept the women.

Mr. Mason: This was really a question in Waesche's mind?

Dr. Stratton: I don't think it was ever a question in Admiral Waesche's mind, but it was a question of getting the Service as a whole to accept them. I would say that the biggest job that I had was that, getting acceptance, getting the doors open. If you could get the doors open so that the women could get a chance to do the jobs they could do the jobs. But to get the doors open that was not so easy. It took a good deal of personal contact, not only with the men officers but with their wives.

Mr. Mason: That's an interesting point.

Dr. Stratton: We knew that that would be where part of our problem would lie, that if we were accepted by the wives that half our battle was won, because we ran a good chance of there being opposition.

Mr. Mason: On what basis?

Dr. Stratton: On a number of bases. A - that some of the women were going to be commissioned officers. Because it was war they were going to be commissioned perhaps as Lieutenant J.G. when it had taken the husbands maybe ten years to get to be Lieutenant J.G.'s. So that problem was built in right away.

Secondly - the SPARS were going to be working directly with their husbands, the husbands of Coast Guard wives. This in itself was a threat.

Then - there was just the question of why should women be in the Coast Guard anyway? This was a man's world, a man's job, and what were the women doing there anyway?

Some of the key wives, who were enthusiastic, helped us a great deal.

Mr. Mason: How did you go about doing this?

Dr. Stratton: We just tried to make friends.

Mr. Mason: But you tried to make friends by design?

Dr. Stratton: Yes, I suppose you could say by design, intentionally. Really that isn't any different from what it is in a university. If the President's wife likes you it helps a lot. This wasn't any different in the Service.

I'll tell you who was a great help to us - Mrs. Forrestal.

Mr. Mason: That's interesting.

Dr. Stratton: Well she was. She, as you know, was enthusiastic about women in the Service. She sometimes flew up to the Academy for the graduation of the women officers, and this helped.

Mr. Mason: She was on that advisory board as I remember.

Dr. Stratton: Yes, she was.

We had to make a decision almost immediately as to where we were going to do our training. We were the only Service that trained the women officers in the regular Academy.

Mr. Mason: But that wasn't at first, was it?

Dr. Stratton: With the women officers it was. It wasn't with the enlisted women.

1 Stratton - 22

Mildred McAfee thought, and I agreed with her, that it would be a saving of the taxpayers' money and that it made sense to train the women together. So we agreed, and the first class of enlisted SPARS were trained at Hunter College with the WAVES.

Mrs. Streeter and I both found out that you had to identify the women with the Service of which they were members. This had to be done because each service has it's own tradition and is very proud.

I don't know whether the Services are more unified now, but they certainly weren't unified in those days. We just had to, for the sake of gaining acceptance within the Coast Guard, separate the training and do our own training. So we had to find some place. By then the Army and the Navy had everything, most of the hotels in the country. Everything was gone.

Mr. Mason: You were sort of 'johnny come lately.'

Dr. Stratton: We were 'johnny come lately.'

By a stroke of good luck we got the Palm Beach Biltmore and made a training station out of it. I went down to look that over. Admiral Donohue, who was Chief of Personnel for the Coast Guard, also came down to look it over. We took it and made a training station out of it. As a matter of fact it was very satisfactory.

1 Stratton - 23

Mr. Mason: How did you happen to come upon the Biltmore down there?

Dr. Stratton: I think the owner of the Biltmore came to the Coast Guard, because he went down on the train with us and wined and dined us. He owned not only the Biltmore, but he owned another big hotel there in Palm Beach where he had his headquarters. I think he made the approach to the Coast Guard, a least that's my recollection.

We used the Palm Beach Biltmore until toward the end of the war, when we used Manhattan Beach.

Mr. Mason: You didn't get the Biltmore until '43.

You said that almost immediately after you were sworn in as Director, you went up to Northampton and secured twelve officers to serve with you. What kind of duties did you assign them when you got them to Washington?

Dr. Stratton: We had SPAR Officer Selection and Recruiting. As you know a great many of the officer were used for recruiting. Then they were used in the assignment of enlisted personnel, and in thinking about how we were going to set up the Coast Guard training and what the Coast Gurad wanted. It wanted some of it's own tradition taught. As I recall it, we assigned some of the officers to Hunter to help with the training there of the enlisted personnel.

1 Stratton - 24

Mr. Mason: With whom did you work most closely in the Coast Guard among the male officers?

Dr. Stratton: I worked a great deal with the male officers since everything was new. It wasn't exactly like a baby learning to walk, because you were learning to walk within a very restricted form, but every step was new.

I worked a great deal with, as he was then, Captain and later Admiral Spencer who was the Assistant Chief of Personnel, and with Admiral Donohue who was the Chief of Personnel, and with Admiral Gorman who was the Chief of Finance, and with Commander Callahan who was the Chief of Training, and with Admiral Pine who was the Superintendent of the Coast Guard Academy.

I went to the Academy for every graduation of the SPAR officers, which was five or six weeks. Admiral Pine and I would always discuss how things were going and if things had gone well or hadn't gone well, and so on, also with Commander Phanamiller there. And with Admiral Michel who was a doctor from the Public Health Service who had charge of the Health Services for the Coast Guard.

Most of all I'd say I worked with Admiral Donohue, and, as he was then, Captain Spencer.

Once in awhile I'd get to see the Commandant, but of course I could only get to the Commandant by going through my boss who was Admiral Donohue.

If there was something really crucial I usually could get to see Admiral Waseche, and then I could get things ironed out very easily.

Mr. Mason: I understand they did with him.

Dr. Stratton: Wonderful man to work for.

Mr. Mason: All the opposition just melted away.

Dr. Stratton: He was never opposed himself. He gave us all the help that he could, and that made all the difference in the world.

Mr. Mason: Did you get ready acceptance yourself with these other men whom you mentioned?

Dr. Stratton: That's hard for me to answer.

Mr. Mason: Based on results as you see it.

Dr. Stratton: I think Captain Spencer was my toughest nut, because he was sure the Navy had palmed off on the Coast Guard the worst they had, and it took me a little while with Captain Spencer. And that wasn't really personal, that was the ingrained feeling that the Coast Guard was going to get the worst of it.

Mr. Mason: That was the way they felt about it.

Dr. Stratton: I won't say 'they.' That's the way many of them felt about it, and that's certainly what Captain Spencer thought. But after I could convince him that I'd been in the Navy only a few weeks and that it couldn't have affected me very much, he accepted me.

I never had any personal difficulties with any of the men officers. They were all very pleasant to work with. They may not have wanted women to come but since they had them they wanted, just the way all the other Services did, to have the best it was possible to have. And, therefore, I didn't have any battles of any kind that I recall with the men officers. In fact, I enjoyed working with them very much. They were good to me.

Mr. Mason: I would think a part of your armament in dealing with them on this question would have been the fact that the girls, the SPARS probably like the WAVES, were not interested in careers, they were only interested in helping with the war.

Dr. Stratton: I'm sure that this was in the back of the minds of everybody since we were sworn in "for the duration and six months after."

Then, like all the other Services, we had a lot of trouble recruiting, which frankly surprised me. I thought that we'd have a rush to the colors, but as you know we didn't.

From early on we had to fight the propaganda - that women were after all just camp followers who weren't really in for any serious purpose. Now we did not get this from within the Service that I know of, but from the public we had this to fight.

I remember Mrs. Hobby's saying to me the day that the newspaper stories appeared on the WAACS that, "I just thought I couldn't hold my head up. I just thought I couldn't hold my head up again. I talked to my husband and he said, "Oveta never pay any attention to anything that isn't true."

Mr. Mason: He was a newspaper man so he knew.

Dr. Stratton: That was hard to battle because, "How could you? How do you?" As Mike Lyon says in her book, THREE YEARS BEFORE THE MAST, "If one SPAR got out of line, just one, then we were all like that."

But I wouldn't say that it constituted a major problem. I don't think it was any more of a problem in the United States than it was in England, but it was part of our problem.

Mr. Mason: And you would solve a problem like that only on a basis of the record, wouldn't you?

Dr. Stratton: As I say the problem was not hard to solve within the Service, because after the men worked with the women and the women worked with the men, they liked each other and respected each other.

But with the public it was harder, because we didn't get the favorable newspaper stories that could have helped us. The newspaper often would look for the lurid story, but I don't think we worried too much about it. We were too busy trying to get on with the job.

Mr. Mason: Would you talk a little about the motivation of the girls who did come into the SPARS?

Dr. Stratton: Of course they all came in voluntarily. They were, most of them, very well motivated. They had mixed motives. There were those whose husbands had been called to service and who were lonely and wanted to get away from it all and do something different. There were those who genuinely felt that at any sacrifice to themselves they would come into the service to make whatever contribution they could. There were those who saw it as a way to, "Join the Coast Guard and see the world." There were those who were just bored and wanted to do something different. There were varieties of motives.

I discovered that, first of all, when I was stationed at the University of Wisconsin, those first few weeks in the WAVES. Some of the women had hardly got in when they wanted out. The Red Cross was extremely helpful on such cases. They helped a great deal.

Mr. Mason: How did they do it?

Dr. Stratton: They would get in touch with the families or get in touch with the husbands or make the family contacts. And very often after they had done this they would either recommend to us, "Yes, the only thing to do is let this woman out," or recommend, "No, we can straighten this situation out and let's go on with it."

Our SPAR rate of attrition was not out of line. I think overall we recruited about 12,000, at peak strength we were about ten. So the rate of attrition was not too bad.

Mr. Mason: In considering that subject, their motivation — I noted in Miss Lyon's book, she has a list of reasons for joining. I wondered about one of them, I rather questioned it. She said, "Self advancement was one of the motivating factors." Would you explain that.

Dr. Stratton: Oh yes, I think she's right on that.

You've got to remember that a lot of women were stuck in dead-end civilian jobs. The advertising did say, Public Relations did say, "there were opportunites for advancement." As a matter of fact there were.

Not only that, another factor which I think was even more important than the women realized was they got training in the Services they never could have got in civilian life, and technical training. This was a route to advancement not only in the Service but, in some cases at least, after their period of service was over. I would say that definitely was a factor, just as it would be with a man who volunteered.

Mr. Mason: I suppose I looked at the emotional side. They wanted to do their bit in the war so they joined.

Dr. Stratton: I wish it had been as simple as that, but it wasn't as simple as that, because the recruiting was tough going for all the services.

As Mike Lyon tells in her book we began recruiting with the Navy. We had exactly the same problem there that I described to you - that the Coast Guard was sure that if there were choices at a Navy Recruiting Station they were going to get the little end of it. So we finally had to set up our separate recreuting stations, and we really worked at it.

1 Stratton - 31

When you come right down to it and you're thinking about going into one of the services you've always heard about the Navy, you haven't always heard about the Coast Guard.

Mr. Mason: Unless certain regions in those days —

Dr. Stratton: Certain regions along the sea coasts of course, but that was a very small part of our total recruiting area.

We did get also daughters and nieces and so on of Coast Guard personnel who wanted to be in the same Service as their fathers or uncles or somebody else.

Mr. Mason: In the same vein and since we're talking about recruitment and reasons for coming in, and you mentioned the fact that they got exceptional training in certain categories, has any effort been made to assess the value of such training in civilian life afterwards to some of these girls?

Dr. Stratton: Not to my knowledge. It could have been done twenty-five years ago, if anybody had been interested and if there had been the money. But as you know as soon as the war was over the rush was on to bring the boys home and get the girls out.

I certainly know as soon as the war was over I couldn't have felt more uncomfortable in a uniform, I couldn't get out fast enough because the whole temper of the times was, "What are you doing in uniform?"

There was no money, there was no interest as far as I know in assessing this. But with the women that I know, and that's very limited, I think that the experience was very useful to all of us. It was hard to put your finger on it, and I don't think it was so much in the technical training, although that was needed in the Service, but the thing that we carried away I think was much more subtle than that. I think with most of us who had three or four years in the Service it was an absolutely unforgetable experience.

At least speaking for myself it gave me a feeling for my country that I never had had as keenly before and I will always feel different about my country for having spent those years in the Coast Guard. I think a great many of us carried that over, but we didn't talk about it. I found out in the later civilian jobs it was best not to talk about it.

Mr. Mason: I was wondering, thinking in terms of a wider field of activity for women – prior to World War II women were somewhat relegated to the educational field and to the clerical field. I wondered, if as a result of their differing experiences in World War II and in the services, if this didn't immediately offer a wider scope to the talents of women?

Dr. Stratton: I'm afraid I don't think so.

After World War II we had this big push, "Back to the homes." The women's magazines, in particular, for the period from the end of the war for the next ten years put on a big push that the only thing was home and children. Betty Friedan exposed this 'crusade' in THE FEMININE MYSTIQUE.

I don't think so, I think the push was all the other way. I always had the idea that the women who served their country during time of need would perhaps be found in the legislative halls, state or national. As far as I know, you can correct me, I don't know of one single woman who was in the Service who's ever been a Congresswoman or in the State Legislatures. The State Legislatures are a guess but I don't know anybody who has. And I certainly don't know any woman who's been either a Congresswoman or a Senator. Yet you would have thought that out of this whole pool there would have been some who would have wanted to do it and would have had that kind of opportunity. It didn't work that way.

As I say I think for the people who were in it, some didn't like it, but those who did give themselves to it felt a great deal of satisfaction. But once the war was over, it was over.

I remember that I had to speak for Dr. Lillian Gilbreth here in New York, at a University Forum, and the question was asked me, "Do you think women should be drafted?"

I said that I felt in the unhappy event we ever had another war, yes they should serve their country and that I saw no objection to the draft. The blast that I got was really something.

Mr. Mason: Predicated on what theory?

Dr. Stratton: This was when I was with the Girl Scouts. Those who opposed service for women, compulsory or volunteer, felt that I couldn't possibly understand what the Girl Scouts were all about if I had that point of view.

Mr. Mason: They made it a personal thing.

Dr. Stratton: In fact when I was with the Girl Scouts I just never thought at all about the fact that I had been in the service. The quieter I could keep about it the better.

Mr. Mason: Let's go back to the beginning of 1943, when your organization was really getting underway. You had your twelve officers delegated to various departments, so to speak. And then you began to bring in the enlisted girls.

What kind of quotas did you have at first and how successful were in in filling those quotas and in training the girls? And what were the problems you ran up against?

Dr. Stratton: I don't remember what the size of the quotas was, what numbers we tried to get. I couldn't tell you that without going back and checking the records.

We didn't fall down on getting what was needed, but we did have a little difficulty getting the SPARS trained fast enough to meet the needs after the Coast Guard began to find they could use them.

It took about three months, as I recall it, to get a storekeeper or a yeoman ready. We had difficulty on that score. We weren't turning them out fast enough. But that wasn't because our recruiting was falling behind, although we certainly did beat the bushes to get the women.

The enlisted training, at first, was pretty standardized: yeomen and storekeepers. Then finally we got the Loran stations opened up for women. That was very hush-hush and I know very little about it myself. I know that the women were allowed to man those stations.

Most of the officers were in Communications, the largest number. That also to me was very hush-hush.

Mr. Mason: There they worked with the WAVES, did they?

Dr. Stratten: No, they worked with the officers and men of the Coast Guard, in the big installation there at Headquarters.

We then had what was called the DCGOs, the District Coast Gurad Offices. There were then twelve around the country, and SPARS were in Communications at all the DCGO offices.

A lot of energy went into marching, which a great many people thought was pretty foolish and im some ways it was. In some ways I think it wasn't because a certain feeling of unity did come out of marching together. The SPARS liked to march, they enjoyed it.

I was down at the twenty-fifty reunion of the SPARS at the Biltmore last year. The SPARS marched down to the beach club, the Sun and Surf Club I think it's called, and marched back because that was their wartime routine and they got a big kick out of doing it again.

They really rather enjoyed the marching and it did something for morale. Of course we stumbled along a lot at the beginning of the training as to how it should be done.

It was the Coast Gurad officers themselves who wanted this marching and all the things that the men did. They just carried it over to the women. If you got a martinet of a Commanding Officer then you had your problems.

We were very lucky at Palm Beach during part of the time, because we had the Kenner 'boys', Willie and Frank Kenner, twins, who were Captains in the Coast Guard. They were absolutely marvelous, but we were not always so fortunate.

Where we did have a CO who was tough and unsympathetic, I had no Command function any more than Mildred McAfee did, I could only try to persuade. This was one, I would say, of the original basic decisions.

There were those who thought that the Women's Reserve should be set up as a separate unit with a Command function, with a Director. There were those who felt it should be integrated into the regular service. And I think that that was the better decision.

Mr. Mason: You think, in retrospect, that it was?

Dr. Stratton: And I thought at the time that it was. I think it was better all around. While it made the job of the Director a little more difficult, perhaps, I think it was much better.

After all if you can't persuade to your point of view, either you're not making a good case for it or you haven't got a good case to start with.

If I had to do it again I think that's the right decision. It gave the women much more of a feeling of belonging to the Coast Guard, and the Coast Guard a feeling that the SPARS were part of the outfit, than if it had been a separate unit.

Mr. Mason: I can see as a separate unit where with some of them it never would have been accepted.

Dr. Stratton: I think from the standpoint of acceptance in the Service, it was important and I believe it was right. It made the position of the Director very anomalous, but very few people knew it.

Mr. Mason: You had to be content with your persuasive powers, but probably you sharpened those powers in the process.

Dr. Stratton: Hopefully.

Mr. Mason: I know that Mildred McAfee told me that she relied heavily on what she called her "coffee clatches" in her office, when she had WAVE officers who were delegated to the various Departments of the Navy meet with her daily for a cup of coffee, but ostensibly to propose ideas. It was kind of a brainstorming thing. These ideas were then carried back to the Departments and planted there, so that when they began to germinate they were the ideas of the male officers.

Dr. Stratton: She had a terrific group of women around her there. Her senior women officers, I thought, were just a terrific group.

Mr. Mason: Did you resort to anything of that sort in order to get ideas?

Dr. Stratton: I don't know whether it was as conscious as that, but we used to do something quite similar. I don't think we did it every day, but once a week probably we'd get the senior women officers at Headquarters together and talk things over and see how things were going. Usually I think ours were more on an ad hoc basis - we've got this situation, how should we deal with it?

You see we had this tremendous advantage of following a little bit along behind the WAVES. So that we could take advantage of so much that the WAVES had already set up.

Mr. Mason: They were the pioneers and you were the settlers who came afterward.

Dr. Stratton: They were a tremendous help. I can't say enough for the help that was given to us by Miss McAfee and by her officers.

Mr. Mason: Was this a matter of consultation between you?

Dr. Stratton: By telephone, or we'd see each other. The SPAR and the WAVE officers would get together and talk things over. Some times we were a little bit of help.

I remember that we did one bulletin on discipline for women officers that Miss McAfee liked. She took that over, pretty much intoto, for the WAVES.

We took an awful lot from the WAVES. Then when the Marines came along we tried to help them. It worked that way - the WAACS helped the WAVES, the WAVES helped the SPARS, and the SPARS helped the Marines.

Mr. Mason: Did you have any problems with the inflexibility of Coast Guard regulations, which were designed primarily for men and applied to women. Can you illustrate that?

Dr. Stratton: Yes.

One of the first questions which we solved differently from the way the WAACS solve it or the WAVES solved it, I don't say it was better or worse, but - what were you going to call the woman officer?

The WAACS called her "Ma'am." The WAVES said, "Good morning, Miss Jones."

We just decided that since women were in the Service we would just say, "Good morning, sir." So we used "sir" for everybody, men and women. That got us over one very awkward hump.

Nobody liked "ma'am" and a lot of people didn't like "sir" either, but you had to do something. So that was our solution.

On some of the Coast Guard regulations about solitary confinement, bread and water in the brig, and things like that - we had to soften things up a little bit.

Mostly we tried not to make any changes if we could possibly help it, because we didn't want to ask for any concessions. We wanted to take it as it came.

Mr. Mason: I know the WAVES, for the sake of morale, very quickly discovered that in the barracks it was best to have cubicles separated by dividers and so forth for the comfort of the girls.

Dr. Stratton: Miss Schleman had been the Director of the Residence Halls at Purdue University and she knew a lot about housing for women. Nobody had to convince her of anything like that, but we had to convince the Coast Guard.

We did build barracks in Washington. I don't know whether we had two women in a room, but we didn't build the open barracks. And that's thanks to Miss Schleman, who was able to make telling points on that. I don't believe we ever built anything that were open barracks.

But what we did have to do on the housing, we had to use awful old hotels in some places. For instance in Atlantic City we had a big contingent of enlisted SPARS there. I was always terrified when I went there, even though the Coast Guard was very very careful about fire, I was terrified of fire in those old wooden buildings.

Mr. Mason: Where were you housed?

Dr. Stratton: It was an old hotel in Atlantic City, I don't recall the name of it, but it was one that would just go up in flames if it caught on fire.

I think the fear of fire in these old buildings worried me as much as anything else, when I was Director, because I felt a very deep responsibility for the lives of the women who'd come into the Service.

We had to take what we could get. First of all the men's units had the good hotels. They were all taken. We had to take what we could get, and a lot of it wasn't very good.

Mr. Mason: Just one disaster and your recruitment would have gone down rapidly.

Dr. Stratton: We never did have a fire. We had, of course, fire drills all the time. This was one the things, like the Navy, that the Coast Guard was very very careful about. Even so I used to worry about it a lot.

Mr. Mason: Tell me about your recruitment standards. Did you have very high ones to begin with and find that you had to lower them or what?

Dr. Stratton: Yes, at first we were going to get perfection. I'm sure we made some modifications in the physical standards, which were a little ridiculous for women since they were not going to man the ships at sea.

Mr. Mason: This was what I had in my mind when I talked about the inflexibility of regulations.

Dr. Stratton: In a way that was our own fault, because they weren't inflexible for women until we set them up that way. If we'd had better sense we could have set up more reasonable ones, I think, in the beginning.

Yes, I think we made changes as we went along. I don't think we made changes as far as mental requirements were concerned, but we did make changes in the physical standards both for officers and for enlisted women.

Mr. Mason: What about the requirements for the officer candidates - were they quite as rigid as they were for the Navy for the WAVES?

Dr. Stratton: I think we probably took them right from the WAVES.

Mr. Mason: I've had various women tell me that the entrance examinations were so stringent that it was just a miracle that they passed, some of the women with high educational qualifications.

Dr. Stratton: Again if you talk to Miss Schleman she can probably tell you a lot more about that than I can. As I recall, you have to remember I'm digging this up out of the recesses, I think it was a general intelligence test. Let's say you are 35 years old, you are not as quick as you were at 18. And even though you may have educational qualifications, if you're taking a general intelligence test designed for college students, you don't react as quickly and you don't get through as much of the test. I think it's possible that that might have been a factor.

I certainly found out in the short time I spent with the WAVES in that first class that I didn't learn as fast as the younger ones did. I think that's possibly a factor.

Mr. Mason: You said earlier that the SPARS were the only group among the women service organizations that actually trained at the service academy. Would you tell me about that, and how it came about?

Dr. Stratton: I was asking Miss Blunt, who was Senior SPAR officer in the Training Division at H.Q., (she was sorry she couldn't meet you today but she had to go to a committee meeting) when we started that and whether we started that right away. She said, "Yes, we did," and she was in the very first class that went up there to the Academy. I said, "Do you remember who had the idea or how we happened to do it?"

It just seemed a good idea, again, if you were going to identify with a Service. It also seemed to be quite a recruitment point for us.

Mr. Mason: In this calendar of dates it says that, "On June 28th, 1943 the Coast Guard Academy assumed complete responsibility for the training of SPAR officers."

Dr. Stratton: Miss Blunt said she was in the January '43 class and she trained at the Coast Guard.

Perhaps the Navy was training some of the specialized officers. The General Duty Officers all went up to the Coast Guard Academy, maybe the Communications Officers were trained by the Navy.

But the decision was made, as the British say, "early on," to do it at the Academy. It was rough for the first group or two.

Mr. Mason: Why?

Dr. Stratton: The standards had all been set for the men. Here were these women, a lot of them in their thirties in the first groups, who were doing all these physical exercises, learning to shoot guns, and doing all the things that they weren't going to be called on to do later.

Mr. Mason: This must have struck you immediately as a real hazard.

Dr. Stratton: I didn't see this, I never did actually see the training with the shooting of guns.

I remember so well when I was Dean of Women at Purdue we had Katherine McHale who was the only woman member we had on the Board of Trustees. She was the General Director of the American Association of University Women. She said to me, "Well, the important thing is to pick your fights. You can't fight them all. Which ones are you going to pick?"

You have to be pretty careful which issues you were going to stand on, because you couldn't make a case out of everything.

I believe for us that was a good decision - training the officers at the Academy, because they got a feel that they couldn't have got anywhere else. If we'd had them in a hotel somewhere, they just couldn't have got that same feeling of the whole history and background of the Coast Guard. That was awfully important.

Mr. Mason: And I suppose the overriding factor was your desire to have them completely integrated into the service and completely accepted, so you had to overlook some of these other details.

Dr. Stratton: There also was the factor probably of expense. It was cheaper to do it there than it would have been to set up a complete unit elsewhere. Although that was not the overriding thing. The overriding thing was of course the integration into the Service itself and to get some feeling of the kind of training the male officers got.

Mr. Mason: You said earlier that you attended every graduation at the Academy. Do you want to say something more about that?

Dr. Stratton: With any Service you've got a personality that represents to the group what it is they're trying to do and what it's all about, and I think it was very important to have personal contact. I knew a lot of these people in civilian life. I wanted to show my interest and I wanted them to know it.

Furthermore, it gave me a chance to chat with them informally and see how they were feeling about things. They could say, "I feel some identification. I don't think Washington is just some place over there that never heard of me."

When you had to send women where the service wanted them to go and not where they wanted to go, it seemed to me to be extremely important to have some feeling of humanness and of individual interest. Furthermore, I enjoyed going.

Mr. Mason: So you went every six weeks?

Dr. Stratton: I don't say I never missed one, but I planned to go every six weeks, and I don't think I missed any.

Mr. Mason: And did you have to speak to the graduating class?

Dr. Stratton: Oh yes, I always spoke to the class.
I'd often take somebody, maybe Congresswoman Margaret Chase Smith, on the trip. She was very helpful. She'd go down to Palm Beach with us, fly down with the Commandant and meet the girls. Then we'd nearly always take a personality, like Mrs. Forrestal or somebody else.

Mr. Mason: Were there any differences in the Cadets at the Coast Guard Academy? Was there any difference in their attitude toward the SPARS coming to school there from what was shown by officers of the Coast Gurad toward SPARS? Was there any more ready acceptance on the part of the Cadets as youngsters?

1 Stratton - 49

Dr. Stratton: I don't believe I can answer that, I don't know.

Mr. Mason: Did they share classes?

Dr. Stratton: No, I think not. I don't believe so.
Now what else are you interested in?

Mr. Mason: Lots of things.
What about the Captain's mast - did you have that procedure? Do you want to talk about that?

Dr. Stratton: Yes, we had it. I can't tell you much about it. I never was present at one. There are people who can tell you, but I can't.

Mr. Mason: Do you have any general cognizance of any disciplinary problems? Would you focus on that perhaps?

Dr. Stratton: Yes, I do.
I thought as a Dean of Women in a university that I'd seen everything, but I hadn't. With the enlisted women we had all all kinds of problems that I had never dreamed of or heard of.
If it was unusual, often it would rattle along until finally it would come to rest on my desk, not necessarily for a decision but for discussion or recommendation.

I think it was the varieties of sexual problems which I guess were an eye opener to me, although I thought I'd seen and heard of everything. But I thought the services were pretty tough on any kind of sexual aberration. I thought that often we dismissed people that if I had had the decision alone or with a psychiatrist I wouldn't have.

I just think it wasn't very realistic to expect, any more than you were going to get 20-20 eyesight, that you were going to get everybody who was perfect in other ways. That's the thing that stands out in my mind on the discipline.

It wasn't little things like whether your hair was touching your collar, or whether your skirt was too long or too short, or whether your hat was squared. At the training stations they'd fuss about those things.

What I had to be concerned about was whether you were going to keep these cases or you weren't going to. I've watched how some of these people have got along in civilian life and they've got along very well.

I must say that I never cared much for these reports that came in from the Intelligence Service. I can't remember the name that we had for it. I just felt that we did an awful lot of snooping into the personal lives that wasn't helping us win the war, which was what it was supposed to be all about.

Mr. Mason: Is this perhaps an illustration of the inflexible regulations which were designed primarily for peace time and here you had a war time situation and war time personnel?

Dr. Stratton: That could be, yes. You were drawing from a much bigger pool than during peace time.

I know nothing about what the situation is now, but I should think we've become much more enlightened in the last twenty years, don't you think, in civilian life anyway? I don't know about the services.

Mr. Mason: I think we have in terms of what one reads in the newspapers and so forth.

Dr. Stratton: In terms of what's acceptable and accepted and what isn't.

Mr. Mason: You said that you were surprised at some of the problems that presented themselves, as Dean of Women you thought you'd seen everything. Is it not possible as Dean of Women in that time you were dealing with girls who were seeking an education who had on the whole pretty high standards, and now in the service you were dealing with enlisted people who had different standards because their educational level was different. Is there some correlation there?

Dr. Stratton: Yes. I'd had no experience really with many girls who hadn't had the educational opportunities, although I'd worked in high schools quite a lot. But at high school they go home at night and I didn't have to worry about that.

I got a liberal education myself.

The most bizarre incidents would come across my desk with the enlisted personnel, not with the officers group. Often it would be of course with the male personnel in the Coast Guard.

I just say in retrospect, and I thought at the time, that we were pretty tough.

Mr. Mason: In the matter of officer assignments - did you also, as did Miss McAfee, attempt to really fit the hand to the glove, so to speak? You were getting talented women officers - did you then attempt to put them in the proper slots where they would be most useful?

Dr. Stratton: We tried very hard.

Mr. Mason: How did you go about this?

Dr. Stratton: Miss Schleman worked a lot with the officer assignments. We knew that if we got women with a lot of ability and they were assigned to jobs that didn't call for ability we were going to have trouble.

That's one reason why we tried to be careful not to recruit too many of the very high-powered ones, because we didn't have the slots for them.

There's nothing that destroys morale faster than people who've got the ability and don't get the chance to use it. We worked very hard on the individual officer assignments.

For every class that graduated from the Academy Miss Schleman went up and talked with the officer candidates and tried to find out what their interests and abilities were, and tried to make individual assignments that would be acceptable all around. We didn't always hit it, but we didn't do it on any mass-produced basis. We did it individually. We had to not only for the woman herself, but for the success of the Service.

Mr. Mason: Then you must have had a pretty detailed dossier on her background.

Dr. Stratton: Oh yes, we did, heavens, yes.

As a matter of fact every time I go out to Purdue now Miss Schleman will say, "What shall I do with these officer files? I didn't know what to do with them when the officers were released from the service. Nobody wanted them, so I've still got these officer files. What shall I do with them?" And I guess she still has them.

There was a lot of talent there. Of course the WAVES got a great many women of very high ability. I guess the Navy had a great many more slots for them than we had.

Mr. Mason: What about the assignments - were they permanent assignments for the duration, or were they switched around?

Dr. Stratton: Oh no, they weren't "for the duration."

For instance - one of the officers whom we got from the Navy was Teresa Crowley. She went to Palm Beach as the Assistant to the CO there, in charge of everything that he wanted to assign to her. Then after that she took our first contingent of SPARS to Alaska. She was always the spearhead.

We had an officer who was Drill Officer and Company Commander at Palm Beach. She took the first contingent out to Hawaii.

The only officers who really did the same thing "for the duration and six months, too," were the Communications Officers. I never knew much about that, because that was very highly specialized and secret training. They were usually the young officers. A lot of them had some experiences in similar civilian lines.

We used many General Duty Officers in charge of the barracks and in charge of the SPARS themselves.

Mr. Mason: What about the enlisted personnel - were they put in a slot and kept there or did they move about?

Dr. Stratton: They moved about. The last groups of SPAR officers were all chosen from the enlisted personnel. They got chances to take specialized training. Then after they got their specialized training, they got their new assignments. They didn't stay in one assignment.

If they were Yeomen, they'd probably stay Yeomen, unless they got a chance to be a SPAR officer. In other words they wouldn't be apt to change from Yeoman to some other specialized rating, like the Loran. They'd stay a Yeoman unless they got to be an officer, but they wouldn't necessarily stay in Atlantic City or wherever it was. They'd move about.

Mr. Mason: You said that you'd like to say something about the relationship between the SPAR and the civil service employee.

Dr. Stratton: We had this in the Coast Guard as I'm sure you had must have had it in the Navy. Working side by side, expecially at the Headquarters, would be a Civil Service person doing a somewhat similar job to what the enlisted SPAR was doing. One was under certain regulations and getting paid a certain amount, and the other was not under any such regulations and getting paid a different amount.

Furthermore there was just a natural built-in questioning between the two because the Civil Service had been there first and the SPARS were described as johnnie-come-lately.

We had a little smoothing out to do in that area. Usually after they got to know each other, again, it worked out pretty well. But for instance the Admiral, Chief of Personnel, had a civilian secretary.

Mr. Mason: She'd probably been there for thirty years.

Dr. Stratton: She'd been there for a long long time, and she knew the ropes. She knew the ropes a lot better than the rest of us did.

This was rather general though — that there was some feeling between civilian personnel and military personnel. I think the civilians envied the military personnel more than the other way around, although the SPARS were the ones who were under more regulations.

Many times the civilian personnel could teach the rest of us a lot, if they were so inclined.

I would like to tell you one thing about how I got indoctrinated into the Coast Guard. I knew I didn't know anyhing about it and that this would quickly become evident, so I asked to have a Coast Guard officer assigned to me. I could ask him anything I didn't know and he would go with me and keep me from making mistakes.

I don't know how happy he was. He was a very handsome Coast Guard officer, Commander Jewell. I don't know whether he liked the assignment, but he was tremendously helpful to me because without him I would have made many more blunders than I did.

I could always call him at any time and ask him, "What should I do about this?" or "What's the protocol for this or that?" or "What does this mean?" or "What does that mean?" And he would tell me. That was, I think, one of the best protective devices I had when I was trying to learn my way around.

I suppose the real question is — "What did we do, if anything, to help win the war? What contribution did we make?"

The recruiting posters said, you know, "Release a man to go to sea." This was good and bad, because some of them didn't want to be released to go to sea. This was a two-edged sword.

I think that during the war period we did make a contribution in carrying the paper work and the routine work and some of the specialized work that certainly had no sex label attached to it. It could be done by any intelligent person.

I also think that it was wise at the end of the war that the Coast Guard did not try to continue a large SPAR contingent. I didn't recommend it, because the Coast Guard is a small service.

While the Coast Guard has kept a few SPARS (and has great loyalty from the SPARS) it can't absorb women the way the Navy can or the Army can. There aren't the openings.

And I think in the Coast Guard it really was best that the SPARS be a wartime organization and just the smallest cadre be kept in the unhappy event that they should ever be needed again.

I think the Coast Guard let its reserve legislation lapse after the war. They probably couldn't afford anybody over on The Hill to keep up with what legislation was being proposed and wasn't. At any rate, why I don't know the legislation did lapse.

The ones who were trying to stay in the reserve lost all their status, and I believe finally got the legislation changed so that the service could be continuous. The number of those who continued in the reserve was not large, certainly not of the ranking officers. None of them did, as far as I know. They had gone into it for the duration, and that's all they wanted to do. As soon as the war was over they were through.

I think that the peacetime mission of the Coast Guard had great appeal, in the fact that during peacetime it does perform a daily mission.

Mr. Mason: Of a humanitarian nature very often.

Dr. Stratton: This had a strong appeal I think to the women who came in.

I tried to think before you came what there was, if anything, that might be different about the SPARS from the WAVES. Essentially of course we were all trying to do the same thing.

I think that I would mention the fact that the officers were trained in the regular Academy, that was a unique feature of the SPARS.

Then finally we got some specialized billets opened up to both the enlisted and the officers that were interesting and gave the women some specialized training.

The problems and satisfactions I think were very similar for all the Services.

Mr. Mason: You were named Captain on the 1st of February 1944. How did you solve the personal problem - a woman, a Captain in the Coast Guard? Which took precedence on some occasions?

Dr. Stratton: That was easy, because we were taught from the beginning that as far as any social courtesies when we were on duty, the rank came first, not the woman. So that I had no problem on that. I knew exactly where I walked and who got into the small boat first, and who went into the elevator first. Life was very easy. Occasionally there'd be an Admiral who wouldn't use his rank. But by and large we all knew exactly where we stood.

You ask me about this business of being a Captain — I had a very funny experience on Pennsylvania Avenue right across from the White House. I was walking along one day and this enlisted man in the Navy came along. He looked at me, put his hands on his hips, and said, "Ha, ha, ha, a Captain in the 'Hooligan Navy'," and he threw back his head and laughed. So I threw back my head and laughed and we passed each other very pleasantly.

Mr. Mason: Without a salute.

Dr. Stratton: The salute — a lot of funny things happened on on that. I remember one time I was down in Norfolk. I had a SPAR driver, a very good driver, who never saluted. So the officer in charge had a little chat with her and said, "Look, this won't do. You're supposed to salute." She said, "Well I'll tell you, I just don't care very much for saluting."

We had a great many very amusing things that happened.

Did Miss McAfee tell you the story about the little woman on the railroad train on the way to the West Coast? She tells it and I tell it, so you can put it down that it happened to either one of us.

The little old lady couldn't stand it any longer. Finally she looked across and she said, "Excuse me, but do you mind if I ask you — are you a WAAC, a WAVE, or a SPAM?"

That story stood me in good stead many times.

Also when I was out in Minneapolis, I was supposed to be making a speech, I was being introduced. My introducer said, "Captain Stratton always lives up to the motto of the Coast Guard - Seldom Prepared but Always Ready."

Mr. Mason: Which was a light note on which to begin.

Dr. Stratton: It was a good start.

Mr. Mason: Did you have a counterpart to Mildred McAfee's Fran Rich who traveled and reported to you?

Dr. Stratton: Not as such.

Mr. Mason: She was actually something of a trouble shooter, I suppose, going to situations where the morale was low and what have you, but constantly, she told me, made nightly long hand reports to Mildred McAfee. So it was a great help to her.

Dr. Stratton: No, we didn't have anything like that. Some times I'd get nightly reports by telephone, but not by my request. I don't think I could have done that, because that would have been too much of an end run.

So, I repeat again, I had no authority. I had only powers of persuasion and nothing else. I would have been in trouble with the Commanding Officer. I could have gone myself, or I could have requested the CO if there was trouble, if I could ask somebody to come and talk with him. But I couldn't have had anybody traveling and reporting to me, because I wasn't in the chain of command.

Mr. Mason: I suppose in her case it was feasible because there were so many WAVES.

Dr. Stratton: Maybe so, but I couldn't because if you're not in the chain of command, you're not.

Mr. Mason: Tell me about morale problems, and how you might have dealt with them.

Dr. Stratton: We had two kinds of morale problems.

The individual problem - where the SPAR was unhappy about her assignment, or unhappy about her roommate, or unhappy about the fact that her husband was sent to sea.

We did have counseling services in the barracks where you could usually deal with individual unhappiness.

We had a morale problem at Palm Beach. We had one CO there --

Mr. Mason: You mean because he was tough?

Dr. Stratton: Tough and unreasonable. That was when I had telephone calls telling me things were bad.

Mr. Mason: From your own personnel?

Dr. Stratton: Yes.

I went down several times myself. I'd rather they'd tell me there was a problem than to tell me there was no problem. You had that kind too - "There's no problem at all. Everything's fine."

I guess all I can say is, just like any other organization, it all depends on who's at the top. If you've got a good person things are all right. You can reason with him.

I didn't feel I could ask to have him removed, I couldn't ask to have him removed. I would only try to go down and do my best to bolster the morale of the officers. If you could keep their morale up you could keep up the morale of the enlisted personnel.

Mr. Mason: You can't change the stripes of a bully, can you?

Dr. Stratton: And we only had one.

We had the show, TARS and SPARS, which was kind of a morale builder which toured the country and went to the Coast Guard installations.

1 Stratton - 64

Mr. Mason: That was a musical, wasn't it? Whose idea was that?

Dr. Stratton: I don't know whose it was. If we could find any of the old scores, we could probably find out who wrote it. I don't remember who it was now, but I know it caused us a lot of headaches.

Mr. Mason: What kind of headaches?

Dr. Stratton: The same kind you have on a college campus when the Glee Club rehearses after eleven o'clock at night and all that. They just never lived by the regulations, they weren't that kind. The ones that go into something like a musical show are not exactly the kind that live up to military regulations. So it was a headache for the people who dealt with the enlisted personnel at Headquarters. But perhaps it was a morale builder, I hope so.

Mr. Mason: That of course naturally leads me to the area of Public Relations, and what kind of policies you formulated in this field. There was a need for Public Relations in terms of recruitment and et cetera. What did you do?

Dr. Stratton: The Director of Public Relations was a regular Coast Guard Captain. We never had very good Public Relations.

Mr. Mason: The SPARS didn't have their own then?

Dr. Stratton: No. We had a woman who was in the Public Relations Department, and she wasn't very much help. I would say that was a very weak area with us, very weak.

Mr. Mason: You didn't have any Madison Avenue types who were enrolled as officers?

Dr. Stratton: No. If we did I don't remember.

The Coast Guard was always great on photographs. They had photographs of everything.

I think probably coming from the Navy you don't know how poor the Coast Guard is and was, how little money they had. They didn't have money to spend on Public Relations. Furthermore, I don't think they would think it was too important. You do your job, and that's that. We didn't have much Public Relations, not because they didn't want to give it to us, they just didn't have it. So we just got along as best we could, the way the whole Coast Guard did. But it was nothing like the set-ups that the Navy had. I would definitely say that was a very weak area with us.

Mr. Mason: The Navy had people like Billy Wilde, who knew something about publicity, and Hazel Markel and people of that sort, who then applied their skills.

Dr. Stratton: And you have a great many men officers in Public Relations.

Mr. Mason: But I think not at the outset of the war. This is a concept which grew. Because as I understand it the old Navy was the silent service and didn't believe in publicizing what they did. This pertained to Admiral King, Admiral Nimitz, and all the top echelon.

Dr. Stratton: The first thing that struck me when I went to the Coast Guard (Not that I'd had much experience with professional PR, I hadn't. The University had a very simple set up) for instance was when it came to getting a name for the SPARS I didn't have anybody to turn to, nobody. I just had to get it or it wasn't going to be.

(Short break in interview here)

Dr. Stratton: As soon as we got the legislation permitting the SPARS to go to Hawaii and Alaska we prepared.

Mr. Mason: Was it a difficult thing to achieve?

1 Stratton - 67

Dr. Stratton: Didn't the Navy and the Coast Guard get that at the same time? Didn't you have to have special legislation for the WAVES? I think we got it in the same bill.

Mr. Mason: I suppose the objections were the same in the Coast Guard as they were in the Navy.

Dr. Stratton: We didn't have any objections in the Coast Guard. It was the Congress which insisted on protecting the women in the naval services and did not want them to go outside the continental limits. We had no objection within the Coast Guard, as far as I know.

As soon as we had the legislation we prepared to send our first contingent over, and four of us went over By Pan Am Clipper to make arrangements.

Mr. Mason: To Hawaii?

Dr. Startton: Yes, to Hawaii. A psychiatrist, the woman who was going to be in charge of the SPARS over there, the woman who did all the assignments of enlisted personnel at Coast Guard Headquarters, and I - four of us went.

We talked to the Coast Guard, looked into the housing, and tried our best to get things set up. The woman who was going to stay over and take charge of the SPARS when they came stayed, she didn't come back.

1 Stratton - 68

Mr. Mason: How large a contingent was needed there?

Dr. Stratton: I'm guessing, I suppose we sent a hundred or so. That's a guess.

I do know that the WAVE officers were already there and they were a tremendous help. Margaret Moon who went over, she was a Senior Lieutenant, was in charge of the SPARS over there. The WAVE officers were very helpful to her.

Miss Schleman went to Alaska and did the same thing in Alaska that we had tried to do in Hawaii. We sent our contingent there. As a matter of fact they didn't seem to mind the cold weather. They enjoyed their assignment there.

But other than Hawaii and Alaska we didn't have any women stationed outside the continental limits.

Mr. Mason: Now tell me about the windup of the wartime service.

Dr. Stratton: The windup, of course, began very shortly after VJ day and proceeded pretty rapidly. We had stations where the returning SPARS were discharged. The officers were "separated."

I got out I believe in February. Miss Schleman stayed and finished up. I think we were all lost when we got out.

Mr. Mason: Lost in what sense?

Dr. Stratton: When you're in the service, as you well know, everything is taken care of for you. You have your medical and dental care, you have the protection of the service. You don't have to worry about your clothes, you know what you're going to wear. You're kind of taken care of, that's the only way I can express it, in a way that you're not in civilian life.

When we got out we all had to find new jobs or go back to jobs that somebody else had held in our absence.

Mr. Mason: Which was your case?

Dr. Stratton: I didn't go back, I never went back. I went to the Retraining and Reemployment Administration and then to the International Monetary Fund. So I never went back to Purdue as Dean of Women, although I was still on leave of absence. I think it was easier not to, than to go back to where somebody else has been holding the job for several years. I don't think that would have been easy.

But we didn't know what kind of clothes to buy. We made mistakes. We looked stranger than other civilians did, because we hadn't bought any clothes for four years. We were just sort of lost and it took awhile for us to find our way back into civilian life.

The people who had given up their jobs had to go back and hunt jobs had a big adjustment to make.

The women who were going back and hadn't seeen their husbands in years, that was a tremendous family adjustment.

There were the ones who were just waiting to get married until they could get out.

The actual separations, the routines were worked out. There is nothing really interesting to tell you.

Mr. Mason: There was no great problem with demobilization then, was there?

Dr. Stratton: I suppose there were a lot of individual problems, but noting unusual at all. But it was the adjustments of all the people who'd been in the service who had to find out how to be civilians again that were the interesting problems that arose. Of course most of those we didn't have anything to do with, but I saw a lot of it in the Retraining and Reemployment Administration, which is a different angle on things.

Do you remember the Baruch-Hancock Report on demobilization and use of personnel after the war and what to do with everybody after the war? The Retraining and Reemployment Administration was set up under the Baruch-Hancock Report.

Mr. Mason: This was a federal agency?

Dr. Stratton: Yes. General Erskine, of the Marines, the one they call the Big E, was our boss. I was his Special Assistant.

That was quite an experience too - working with a Marine General. We saw a lot of the readjustments to civilian life.

Mr. Mason: How did you tackle the problem?

Dr. Stratton: We were supposed to coordinate all the activities of the Federal Government. You know how anybody in the Federal Government loves to be coordinated. We were supposed to coordinate the activities of all of the agencies dealing with retraining and reemployment. The whole agency had just gotten out of one service or another. We didn't know as much as the people that we were trying to coordinate. So we had a very interesting couple of years at that.

How we went at it was - there was quite a Public Relations program on the reemployment. Of course the veterans had preference for jobs. We had a Field Service, which would go out and see how things were going. Actually we didn't turn out to have as big a reemployment problem as Baruch-Hancock had expected. There had been such a shortage of goods and material during the war that there was this buying surge.

Mr. Mason: No depression, there was an upturn in the economy.

#1 Stratton - 72

Dr. Stratton: Tremendous, so people could get jobs.

I thought it ran surprisingly smoothly, in view of what had been expected to be a tremendous reconversion problem.

Mr. Mason: How long did you stay with that outfit?

Dr. Stratton: I think I was there about eighteen months.

Mr. Mason: And then you became a banker?

Dr. Stratton: I didn't really become a banker. I wish I could say that I knew how to be one. I just happened to go to the right cocktail party.

The International Monetary Fund was looking for somebody in the field of personnel. To deal with exchange rates they had mostly international economists. I didn't have anything to do with the economics of the Fund. I had to do with the Personnel. We recruited from all over the world economists from a great many nations. I had a Belgian Managing Director. I had a pretty hard time to convince him that a woman could do anything.

Mr. Mason: That was an unfortunate choice of a boss, wasn't it?

Dr. Stratton: Maybe he thought the other way around.

Anyway, I had a very interesting experience there in working in a completely new area from anything that I had worked with before. But this had many similarities too, because the staff would all want to come and talk about their problems.

They all had housing problesm and they all had problems of educating the children. They all had health problems -- where were you going to get a doctor and a dentist?

It was Personnel, that's what I did. It was not really, in lots of ways, too different. But I didn't have anything to do with the "substantive," as the United Nations calls it, work of the Fund. I was supporting service to the staff, that's what I really was.

I tried to learn some Economics, but I don't think I learned much.

Mr. Mason: How long were you with that?

Dr. Stratton: I was there three-and-a-half years.

Mrs. Mason: And then you went to the Girl Scouts?

Dr. Stratton: Then I went to the Girl Scouts, and I was there ten years.

1 Stratton - 74

Mr. Mason: You were Executive Director of the Girl Scouts. Was that a satisfying experience?

Dr. Stratton: Very. Very interesting and very different working with volunteers, which was a new experience to me.

Mr. Mason: That has its built in headaches.

Dr. Stratton: It has a few headaches built in, yes.

After I finished with the Girl Scouts, I represented the International Federation of University Women at the United Nations for six years.

Mr. Mason: Tell me a little about that.

Dr. Stratton: The Charter of the United Nations provides that Non-governmental Organizations have consultative status at the United Nations. The Non-governmental Organizations are "we, the people." The rest of it is all governmental. The Non-governmental Organizations, in consultative status with the Economic and Social Council, may attend all sessions of the Economic and Social Council and its subsidary organs. That means The Commission of the Status of Women, The Commission on Social Development and The Commission on Human Rights.

You attend these sessions and you report back to your organization in writing, especially on what the United Nations wants these organizations to be doing. If they think you have special competence, or your organization has special competence, they might possibly consult you about something. But really they have such a highly specialized staff now that it works mostly the other way. In other words the Non-governmental Organizations try to further the program of the United Nations.

The University Women had branches in different countries, so we had to get the information out to fifty-two countries. During those six years I traveled at least half the time.

Mr. Mason: World wide? Fastinating job.

Dr. Stratton: Yes.

Mr. Mason: Was my friend, Mary Lord, attached there then?

Dr. Stratton: Mary Lord was above the SALT, I was below it. She was a delegate, I was an N.G.O. She served under Eisenhower, as I recall it.

Mr. Mason: Yes, she did.

Dr. Stratton: I know her, but she served before I was there.

Mr. Mason: She was our appointee on the Commission on Human Rights. She succeeded Eleanor Roosevelt.

Dr. Stratton: That's right, she did.
    Mrs. Tillett was on the Status of Women.

Mr. Mason: Thank you very much.

Dr. Stratton: You're welcome. It has been a pleasure to recall "the old days." I don't know whether I've been able to tell you anything that's of interest, but this is the way I remember it.

Mr. Mason: Indeed you have.

Index to Interviews with

DOROTHY STRATTON

Baruch-Hancock Report, 70-71.

Biltmore Hotel, Palm Beach, Fla., 22-23.

Blunt, Miss Virginia, 44.

Crowley, Teresa, 53.

Donahue, Admiral, 22, 24-25.

Dykstra, Dr. Clarence, 8.

Erskine, Gen., 70.

Forrestal, Mrs. James, 21, 48.

Friedan, Betty, 33.

Gilbreth, Dr. Lillian, 2, 33.

Gildersleeve, Dean Virginia, 3.

Girl Scouts of America, 34, 73.

Hobby, Ovita C., 27.

International Federation of University Women, 74.

International Monetary Fund, 69, 72-73.

Kenner, Willie and Frank, 36.

Lyne, Mary (Mike), 27, 30.

McAfee, Mildred (Mrs. Horton), 10-11, 15, 21, 36, 38-39, 60.

McHale, Katherine, 46.

Moon, Margaret, 67.

Pine, Admiral, 24.

Retraining and Re-employment Administration, 69-71.

Schleman, Miss Helen B., 17, 41, 43, 52-53, 68.

Shelly, Mary Jo, 5.

Smith, Margaret Chase, 48.

SPARS: Legislation, 11; nucleus of Wave officers, 11; question of a name, 13; question of a uniform, 14-15; Stratton task of getting acceptance for, 16, 19-20; training at Hunter College, 21; initial officer assignments, 23; problems of recruitment, 27, 30; standards for recruitment, 42; motivations for enlistment, 28, 30-31; Loran stations, 35; 25th reunion, 36; integration into regular C.G., 37, 46; experience of WAVES useful, 39; mode of address, 40; Coast Guard Regs, 40; training at C.G. Academy, 44-45; discipline, 49-51; assignments, 53; SPARS vs Civil Service employees, 54-55; Did they help win the War?, 56; contrasts between SPARS and WAVES, 58; saluting, 59; morale problems, 61-62, 63; Tars and SPARS, 63-64; public relations, 64-65; SPARS to Hawaii, 66-67; demobilization, 68.

Spencer, Capt., 24-26.

Stratton, Dr. Dorothy: Helped with WAAC officer candidates, 2; feeling that women should serve, 3; leave of absence from Purdue U., 4; commissioned as Lieutenant in WAVES, 4; Smith College training, 5; University of Wisconsin radio operators school, 6; Coast Guard interview, 9; commissioned Lt. Cdr. on assuming directorship, 17; difficulties with male officers, 25-26; later value of service to women, 31-32; views on the draft, 33-34; attendance at C.G. graduation ceremonies, 47; her indoctrination into Coast Guard, 56; rank of captain, 58.

Streeter, Mrs. Ruth, 18, 22.
Underwood, Captain Herbert W., 6.
Waesche, Admiral Russell, 9, 16, 25.

www.ingramcontent.com/pod-product-compliance
Lightning Source LLC
Chambersburg PA
CBHW080626170426
43209CB00007B/1524